POLICING AND
GENDERED JUSTICE

POLICING AND GENDERED JUSTICE EXAMINING THE POSSIBILITIES

Marilyn Corsianos

UTP

University of Toronto Press

LIBRARY AND ARCHIVES CANADA CATALOGUING IN PUBLICATION

Corsianos, Marilyn
   Policing and gendered justice : examining the possibilities / Marilyn Corsianos.

Includes bibliographical references and index.
ISBN 978-0-8020-9679-1 (pbk.).—ISBN 978-1-4426-0135-2 (bound)

1. Policewomen — Canada. 2. Policewomen — United States. 3. Sex role in the work environment — Canada. 4. Sex role in the work environment — United States. 5. Discrimination in law enforcement — Canada. 6. Discrimination in law enforcement — United States. I. Title.

HV8023.C67 2009   363.2082'0971   C2008-907830-6

We welcome comments and suggestions regarding any aspect of our publications—please feel free to contact us at news@utphighereducation.com or visit our internet site at www.utphighereducation.com.

North America
5201 Dufferin Street
Toronto, Ontario, Canada, M3H 5T8

2250 Military Road
Tonawanda, New York, USA, 14150

ORDERS PHONE: 1-800-565-9523
ORDERS FAX: 1-800-221-9985
ORDERS EMAIL: utpbooks@utpress.utoronto.ca

UK, Ireland, and continental Europe
NBN International
Estover Road, Plymouth, PL6 7PY, UK
TEL: 44 (0) 1752 202301
FAX ORDER LINE: 44 (0) 1752 202333
enquiries@nbninternational.com

This book is printed on paper containing 100% post-consumer fibre.

Recycled
Supporting responsible use
of forest resources
FSC www.fsc.org Cert no. SGS-COC-003153
© 1996 Forest Stewardship Council

The University of Toronto Press acknowledges the financial support for its publishing activities of the Government of Canada through the Book Publishing Industry Development Program (BPIDP).

Designed by Daiva Villa, Chris Rowat Design.

Printed in Canada

This book is dedicated with love and admiration to my mother Rena Corsianos and in memory of my father Demetre Corsianos for being exemplary role models.

Contents

Acknowledgements

I am indebted to the many police participants in my research projects, from the front-line officers, to the members of upper management, who shared their stories with me over the years, gave me access to conduct the necessary field research, and who provided me with invaluable information that made this book a reality. Also, numerous others invested their time and energy in answering questions and providing material at different stages of this endeavour. I would especially like to thank Penny Harrington; Lenna Bradburn; Chris Mathieson and Joanna Hayman from the Vancouver Police Historical Society and Centennial Museum; Liza Pormady and the Ralph and Mary O'Hara Portland Police Officer Archive and Collection; Anjali Vohra and Nova Scotia Archives and Records Management; Myra James and Ontario Women in Law Enforcement; the Toronto Police Museum and Media Relations Office; the Los Angeles Police Historical Society Inc.; and the Canadian Police College Media Relations Office.

I am grateful to the University of Toronto Press for their support of this scholarship. I would especially like to thank my editor Anne Brackenbury for her commitment to this project and for being a wonderful person to work with. I would also like to extend my many thanks to Kirsten Craven for her copy-editing and to the academic reviewers who offered constructive criticism and detailed suggestions. I also wish to express my appreciation to Sharon Crutchfield for her helpful editing and much needed queries on the rough draft of the manuscript.

A number of colleagues have provided encouragement and inspiration. I would like to express my gratitude to my former colleagues at Central Michigan University for their words of wisdom, critical discussions, and commitment to social justice. In particular, I would like to acknowledge Athena McLean, Angela Haddad, Gil Muşolf, Larry Tifft, Alice Littlefield, Larry Reynolds, Blaine Stevenson, Harry Mika, and Brigitte Bechtold. I would like to express appreciation to my colleagues at Eastern Michigan University, especially Kristine Ajrouch, Gregg Barak, Marilyn Horace-Moore, Paul Leighton, and Barbara Richardson. My appreciation is always extended to all of the critical and feminist criminologists who have conducted invaluable research in the area of gender, crime, and the criminal "justice" system and whose work we have benefited from.

I wish to thank Colleen Anne Dell for her constructive criticism of the original book proposal, and Peter Manning and Ray Morris for their support and encouragement over the years. I would also like to thank Robert Holkeboer and the graduate school at Eastern Michigan University for a sabbatical leave in 2007 that provided time away from teaching in order to write the book. Special thanks to my graduate assistant, Jess Klein, for her timely searches, e-mails, and phone calls, and for her great attitude and her inspirational music. Let's hear it for the "Fallsway Downs!" Also, many thanks to my graduate assistant, Amanda Reynolds, who helped retrieve numerous articles and books. Also, to all the members of Empowering Women Everywhere, I would like to acknowledge their commitment to making the world a safer place for all women and I thank them for all the wonderful memories. I will never forget our trips to New York City and Washington, DC, and our weekly discussion sessions. A special thanks to Courtney Gillaspy and Darlene Rosteck—"EWE Grrrrrls Rock!"

To my friends—my personal support system—who have been with me since "way back," I want to thank them for their love and loyalty. I consider myself privileged to have this sense of history with so many incredible women whose friendships are irreplaceable. I extend much gratitude to Afrodite Triantafillou, Julia Easson-Meyer, Shawna Findlay-Thompson, Frances Nicitopoulos, Vivian Silverson, Mari Bardavilias, and to the late Robynne Neugebauer, who I miss dearly. Robynne's love, generosity, and gentle spirit will never be forgotten and I am a better person for having known her. Her scholarship and commitment to social justice and policing, and to eradicating gender, race, and class inequalities were, and continue to be, inspirational. She was like a sister to me and I wish we could have had the opportunity to write this book together. I am humbled by her compassion, honesty, and activism, and she has motivated me to press on and work for change, despite the disappointments along the way. Also, I thank Christopher Downer for being such a dear, compassionate, and resourceful friend and for always displaying wit and charisma like no other. Furthermore, my deepest gratitude I extend to Becky, Alan, and Laura Turanski for their love and support and for becoming part of our family and welcoming us into theirs.

My primary debt is owed to my parents, Demetre and Rena Corsianos, for their love, support, and encouragement over the years and for teaching me to embrace life and all of its challenges and to never give up. Without them I would not be where I am today. As immigrants to Canada, they worked hard to provide for their family and give their children the opportunities they never had. I am so proud and privileged to have been raised by them and I thank them for everything! I am grateful to my brother George for always being there for me, for our frequent talks that always make me laugh, and for bringing love and a sense of peace to my life. I am also thankful to my brother Terry for his love and unconditional support and for the many wonderful memories.

As for my strongest supporter, Spiro Vlahos, I consider myself very lucky to have met him, and to have experienced the incredible journey we have had together. I thank him for being my most constant and loving supporter and for persevering alongside of me as I completed this project amidst giving birth to our second child. I am grateful for his patience, humour, love, and his commitment to our family and to social justice in the world. To my children, Rena and Demetre, I thank them for making Mummy laugh on a daily basis, for being so darn cute, and for questioning "authority" every chance they get!

Marilyn Corsianos

Preface

The research on gender and policing has not experienced a significant increase in the academic world; in other words, most policing research continues to ignore gender from its analysis. Some policing scholars have noted that the reason for excluding gender is because women continue to make up a small number of sworn officers in both Canada and the United States. This response is disappointing, but certainly not surprising. To date, only a handful of academic books have focused on the relationship between gender and policing globally, let alone within a North American context. This book, on the other hand, offers a feminist critical analysis of gender and policing as it relates to the US and Canada. It examines the experiences of women in the field of policing and critically examines the interconnectedness of the police organizational structure, culture, history, and politics, as well as its socio-economic order and dominant ideologies. Furthermore, it enhances the body of knowledge on gender and policing by bridging the gap between theory and practice, and by using different approaches to present information and engage readers.

This book is divided into eight chapters. Chapter 1 examines the early roles of women officers, beginning in the early 1900s in both Canada and the US, and evaluates the impact that the first phase of the women's movement had on the creation of the "policewomen" positions and their particular roles. It also discusses the legal changes that followed with the second "wave" of the feminist movement and its effects on women and policing.

Chapter 2 details the importance of feminist inquiries into criminological knowledge and the profound contributions feminist studies have made to our understanding of gender and criminology. It also highlights some of the early work that focused initially on female offenders and female victims of crime, and subsequently on women working as criminal justice agents such as the police. Chapter 3 introduces the six main feminist theories (liberal, socialist, Marxist, radical, antiracist/multiracial, and postmodern) and provides suggestions on how to change the current problems relating to gender and policing from each of the different theoretical frameworks. The point of this exercise is to offer readers some concrete examples of the possibilities for change and encourage readers to think through some of their implications.

Chapter 4 evaluates the different forces that affect/influence and to a larger extent define police culture. The sociology of police culture cannot be separated from an analysis of the dominant ideologies that produce and reproduce gender inequalities, as well as other inequalities including race/ethnicity, class, and sexual orientation. Expanding our understanding of the different dynamics of the police culture helps us gain a better understanding of particular types of "knowledge"; for example, officers' perceptions of their roles as police officers; the types of policing styles that are promoted within policing circles; what constitutes "criminality," etc. Chapter 5 introduces readers to the literature on "community policing" (CP), presents arguments made by both its supporters and opponents, and identifies problems with particular CP approaches. The second part of the chapter discusses some of the gendered experiences that officers are confronted with under the current crime control model (despite some organizational attempts at CP) and critically explores the possibility of using CP initiatives as feminist "tools" to encourage social and structural changes. A key question addressed is whether we can encourage emancipatory politics within policing, specifically freedom from sexist ideologies using the CP model.

The first part of Chapter 6 presents readers with a more descriptive account of the organizational structure, operational systems, and culture of detective units in Canada. This is intended to help readers gain a better understanding of detective work, and to also better evaluate the information presented in the second part, which addresses the gendered differences relating to detectives' discretionary powers and decision-making. The purpose of Chapter 7 is to engage in a theoretical exercise to demonstrate how the category "women" or "woman" ensures shared experiences of "oppression" for all female officers, regardless of whether individual female officers identify them as such, and regardless of the different social categories they may represent (e.g., race, ethnicity, sexual orientation, age, etc.). Female officers do not necessarily have the exact same experiences, nor are they all "oppressed" in the same way, but they share experiences of oppression. An experience can still be considered "oppressive" even if not recognized by the individual as such because there are accompanying effects to that oppression.

The last chapter, Chapter 8, addresses the importance of feminist methods in identifying exclusionary practices in the production of "knowledge" as they relate to policing, as well as the need for action research that aims to make a positive difference in the lives of many people.

CHAPTER 1

The History of Women in Policing in the United States and Canada

This chapter begins with a brief history of the first "wave" of the women's movement during the mid-1800s to the early 1900s, followed by a closer look at the relationship between the movement and the early women in policing in both the United States and Canada. The changes in women's participation in law enforcement following this period are also discussed and evaluated in relation to the second "wave"/phase of the women's movement. It is important to study the history of particular organizations such as the police in order to gain a better understanding of the purpose and operation of policing systems today. As pointed out by Foucault (1977), one must study the history of particular social phenomena in order to be able to write "the history of the present." Gaining insight into the history of various aspects of policing can shed some light onto current police practices and social experiences and can provide direction on how to address current challenges and inequities.

The First Wave of the Women's Movement

In Western societies, it is generally agreed that the women's movement, also referred to as the feminist movement, has experienced two distinct phases, the first taking place between the mid-1800s to early 1900s, and the second starting in the 1960s. More recently, some writers and academics have referred to the feminist/women's movement from 1980 to the present as the third "wave" of the feminist/women's movement (Denfield, 1996; Heywood and Drake, 1997; Walter, 1999).

There have been different forms of resistance by individual women against gender discrimination over the centuries, but beginning in the mid-1800s, there was noticeable organized action taking place. Women began to work collectively and protest against exclusionary and discriminatory practices and significant changes were being made. It was defined as a "movement" due to the level of action and change. Efforts were focused on changing marriage and property laws, improving working conditions, and gaining access to education and politics. As women lacked political clout, time and energy were initially dedicated to obtaining the right to vote.

It is also generally agreed that the Seneca Falls Convention in New York in 1848 marked the beginning of the women's movement in the US. The movement was partly born of the abolitionist movement, since women who attended the World Anti-Slavery Convention in London in 1840 were not allowed to vote. American women began to organize and work collectively partly in response to their exclusion from the anti-slavery meeting. They realized that without the power to vote, they lacked political clout to accomplish particular goals and enact change. After the American Civil War, the movement split over a disagreement as to whether to concentrate efforts on suffrage. In 1890 women's organizations regrouped and collectively concentrated their initial efforts on the right to vote.

The women's movement in Canada, on the other hand, was influenced by both the US and British movements. Many Canadian women attended the Seneca Falls Convention and subsequently started to form associations and exchange ideas with suffragettes and organizations in both the US and Britain. These events contributed to the beginning of the suffrage movement in Canada, which is said to be marked by the founding of the Toronto Women's Literary Club in 1876 by Emily Stowe. Its name was strategically chosen to avoid public criticism, but was later, more appropriately, renamed the Women's Suffrage Association (Wilson, 1996).

This period between the late 1800s and the early 1920s is referred to by historians as the social reform era, or the social purity reform movement because it sought to respond to the vast changes brought about by industrialization and urbanization. The Industrial Revolution attracted a huge influx of immigrants and people from rural areas to the urban centres to find employment predominantly in the vast array of factories. The explosion in population lead to a series of social problems that included increased criminal activity, alcoholism, overcrowded streets, homelessness, pollution, and poor hygiene and sanitation issues (Macionis, 2005).

As a result, many women's organizations were created to address these issues and commit to reform. According to Wilson (1996), some focused their efforts on preparing young single women for employment while at the same time ensuring that "traditional values" were preserved; some focused on improving working conditions for women and children and/or eliminating child labour; and others concentrated their efforts on health and welfare reforms. For Bashevkin (1985: 5), "Organized pressure for the vote was thus allied with a broader reformist response to the rapid pace of industrialization, urbanization and the perceived decline of traditional values."

Many of the women who participated in the reform movements represented the middle and upper classes. The prevailing ideology was that women were morally superior to men, and women's "proper" roles were viewed as "nurturing," "pure," "morally conservative," and "civilized." It was believed that this role division was the result of innate differences between the sexes. Women were responsible for ensuring family stability and providing moral guidance to family members (Ginzberg, 1990). Thus, many economically privileged women grew increasingly concerned with the variety of "dangers" that were associated with the growing industrialized cities. All single women searching for employment in blue-collar, white-collar, or domestic work were seen as vulnerable and thus posed a serious threat to the preservation of "traditional appropriate feminine" behaviour and the "traditional family unit" (Myers, 1995).

Women representing racial minority groups and immigrant women also participated in the women's movement during this period. Working-class women and recently employed immigrant women took part in suffrage parades to protest against the current working conditions, their inability to vote, and other restrictive laws (Schrom, 1980). Similar to the clubs started by American women of European descent (Gere and Robbins, 1996), African-American women formed organizations and fought against sex and racial discrimination (McKinley-Floyd, 1998; Meis Knupfer, 1996). Similarly, African-Canadian women organized against gender, race, and class oppression. In 1878 they formed the Women's Home Missionary Society, and in 1882, the Ladies' Union Aid Society was established. Other examples included the Coloured Women's Club in Montreal in 1902. The majority of these organizations were local, but, in 1951, the Canadian Negro Women's Club was started in Toronto, which sponsored the Congress of Black Women with chapters all across Canada (Hamilton, 1993).

The fight for the vote was tied to the fight to preserve "traditional values." The early feminists, often referred to as the "maternal feminists," believed that the right to vote would provide them with the necessary political voice to preserve the "separate spheres" of women and men. Canadian women finally won the right to vote at the federal level in 1918 (Wilson, 1996), and in the US women were able to vote in 1920 with the Nineteenth Amendment to the Constitution (Macionis, 2005). However, gaining the right to vote was only one small step towards achieving gender equality. Multiple structural, systemic, and ideological barriers to gender equality remained. Many battles had to be fought and continue to be fought, including several in the area of policing.

Introduction to Policing

Sir Robert Peel is recognized for his success in passing the Metropolitan Police Act in 1829 in London, England, when he served as Home Secretary, leading to the creation of the first "modern police force." According to Peel, the purpose of the police was to enforce the laws, maintain peace, and to ensure individual liberties in the process. For Peel, the police were the public and the public were the police; the police at that time being only members of the public who were paid to conduct duties that were incumbent on every citizen in the interests of community welfare (Langworthy and Travis III, 2003). The English policing system significantly influenced the development of police agencies in both Canada and the US. One cannot say, however, that, since its inception in either of the three countries, the "police are the public." This is evident in the types of behaviours and groups of people that are disproportionately policed (Reiman, 2007; Websdale, 2001; Forcese, 1999; Neugebauer, 1999; Russell, 1998; Visano, 1998; Mann, 1995; Arnold, 1995), and in the gender, race, ethnic and class composition of the police officers themselves (Schulz, 2004b; Langworthy and Travis III, 2003; National Center for Women and Policing, 2003; Forcese, 1999). With regard to gender specifically, the public has consisted of approximately equal numbers of women and men, but the same cannot be said about police organizations. Women started to work as police officers in the early 1900s, but their numbers were disproportionately low. Women were certainly not represented equally in police agencies and their experiences were gendered in many different ways.

History of Women in Policing in the United States: The First Wave
In the early nineteenth century in the United States, women were initially employed in the criminal justice field as prison and jail matrons working with women and girls. They were primarily upper-middle-class women, and by the 1880s, they had succeeded in creating a new position for women in the criminal justice system—the police matron. The police matron was initially assigned to work with female prisoners and women and children who had been arrested by the police.

However, the position of "policewoman" would be introduced later. In fact, the identity of the first woman to be sworn in as a police officer is debatable. In most criminological literature, Alice Stebbins Wells is listed as the first female officer in the US in 1910 (Feinman, 1986; Hale and Bennett, 1995; Segrave, 1995). She was appointed at the rank of detective by the Los Angeles Police Department, which officially gave her the classification of "policewoman" (Van Wormer and Bartollas, 2000).

However, other sources list Portland's Lola Greene Baldwin as America's first policewoman in 1908. Baldwin was sworn in to "perform police service" for the city of Portland, Oregon. She became the first woman hired by an American municipality to carry out law enforcement duties (Myers, 1995). The role of "policewoman," however, was very different from that of "policeman" as will be discussed below. Interestingly, in the case of Baldwin, her work as a policewoman was not the result of any proactive efforts on the part of the Portland police organization. Rather, "she had forged the role herself and, with the aid of women's organizations and male sympathizers, successfully convinced authorities that it was a necessary adjunct to Rose City policing" (Myers, 1995: 1).

Moreover, the first African-American woman appointed to policing was Georgia Ann Robinson. In 1915 a delegation of African-American women petitioned Mayor Charles Sebastian and Chief of Police Clarence Snively to hire black female officers to serve the black community. Similar to white female activists, black female activists were concerned about various "moral issues," including the sexual exploitation of

Alice Stebbins Wells: The First Woman Sworn in as a "Policewoman"

Alice Stebbins Wells was appointed as a "policewoman" at the age of 37 by the Los Angeles Police Department (LAPD). She petitioned the city's Police Commission to become the first policewoman, and the commission passed the ordinance under Mayor George Alexander. She was sworn in on September 12, 1910.

Her duties were to work with women and juveniles and to investigate the social conditions that led some women and children to commit crime. Wells never carried a firearm and mostly worked with the juvenile and crime prevention units. She organized the International Association of Police Women and the Women's Peace Officer Association in California in 1913. By 1916, 20 states had women working as "policewomen" and Wells was instrumental in persuading the University of California to offer the first-ever training class for policewomen.

Wells retired from the LAPD in 1945 at the age of 72, following 35 years of service. She passed away in 1957 at the age of 84 (Los Angeles Police Historical Society; Appier, 1998).

Lola Greene Baldwin: The First Woman Sworn in to "Perform Police Service"

Lola Greene Baldwin was sworn in "to perform police service" for the city of Portland, Oregon, on April 1, 1908. Many consider her the first policewoman in the US since she was the first woman hired by an American municipality to carry out regular law enforcement duties. In 1905, during the Lewis and Clark Exposition, she was hired by the Portland Travelers' Aid Society to ensure the safety of women and juveniles since these groups were perceived as being "vulnerable." Her work was recognized by the mayor, the city council, and the police chief and she ultimately secured a permanent position with the Portland Police Bureau.

In 1908 she passed a specialized "female detective" civil service exam and was then hired to serve as the "Superintendent of the Women's Auxiliary to the Police Department for the Protection of Girls" (later known as the Women's Protective Division). Her duties emphasized crime prevention and social work and she primarily worked with women and children. She did not wear a police uniform, or carry a firearm. On May 1, 1922, Baldwin resigned at the age of 62 after serving for 17 years, 14 of them as a paid policewoman. She passed away in 1957 at the age of 97 (Myers, 1995).

Photo Source: Photo issued by Portland Police Historical Society, WPD Collection.

Georgia Ann Robinson: The First African-American Woman Sworn in as "Policewoman"

In 1919 Georgia Ann Robinson became the "first black policewoman" in the US. She was initially hired by the LAPD as a matron after meeting all of the qualifications required to become a policewoman, which were as follows: "Policewomen" were expected to be 30 to 44 years of age; be married and preferably with children; hold a college education in teaching, nursing, or sociology; and pass a civil service exam. The requirements for women were much higher than those set for policemen.

Policewomen were considered civilian employees and they did not wear uniforms. Thus, Robinson received no formal training and no pay. However, three years later, on June 10, 1919, Robinson was appointed as a "regular policewoman" with pay and was later assigned to work on juvenile and homicide cases. She was so committed to her work that she frequently brought young girls who had no place to stay to her home, and she helped create the Sojourner Truth Home for destitute women and girls.

Robinson retired from the police department in 1929, after 13 years of service. However, she continued to work with women at the Sojourner Truth Home, and with Dr. Claude Hudson on several civic projects, including the desegregation of both the local beaches and the hiring practices in the Los Angeles public schools. Robinson passed away in 1961 at the age of 82 (Ryan, "In Memory of Georgia Ann Robinson").

their young girls. "For black women, however, the prevalence of racist myths regarding black female sexuality gave the issue of sexual exploitation a special urgency" (Appier, 1998: 129). The activism of these women in Los Angeles during this time played a key role in the hiring of Robinson (Appier, 1998), who was appointed as a matron to the LAPD in 1916, and became a police officer in 1919, working in the same department (Schulz, 1995).

A. Proactive and Preventive Policing

Beginning in the late nineteenth and early twentieth centuries, female officers were hired to work with women and children and were paid less than their male counterparts. These female officers represented what many historians refer to as the social purity reform movement that sought to protect police women's "social morality." Women were generally viewed as nurturing, pure, morally conservative, and civilized. Upper- and middle-class women were concerned with the "inappropriate" and "unfeminine" behaviour of many of the poor women who moved to large cities across the US to find jobs, and felt it was their duty to offer moral guidance and act as "municipal mothers" to those whose lifestyles they believed needed to change (Ginzberg, 1990).

Although policewomen primarily policed poor women and girls, all females of all ages and classes were perceived to be vulnerable in large industrialized cities, regardless of whether they worked in blue-collar, white-collar, or domestic jobs. Many employed women were unmarried and had limited skills. Thus, policewomen took on the role of municipal mothers and "urban reformers," keeping a "watchful eye" over them (Myers, 1995). Their efforts were primarily focused on proactive and preventive policing, but they also conducted interviews with female suspects and made sentencing recommendations (Martin and Jurik, 2007). Additionally, these women offered assistance to girls and women working in places that were illegal and/or perceived to be improper, such as dance halls, saloons, and brothels. They helped them to find paid work that was reflective of "proper" women's domestic roles and "femininity," as well as safe housing away from illegal operations (Myers, 1995).

As noted above, the industrialization of cities during this period brought significant increases in population, pollution, competition for jobs, alcoholism, crime, and a number of other social problems. The high influx of immigrants produced anxiety for many of those representing the middle and upper classes, who blamed the former for various societal problems (Langworthy and Travis III, 2003), including the spread of venereal diseases, and perceived them as "immoral" and "criminal" (Myers, 1995).

The first "wave" of the women's movement shaped and influenced the roles of early policewomen. The climate of "social hygiene" was also an important force. During the early twentieth century in the US, several concerns were identified by physicians and government, and there was an urgency to control them in order to promote "cleanness," "morality," and "physical safety." Thus, efforts were focused on sanitation and public health programs, venereal disease control, and vice and prostitution abatement. The threat of venereal disease was a sign of social degeneration for the self-defined "moral reformers," who called for the promotion of sexual abstinence for both sexes. Prostitution, for instance, was defined as a public health problem, which empowered the police to concentrate their resources on fighting urban vice. Moreover, the moral reformers viewed homosexuality as a sign of social degeneration. Early policewomen tried to address alternatives to incarceration and address the overcrowding of jail facilities after reports of lesbian activity among incarcerated females became public (Myers, 1995).

The policing of the female sexual delinquent became the priority, as did female-to-female preventive solutions. Criminological research shows the overwhelming preoccupation during this time with policing the sexuality of girls and women (Tappan, 1947; Vedder and Somerville, 1970; Shelden, 1981; Chesney-Lind and Rodriguez, 1983; Brenzel, 1983; Odem and Schlossman, 1991; Chesney-Lind, 1995; Chesney-Lind and Shelden, 2004; Balfour and Comack, 2006). The criminal justice system aimed to enforce girls' conformity to sexual norms, while at the same time the behaviour that was condemned in girls was supported in boys (Chesney-Lind and Shelden, 2004; Chesney-Lind, 1995). The label of "sexual delinquent" was attached to women and/or girls for engaging in many different types of behaviour that included choices of dress, use of language, violating curfews, being a runaway, and engaging in sexual intercourse. As Myers (1995: 76) states:

> Although some delinquent girls literally were sex offenders, others simply offended their sex. Any outward signs of "precocious sexuality" rebuked traditional female moral standards ... As government became involved in reform to clean up the city, it was natural that the policewoman, with her determined mission of keeping young women from prostitution and related vice, would play an enhanced role.

Women who were labelled as sexual deviants by the criminal justice system, and women who were convicted of other types of crimes were often viewed as fallen women, unnatural, unfeminine, evil and/or mentally or socially ill (Balfour and Comack, 2006; Dell, 1999; Klein, 1973; Morris, 1988; Smart, 1976). Moreover, the use of I.Q. tests on inmates by biological determinists did not help matters. The low scores of female sexual delinquents were perceived as "evidence" of their being "mentally defective" and "feeble minded": "Even girls who had not yet committed moral offenses could be institutionalized as a protective measure. On the basis of a mere tendency to immorality, courts could place females under indeterminate or permanent custodial care" (Myers, 1995: 78). The behaviour of women and girls was frequently medicalized and assumed to be the result of heredity, hormones, premenstrual syndrome and/or mental illness (Lloyd, 1995; Ogle, Maier-Katkin, and Bernard, 1995; Singer et al., 1995; Walklate, 1995; Maden, Swinton, and Gunn, 1994; Ussher, 1992; Kendall, 1991).

Emphasis was placed on proactive policing in order to try and prevent many women and girls from committing crimes and/or becoming victims of crimes, particularly "sex crimes," and from being "sexually exploited." This meant that policing efforts were concentrated in public spaces, such as restaurants, hotels, amusement parks, massage parlors, theatres, and concert halls. The social climate was changing to the point where one could frequently find single men and women in public spaces participating together in a variety of leisurely activities. Places that encouraged the "mixing of the sexes" were policed closely by the municipal mothers, as were areas that encouraged "immoral dress." For instance, public swimming pools and dance halls were identified as areas where inappropriate clothing was often worn. In addition, policewomen monitored local help-wanted ads that offered large wages to women and girls for questionable employment; found temporary shelter for those in need of housing; dealt with creditors to negotiate small payments from debtors in order to protect women and girls from various forms of coercion; helped women and girls enroll in classes (e.g., "beauty school," and sewing and typing classes) in order to learn needed skills to find "legitimate" employment; and worked to collect money from delinquent employers who failed to pay their female employees on time and/or the amount agreed upon. In the case of Portland, Oregon, Baldwin frequently advertised her office location and phone number in the "Help Wanted" section offering free employment advice (Myers, 1995: 33).

B. Differences between American "Policewomen" and "Policemen": The First Wave
Policewomen, such as Baldwin, "embodied the American woman's transition from Victorian seclusion to post-Victorian acceptance as a traditionalist, nurturing, morally conservative activist in the public sphere" (Myers, 1995: 3). Moreover, they not only represented the upper-middle class in comparison to men but were more educated than their male counterparts. Typically, policewomen were required to have a college education, whereas policemen overwhelmingly represented the working class (Martin and Jurik, 2007). Similarly, some African-American women who had comparable socio-economic backgrounds as their white female counterparts were hired in large cities to work with African-American women and girls. They were often social workers, teachers, or ministers' wives and therefore were perceived as individuals with "status" in their communities (Schulz, 2004a).

The early women in the field formed two professional organizations that set high entry standards and ongoing training far in excess of male officers' requirements. They did not view themselves as female versions of policemen. Rather, they considered the male officers as being inferior, given their distinct differences in class and education. However, policewomen chose to use the title "police" in order to ensure their legal authority and the cooperation of male officers (Schulz, 2004a).

Most of the women were paid less than male officers, but there were exceptions. Baldwin, for instance, served as a female detective but was given the official title of

Superintendent of the Women's Auxiliary to the Police Department for the Protection of Girls. The police committee recommended a salary of $150 per month for the female detective. Since specific divisions within the department were headed by officers at the rank of captain or above, the committee offered her this rate of pay, which was $35 more than that of a male detective (Myers, 1995).

Not surprisingly, policewomen's supporters and peers were not male police officers, but rather social workers, feminists, temperance leaders, and members of women's civic clubs. In 1915 the International Association of Policewomen (IAP) was established to provide support for policewomen and direction for the future of women in policing. IAP was modelled after and affiliated with the National Conference of Charities and Correction (later the National Conference of Social Work). The International Association of Women Police (IAWP) was later formed in 1956, but was not closely aligned with social work organizations as was the previous IAP (Schulz, 2004a; 2004b).

Moreover, policewomen encountered different physical standards compared to the men. As was mentioned earlier, they often did not wear uniforms or carry guns (Martin and Jurik, 2007). They were strongly opposed to uniforms and for those who were permitted to carry guns, most chose not to arm themselves (Schulz, 2004a). Baldwin was opposed to wearing a uniform because she felt it would serve to alienate and deter women and girls from seeking police assistance. She also kept her badge hidden in her purse. Her commitment to this manner of dressing influenced women on the Portland Police Department to continue their work in plain clothes until 1972, 50 years after Baldwin's retirement (Myers, 1995).

To avoid tension and opposition from male officers, leaders of the policewomen's movement in the US created Women's Bureaus that were separated administratively, and sometimes physically, from the rest of the police department (Martin and Jurik, 2007). Others set up their offices away from the police department in the hopes of making their services more accessible to women and girls by seeming less intimidating (Myers, 1995).

C. Changes in the Number of Women in Policing in the US

From 1910 to 1917, there were approximately 125 policewomen employed in about 30 cities across the US (Schulz, 2004a; 2004b). By 1929 there were almost 600 women working as policewomen serving 150 to 175 cities (Rockwood and Street, 1932). However, between 1929 and 1931, the numbers started to decrease and by 1940, there were no more than 500 policewomen (Schulz, 2004a; 2004b).The 1930s was also the decade where the image of the police as crime fighters began to be promoted, a direct contrast to the image of policewomen as social workers.

Following World War II, in the late 1940s, there was a shift in the representation of women entering policing; this group of women often differed in their socio-economic backgrounds and ideological beliefs. They were middle-class careerists, not upper-class "reformers" interested in "saving" individuals and preserving "morality" (Schulz, 2004a). They continued to be more educated and were wealthier in comparison to male officers, but were more similar to policemen than their predecessors. Also, they were not hired during World War II to replace men who were away fighting in the war. Unlike the high number of women who gained entry into previously male-dominated occupations, women's gender-specific roles in policing were not altered by the war and therefore women continued to be hired to fulfill traditional policewomen's roles (Schulz, 2004a). These groups of women were interested in integration and serving in a variety of different units. However, despite this, the number of females recruited was small and few policewomen were hired to work in detective units, vice, or crime lab units. Most were hired to work with juveniles or to perform secretarial duties (Martin and Jurik, 2007). By 1950 there were approximately 2,500 publicly employed policewomen (US Census Bureau, 1950), and by 1960 the number had increased to 5,617 (Schultz, 1995), which meant that they comprised less than 1 per cent of the total sworn personnel in the country (Martin and Jurik, 2007).

D. American Women in Top Command Positions: The First Wave

Few women led police departments in the US prior to the 1970s. To date, three can be confirmed as having served as chiefs. One of these women was Lydia Overturf who was appointed by the mayor of Buckner, Illinois, to serve as police chief around 1920. Buckner was a very small, poor mining community. Common complaints from locals related to gambling, alcoholism, and bar fights. Overturf was appointed to deal with these problems. She was described as a "tough" woman who "marched into taverns" to settle disturbances at all hours of the day and night, and kept the jail full (Schulz, 2004b). She was a poor woman who raised her children on her own. She also ran a small boarding house where many travelling salesmen stayed and where locals went for family-style dinners. According to a local historian, Overturf's work attracted some national attention. On one occasion, she organized a group of people to track down gambling bandits, but the pursuit turned into a wild chase and shootout that was subsequently reported by the *New York Times* (Schulz, 2004b).

The second known woman to head a US police department prior to the 1970s was Kate Shelley Wilder. She served as police commissioner of Fargo, North Dakota, from 1919 to 1921. Unlike Overturf, Wilder was a wealthy woman who came from a prominent family, was well-educated, and was married to an attorney. She was also actively involved in the reform movement. As an early leader of the North Dakota League of Women Voters, she took part in women's suffrage campaigns and was an active member of several civic and women's groups. For instance, she was a member of the Florence Crittenden Circle and served on the national board of directors for the Woman's Christian Temperance Union (WCTU) (Schulz, 2004b).

Both these groups were early and active supporters of policewomen. In 1909, members of the Grand Forks chapter of the Crittenden Circle, concerned over conditions involving transient men and local women, had advocated giving women police powers to stem female delinquency. In May 1910, the Crittenden Circle successfully lobbied the city council to pass an ordinance creating a position for a police matron. This was four months before the Los Angeles Police Department appointed Alice Stebbins Wells as the first woman in the United States to be called a policewoman. By 1915, Fargo also employed a policewoman, making it and Grand Forks among the smallest of the nation's towns to employ women in their police departments (Schulz, 2004b: 47).

Wilder fought for women's suffrage and for women's participation in public institutions such as policing. However, she, like the "maternal feminists" of the period, supported separate institutions for women where policewomen solely could provide policing and social work services to other women and children.

The third woman to be in charge of a police department prior to the 1970s was Florence Grall. However, she played a limited role in actually leading the agency. She was appointed safety director of Lorain, Ohio, in 1926 by the mayor who happened to be her husband. She was an interim replacement who was given the task of hearing charges against a lieutenant whom the mayor wanted to remove (Schulz, 2004b).

First Women Police Chiefs in the US

1919-1921   Kate Shelley Wilder becomes the police commissioner of Fargo, North Dakota

1920-1921   Lydia Overturf is appointed chief of police of Buckner, Illinois

1926   Florence Grall is appointed safety director of Lorain, Ohio

The first wave of the feminist movement influenced the creation of specific gendered roles for American women in policing. In Canada similar demands were made and met with respect to the creation of policewomen positions during this time.

History of Women in Policing in Canada: The First Wave
The literature on the history of Canadian women police is scarce. Some information can be found in police departments' literature describing their histories; police museums; and in police periodicals such as the *OPP Review* and the *RCMP Gazette*. It is important to note that Canada's population is about 10 per cent that of the US, but the size of the country is comparable. Therefore, the sparse population in relation to the country's size and recent history has meant that women's participation in the feminist movement and women's advancement in policing have not been as noticeable as that of American women. Moreover, there are significantly fewer

Canadian academics in the field to conduct the necessary research. As a result, much work remains to be done in this area.

From what we know to date, the first woman recognized for taking on policing duties in Canada was an African-American woman named Rose Fortune. She was born into slavery in Virginia in 1774 during the American Revolutionary War. In 1783 she and her family escaped to New York City and then to Canada where they settled in the Annapolis Valley in Nova Scotia. Fortune's parents were black Loyalists who joined the British Army during the American Revolution in the hopes of finding freedom (*The Canadian Encyclopedia: Historica*, 2007).

However, earning a living was not easy for black Loyalists. Over time, Fortune started her own business transporting the luggage of ship passengers to their homes or hotels using a wheelbarrow. Her entrepreneurial efforts became very lucrative and she replaced her wheelbarrows with horse-drawn wagons. She also set up a "wake-up call" service for travellers staying at hotels to ensure that they did not miss their ship. Fortune appointed herself as the police department of Annapolis Royal and maintained order at the wharves and surrounding areas by imposing and enforcing curfews. As a result, many consider her "the first policewoman" in Canada. She achieved a great deal of success in both her entrepreneurial pursuits and in her policing duties before her death in 1864 at the age of 90 (*The Canadian Encyclopedia: Historica*, 2007; Nova Scotia Records and Archives Management, 2007).

Rose Fortune
Image issued by Nova Scotia
Records and Archives Management.

The first Canadian woman to officially hold the title of "police matron" was Mrs. Whiddon, as she was referred to, with the Toronto police in 1887. Police matrons had to be 25 to 30 years of age and, like their American counterparts, were well-educated (Toronto Police, 2007) and were initially assigned to work with female prisoners and women and children who had been arrested by the police. Similar to the American police matrons, they were expected to serve as moral regulators, policing social arenas that were perceived as dangerous to society generally, and to women more specifically.

Canadian women did not serve as policewomen until the 1910s. The first women to serve in this capacity were Lurancy Harris and Minnie Miller in Vancouver, British Columbia, in 1912, and Annie Jackson in Edmonton, Alberta, also in 1912 (Moore, 1997). In 1913 the Toronto Police Department hired its first two female officers, Mary Minty and Margaret Leavitt. After their retirement in 1919, three other women were hired, and in 1921, another two were appointed. By 1933 policewomen in Toronto became an integral part of the Morality Bureau and worked undercover in criminal investigations (Toronto Police, 2007).

Lurancy D. Harris and Minnie Miller: The First Women in Canada Sworn in as "Policewomen"
In 1912 Lurancy D. Harris and Minnie Miller were hired as the first policewomen in Canada. They were sworn in with "full police powers" and assigned to work with Vancouver, British Columbia's detective department at the rank of Fourth Class Constable. Vancouver created a Women's Division for the purpose of rendering "assistance to young girls and women in the city." This was largely the result of local mission and church groups who were concerned with the growing number of women who were both perpetrators and victims of crime, especially in the area of vice. Both Harris and Miller were proactive in patrolling dance halls, pool halls, parks, beaches, cabarets, and "any areas of amusement where women might get into trouble" (Mathieson, 2005: 2).

Harris received much publicity when working on her first "big case" involving Lorena Mathews. Mathews had fled from Oklahoma to Alberta and then to Vancouver after being accused of murdering her husband. She was arrested in Vancouver and Constable Harris was assigned to escort her back to Oklahoma to face charges. After Harris's return to Vancouver, she was promoted to sergeant and given authority over the Women's Division. She retired 17 years later at the rank of inspector (Mathieson, 2005).

Photo Source: Pictures issued by the Vancouver Police Museum.

Lilian Clerihew became the first policewoman in Montreal in 1915. Clerihew was hired to do "protective-preventive work with women and girls." Her hiring was the direct result of the efforts of the Montreal Local Council of Women, who lobbied the mayor, the city council, and the chief of police, Campeau. Members of the Council of Women convinced local politicians, as well as the chief, that women and girls required the careful nurturing attention of women officers. In 1917 they joined forces with the women's auxiliary of the local Federation Nationale Saint-Jean Baptiste and demanded that the municipal administration create an entire unit of policewomen. Their combined efforts led to the hiring of four female sworn officers in Montreal in 1918; two francophone and two anglophone (Moore, 1997). Other cities, including Winnipeg, hired their first female officer during this period. However, the first troop of female officers to be employed at the federal level, by the Royal Canadian Mounted Police, did not occur until 1974. Prior to that, there were some instances where female office staff was recruited for operational police services in undercover work. Women were positioned with undercover male officers in order to make settings and/or transactions appear "real" (Busson, 1997).

Similar to the United States, the push to hire women police during the first wave of the feminist movement came from middle- and upper-class well-educated women who were concerned with enforcing conservative standards of morality and providing protection for women and children. Many of these privileged women represented organizations such as the Council of Women, and the WCTU, and worked to ensure that the roles of the early Canadian policewomen were gender-specific, centred on work with women and children. The Local Council of Women and other local women's groups were involved in the recruitment of women police during these early years starting in 1912.

Members of minority racial groups and immigrants also took part in the women's movement by organizing against gender, race, and/or class oppression, although their efforts did not seem to be focused directly on policing. African-Canadian women organized through churches, benevolent societies, missionary societies, and through overt political organizations (Hamilton, 1993). White and non-white immigrant women also fought against many barriers that included discrimination in the workplace, poor working conditions, racial prejudice, social isolation, and language barriers (Cassidy, Lord, and Mandell, 1998; Frager, 1993; Elliott and Fleras, 1992; Goudar, 1989). The prevailing negative image of the "immigrant woman" was a struggle for many women during the first phase of the movement, but it continues to remain a challenge for many women today. According to Bannerji (1993), the stereotype of the immigrant woman has been that of someone who is passive, inarticulate, dependent, sad-eyed, and who speaks with an unintelligible accent, or "broken" English. According to Iacovetta (1993), immigrant women are often portrayed as victims of "triple oppression"; that is, as being oppressed by labour markets, racist societies, and by their dominating husbands. However, these common images deny these women individual agency—they fail to convey how these women define themselves and come to understand their experiences.

A. Differences between Canadian "Policewomen" and "Policemen": The First Wave

The first wave brought about changes in many areas. Progress was being made, albeit slowly. Thus, "policewomen" similar to the "police matrons" primarily patrolled public spaces that were believed to attract "immoral" behaviour and cause harm to women and juveniles. These public spaces included tourist areas, dance halls, amusement parks, beaches, train stations, carnivals, and theatres. Moreover, they worked with women and children who had been arrested, and made sentencing recommendations. Like their male counterparts, policewomen were also empowered to make arrests and could arrest any person, female or male. One of the first arrests made by a Canadian woman was by Minnie Miller of the Vancouver PD on August 5, 1912. She arrested William Borden for making himself "objectionable" to women at a public beach (Halliday, "Many Minnies Later").

Similar to American policewomen, Canadian policewomen were more educated and tended to be older than their male counterparts. The majority seemed to be in their 40s, since it was considered appropriate for only older women to be subjected to settings where criminal activities took place. They did not wear uniforms, but did carry police badges to identify themselves as police officers. Typically, they had previous paid and/or voluntary social work experience that included working as probation workers or with religious groups (Halliday, "Many Minnies Later").

The number of women in police work gradually increased, but between 1920 and 1945, Canada experienced a decline in its number of policewomen. In Vancouver a decline was reported in the 1920s compared to the decade earlier. In an article published in 1928, Police Constable Evelyn LeSueur stated: "In 1919 there were in our city four women with police powers and one matron on duty in the jail; that quietly and unostentatiously those in authority have so reordered matters that we now have two women constables, and three police matrons without police authority" (12). According to Moore (1997), the decline seemed to be the result of a number of factors that included a continuous rise in the use of the crime control model of policing and the use of force, a decline in the women's movement, the high unemployment rates that existed after World War I, and the continued opposition by male officers to women police.

After World War II, between the 1940s and 1960s, Canada once again experienced a slow but gradual increase in women officers. However, their roles remained comparable to those of policewomen in the early 1900s. For instance, a recruiting brochure issued by the Vancouver Police Department in 1969 provided a list of duties for policewomen that included conducting searches, dealing with female and juvenile suspects, conducting interviews, doing undercover work with the liquor, drug and morality squads, and doing some patrol work with the Special squad (Moore, 1997). Beginning around the 1950s, some police departments, such as the

Toronto police, established women and youth bureaus that were staffed almost entirely by women (Toronto Police, 2007), and up until the 1970s, women continued to be seen as auxiliary personnel (Moore, 1997). In addition, women did not initially receive pay equal to their male counterparts. In Toronto women were not paid the same as men until 1945 (Toronto Police, 2007).

Standard uniforms for women police started to be introduced in the 1940s. In Toronto women started to wear a police uniform in 1945 (Toronto Police, 2007), but it differed from the one worn by male officers, since women's uniforms consisted of a skirt and jacket, and women did not wear the forage cap like the men until 1991 (personal communication with Lenna Bradburn, 2007; Bradburn, 1997). In Vancouver Nancy Hewitt, a former captain in the Women's Army Corps., was hired to serve as an inspector with the Vancouver Police Department in 1946, and she was successful in creating standard uniforms for women the following year (1947). By 1946 there were 15 policewomen working for the Vancouver Police Department. However, it wasn't until 1973, during the second wave of the feminist movement, that the British Columbia Police Commission gave women the right to carry a firearm and be assigned to regular patrol duties like their male counterparts. In Toronto, however, women began to patrol in marked cars much earlier, beginning in 1959 (Toronto Police, 2007).

Undoubtedly, the roles of policemen and policewomen were gendered in both Canadian and American police departments in accordance with what is referred to as the "equal but separate" model. However, changes would soon follow with the second wave of the women's movement.

The Second Wave of the Women's Movement

After the vote was won, women continued to fight for women's rights in other areas, but it was not until the 1960s that the movement regained its earlier collective spirit, strength, and organization. The movement encompassed women across the US and Canada. It became a universal phenomenon and is referred to as the "second wave" of the feminist movement, or women's movement (Wilson, 1996). According to Wilson (1996: 146), there was

> a growing awareness of the contradictions of an affluent society combined with a general radicalism of the 1960s. Postwar optimism turned to skepticism in the 1960s … Economic and demographic changes in the early postwar years created opportunities for women in education and employment. But women faced blatant discrimination at work and received low pay relative to equally qualified and experienced men. There were few social supports for employed mothers, and, at home, women continued to do the bulk of the housework and child care. These contradictions had existed for some time but came to a head in the 1960s when women in all Western countries became increasingly vocal in their criticisms.

The activists were committed to many areas that included equality in the work-place, equal pay, health welfare and reproductive freedom, recognition of the value of traditional work in the home, and challenging the gender stereotypes and traditional definitions of masculinity and femininity (Wilson, 1996; Davies, 1994; Caputi, 1992; Schneider, 1992). In both the US and Canada, the movement was shaped by both feminists representing different organizations, as well as feminists working at the grassroots level (Ferree and Hess, 2000; Adamson, Briskin, and McPhail, 1988; Hess and Ferree, 1987; Freeman, 1984). American organizations such as NOW (National Organization of Women), and the Canadian organization NAC (National Action Committee on the Status of Women) brought together hundreds of women's organizations to fight for various issues. They were able to achieve a political voice via their large membership, level of organization, and by virtue of the media's frequent coverage of their activities. NOW, for instance, focused its attention on legal and economic barriers to women's equality.

Women working through grassroots groups avoided traditional organizational structures and often provided a voice to women who continued to be marginalized, both politically and economically. Through their efforts, significant contributions were made. According to Ferree and Hess (2000), typically few working-class women can participate in organizing via the networks established by educated urban activists. As a result, they, along with racial and ethnic minorities, organize in ways that address the barriers faced by individuals in their communities. Grassroots organizing has served as an effective political tool in the struggle for social change. For example, individual women police officers working at the community level have brought attention to issues of intimidation, sexual harassment, and discrimination in hiring and promotions within police agencies. Issues such as these are often first voiced by women working at the grassroots level and then addressed by women's organizations nationally. Their combined strategic and organized efforts have contributed to changes in legislation that served as a first step to formally opening the doors for women in fields such as policing.

The US and the Second Wave of the Women's Movement
The second wave of the feminist movement led to the integration of women in policing beginning in the late 1960s and 1970s. Changes in legislation were needed to formally open the doors to women, but lawsuits were also necessary given the discrimination and resistance many women faced. Specifically, lawsuits challenging recruitment and promotion practices were needed in order to allow women to begin to gain entrance and create equal opportunities in policing (Martin and Jurik, 2007).

In the US Congress passed the Civil Rights Act in 1964, and the Civil Rights Bill became law in July 1965. Title VII of this legislation dealt with discrimination in employment on the basis of race, colour, religion, national origin, and sex. Following this, in 1968, two women representing the Indianapolis Police Department, Betty

Blankenship and Elizabeth Coffal, became the first women to be appointed to regular police patrol duties as male officers, which included carrying a firearm, wearing a uniform, driving a marked police car, and answering all police-related calls. They patrolled on an equal basis with their male counterparts (National Center for Women and Policing, 2005a; Lord, 1995). In addition, the Law Enforcement Assistance Administration (LEAA) was created under the Omnibus Crime Control and Safe Streets Act of 1968. About 40 per cent of LEAA's funds for the improvement of law enforcement went to local governments and they pushed police agencies to accept equal employment (Schulz, 2004a).

Despite these advances, women continued to face discrimination in hiring. The Civil Rights Act did not apply to municipal governments and therefore many local laws and ordinances continued to prohibit the hiring of women for patrol work. However, in 1972, Title VII was amended to apply to state and municipal governments. The passage of the Equal Opportunity Act of 1972 extended to local police agencies provisions of the Civil Rights Act and enabled the Equal Employment Opportunity Commission to enforce Title VII. This meant that women could now pursue careers as police officers in local and state police agencies. Also, in 1972, Congress passed the Revenue Sharing Act which prohibited discriminatory use of revenue-sharing funds. Additionally, the Crime Control Act of 1973, which amended the Omnibus Crime Control and Safe Streets Act of 1968, stated that LEAA fund recipients were prohibited from discriminating in employment practices unless they wanted to risk losing their federal grants.

Later, the Civil Rights Act of 1991 was passed in response to a number of United States Supreme Court decisions limiting the rights of employees who had sued their employers for discrimination (e.g., *Wards Cove Packing Co. v. Antonio*, 491 U.S. 164). Several changes were made by the act. For instance, Congress amended the statute to expressly recognize that Title VII prohibits "disparate impact discrimination." Employees could prove discrimination by showing that an individual practice or group of practices resulted in a "disparate impact on the basis of race, color, religion, sex, or national origin, and the respondent fails to demonstrate that such practice is required by business necessity." Changes in legislation and lawsuits would have a significant impact on women and policing as will be discussed below.

A. Women Police in the US: From "Policewomen" to "Police Officers": The Second Wave
By the 1960s, the requirement that women in policing have higher education continued yet they could not compete against the men for promotions (Milton, 1972). However, in 1961, two policewomen successfully sued the New York City Police Department after they were prevented from taking the promotion test for sergeant (*Shpritzer v. Lang*, 32, Misc. 2d 693, 1961, modified and affirmed, 234 NYS 2d 1962). Yet, despite being given patrol assignments, the first group of female patrol officers wore skirts and carried their guns in their pocketbooks. They were also expected to

have short hair, or put their hair up under their hats (Martin and Jurik, 2007). By the early 1970s, the average age for female officers in the US was 35, most had university or college training, and 20 per cent were visible minorities. Their roles continued to be limited to working with women and children and working in support roles such as clerical work. Most female officers also continued to have previous work experience in fields such as nursing, social work, and education/teaching (Perlstein, 1971; 1972).

Although women started to be hired to do regular patrol work, they were confronted with resistance that was frequent, organized, and at times, life threatening (Bloch and Anderson, 1974; Martin, 1980; Hunt, 1984). New female hires were often not taught the necessary work-related skills and were often assigned to work alone on dangerous foot patrols, whereas the men were assigned to work in pairs. Women officers also had male colleagues refuse to respond quickly or assist them on calls. They received negative performance evaluations, experienced sexual harassment, and were subjected to an overenforcement of rules (Martin and Jurik, 2007). Also, many police departments had height and weight restrictions and physical fitness standards as prerequisites to hiring applicants that excluded a disproportionate number of women, as well as members of various ethnic and racial groups. Some departments, for instance, required officers to be between five feet seven inches and five feet ten inches tall as a minimum, and many had physical tests that placed a great deal of emphasis on upper body strength (Fyfe et al., 1997).

As a result of these practices, police departments began to be sued for gender and race discrimination. In 1971, in *Griggs v. Duke Power Company* (401 U.S. 424 [1971]), the US Supreme Court ruled that a policy or practice may be discriminatory if it has a disproportionate effect upon a particular group of people and is not job-related or justified by job necessity. Therefore, height, weight, and physical fitness standards that discriminated against women violated Title VII because they did not meet "the test of Griggs." Gradually, almost all police departments eliminated height and weight restrictions and made some changes to their physical tests used for hiring because they disproportionately discriminated against particular groups (Langworthy and Travis III, 2003). Moreover, following legal changes that mandated the hiring of women and men on an equal basis, departments replaced the titles of "policemen" and "policewomen" with "police officer" (Schulz, 2004a).

The Title VII lawsuits launched against police departments frequently resulted in court orders or consent decrees. Consent decrees attempt to remedy the discrimination in hiring and employment practices experienced by women and other minority groups by establishing affirmative action programs. These mandate the hiring and/or promotion of women and persons of colour through the use of quotas and timetables. By 1987 more than 50 per cent of police organizations serving populations larger than 50,000 had implemented affirmative action programs (National Center for Women and Policing, 2003).

It is important to note, however, that in the United States, the Department of

Justice's Civil Rights Division is the primary institution within the federal government that enforces federal statutes prohibiting sex discrimination. The Department of Justice is the nation's largest law enforcement agency and the Civil Rights Division can be considered the country's largest civil rights legal organization. Citizens rely on the division to bring lawsuits against police departments that continue to apply discriminatory practices and negotiate consent decrees. Yet, some of the division's recent decisions have been disappointing. For instance, over the last few years, many consent decrees have expired and are not being renewed at comparable rates. The National Center for Women and Policing (2003) reports that eight consent decrees expired between 1999 and 2002, but only two decrees have been implemented since 1995. Also, from the 247 agencies with more than 100 officers, 40 had been under a consent decree at some point in time, but only about half (22) of those have remained in effect. The Department of Justice is the agency that obtained some of these decrees and therefore can influence police departments to voluntarily agree to extend, change, or renew the decree, or else go to court.

Also disappointing is that the Justice Department failed to support the female plaintiffs in the *Lanning v. Southeastern Pennsylvania Transportation Authority* (SEPTA) case (2000 WL 1790125) by suddenly dropping its support for the lawsuit in 2001 (American Civil Liberties Union [ACLU], 2007). The plaintiffs in the case claimed that SEPTA's requirement that applicants run 1.5 miles in 12 minutes eliminated a disproportionate number of women and that it was not consistent with job performance requirements nor was it a business necessity (National Center for Women and Policing, 2001). Five female applicants sued SEPTA, the law enforcement authority that patrols the subway system in Philadelphia, under Title VII. The plaintiffs alleged that SEPTA's fitness requirements used for hiring constituted "disparate impact discrimination," since very few women were hired to work as transit officers.

Evaluating "disparate impact discrimination" involves a three-step process by the court. As Grossman (2002: 2) explains:

> First, the court asks, Has the plaintiff-employee made out her prima facie (that is, threshold) case, by showing that the application of a facially neutral standard has resulted in a discriminatory hiring pattern? If so, the court asks, Has the employer, who now bears the burden, proven that the particular standard or practice is justified by "business necessity"?
>
> That leads to another important question, though: What constitutes "business necessity"? After Griggs, an increasingly conservative Supreme Court weakened the standard so that almost any job requirement could be justified as a business necessity.
>
> But then, in the Civil Rights Act of 1991, Congress overruled the Supreme Court and went back to the initial, stringent standard, under which "necessity" truly means necessity — not, say, convenience. After that, appellate courts had to re-interpret the standard consistent with Congress' direction.
>
> If the employer has not borne its burden to show "business necessity," the plaintiff wins.

If it has, the court goes on to yet another question: Has the plaintiff proved that the employer rejected an alternative employment practice that would both have a less disparate impact and satisfy its legitimate business interest? If so, the plaintiff still wins.

The Lanning case went to the appeals court twice, in 1999 and again in 2002. The first appellate decision addressed the question of whether SEPTA proved that the fitness test was "consistent with business necessity." The appellate court concluded that employers must prove that set standards (e.g., fitness test standards) enforce a "minimum qualification necessary for successful performance of the job in question in order to survive a disparate impact challenge" (*Lanning v. SEPTA*, 181.3d 478 [3rd Cir. 1999]). The courts remanded the case back to the district court to determine whether running 1.5 miles in 12 minutes was a "minimum qualification." On remand, the district court reached the same conclusion it had reached previously. The plaintiffs then appealed to the Third Circuit appeals court once again. In 2002 the US Court of Appeals for the Third Circuit upheld the district court's conclusion that applicants who fail the fitness test would be less likely to "successfully execute critical policing tasks" (*Lanning v. SEPTA*, 308F. 3d 286 [3rd Cir. 2002]).

The decision in *Lanning* was very discouraging for many reasons. The fitness test was not used to disqualify existing transit officers who could not pass the test. Already employed officers were given incentives to satisfy the set minimums, but there were no consequences for failing, and the ones who failed were still shown to be effective officers capable of completing their everyday police activities. Also, passing the test was a requirement only for individuals applying to become SEPTA officers and only during the actual application process (which sometimes occurred two to two-and-a-half years before the job actually began). Thus, this proves that the fitness test, currently still in practice, does not establish "minimum qualification" necessary for job performance. If the test did indeed measure "minimum qualification," then all new hires would have to be retested just before beginning work, and then requalify periodically. Also, those who did not pass would have to be terminated (Grossman, 2002). Unfortunately, this "standard" will continue to result in fewer women being hired by SEPTA. This performance "requirement" remains a challenge, as do other areas in relation to women and policing.

B. Pregnancy and Policing in the US

In the US, police departments have varied with respect to their treatment of pregnant police officers. In some departments, there has been a lack of support and/or lack of choice in decision-making given to pregnant officers. Some departments have unlawfully discriminated against pregnant officers by removing them from their policing positions after they reported their pregnancy to management. Alternatively, other agencies have refused to provide pregnant officers with any light-duty assignments, instead forcing them to take unpaid leave until their child is born. Still others have required women to report their pregnancies and then have removed them from their current positions for the "safety of the fetus" (Harrington and Lonsway, 2004).

Police departments that discriminate against pregnant officers are acting unlawfully as this constitutes discrimination on the basis of sex. Police agencies cannot force a pregnant officer to take disability leave as long as she is still physically fit to work, nor can the department change the officer's work assignment against her will. In other words, by law, a pregnant officer can continue to work in her current policing assignment as long as she wants to, providing she is still physically fit to conduct her work. Also, the department must accommodate pregnant officers who request "light-duty" assignments, or "nonpatrol" status during their pregnancies. This request should not be considered any different than when a male officer injures himself (e.g., breaks his wrist or leg) and is placed on "light duty." These types of assignments may include a transfer to different duties, or some type of modification in the officer's current duties. According to the National Center for Women and Policing (2005b), "The best light duty policies are flexible; have no time limit on how long a pregnant woman can be assigned to light duty; leave the decision as to when to commence a light duty assignment with the pregnant officer and her physician; and stipulate that officers on light duty will continue to receive normal promotion and pay increases while in that status, and that retirement benefits will not be affected."

Recently, in 2006, a federal court ruled that the Suffolk County New York Police Department had discriminated against six pregnant officers by not allowing them to work in "light-duty" assignments. The women were denied desk-duty positions, but those same positions were offered to chosen male police officers. All six women were at some point forced to go on unpaid leave after they had exhausted all of their sick days. The department further refused to provide the pregnant officers with adequately sized equipment, such as bullet proof vests and gun belts that would accommodate their changing bodies (Feminist Daily News Wire, 2006). According to the Women's Rights Project of the ACLU (Women's Rights Project, 2006), the six officers were forced to choose between not working and using up their sick and vacation days and then going without pay, or continuing their patrol work without vests and gun belts that fit. As a result of the court's ruling, the Suffolk County Police Department was ordered to change its policies in order to provide equal employment opportunities for all of its members.

Even more recently, in a similar case in May 2008, decorated Ocean County (New Jersey) police officer, Sonia Henriques, who was two months pregnant, was denied a request to go on light duty despite a recommendation from her physician. Police Chief Antonio Amodio was quoted as saying that the police department did not have a policy for maternity leave or light-duty leave (Dahler, 2008). Management told Henriques she could continue her patrol work or take an unpaid leave of absence despite a number of desk jobs available at police headquarters (Larsen,

2008b; Feminist Daily News Wire, 2008). However, unlike the Suffolk county case, after much pressure from the Police Benevolent Association and national media exposure, an agreement was reached between the township and the police union granting the pregnant officer light-duty assignment only days later. In the meantime, the chief stated he was committed to creating a maternity policy for potential future pregnancies in his department (Larsen, 2008a).

In addition to making light-duty assignments available, it is important for departments to provide maternity uniforms for pregnant officers and to provide them with police equipment that can accommodate their changing bodies. Some departments that provide light-duty assignments to pregnant officers involving work at the station (e.g., desk duty), often allow them to wear civilian clothing. Regardless, maternity uniforms and suitable police equipment must be made available to all officers working with citizens.

The federal Pregnancy Discrimination Act (PDA) "requires that pregnant women and women disabled by childbirth or related medical conditions be treated at least as well as employees who are not pregnant but who are similar in their ability or inability to work" (National Center for Women and Policing, 2005b). Therefore, a police agency cannot refuse to preserve a position for an officer on maternity leave, deny seniority status upon return from maternity leave, or refuse to grant pension service time for the maternity leave period when it offers these protections to other officers who are temporarily disabled (Kruger, 2006). The PDA does not prohibit the provision of "additional benefits to pregnant employees" (National Center for Women and Policing, 2005b). Also, the US Supreme Court, in *UAW v. Johnson Controls* (499 U.S. 187 [1991]), ruled that employers were prohibited from implementing any policies that prohibited women of child-bearing age from certain hazardous jobs. Thus, the *Johnson* decision prevents police departments from forcing pregnant officers, who are physically fit to work, to take disability leave.

Another important issue relating to pregnancy and policing relates to range qualification. Some officers have been fired or forced to take unpaid disability leave because they refused to qualify on the shooting range during their pregnancy. They refused because of concerns regarding the possible harm to the fetus resulting from the high noise level and lead pollution. Typically, officers have to undergo this weapons test every six months in order to requalify. However, over the years, many departments have eliminated range qualification for pregnant officers until after they have their child. The New York State police, for instance, eliminated the range qualification until the pregnant officer returns from maternity leave. Other departments have created safeguards, or are in the process of implementing changes that allow pregnant officers to complete this test during their pregnancy. Some of these safeguards may include substituting live fire shooting with dry fire; using firearms simulation technology such as lasers; providing lead-free ammunition; and providing sound silencers for the weapons used on the range (National Center for Women and Policing, 2005b).

Unlike Canada, which has federal parental benefits including one-year paid maternity leaves, the US federal government passed the Family and Medical Leave Act in 1993, which allows employees to take only up to three months of unpaid leave from work for the birth or adoption of a child. The Family and Medical Leave Act (FMLA) contains provisions on issues such as entitlement to leave, employer coverage, employee eligibility, heath care benefits during leave, and job restoration after leave. The FMLA provides minimum guarantees for private, state, and local government employees. Yet, some state laws provide greater protections for pregnant and parenting employees. Also, employers or collective bargaining agreements may provide employees with additional benefits. For instance, the New York State police allows employees up to one year of unpaid leave, which provides a five-month extension to the state's permitted leave of seven months. Moreover, some states such as California, Hawaii, New Jersey, New York, Rhode Island, as well as Puerto Rico, which is an unincorporated territory of the US, provide temporary disability insurance to officers who cannot work for medical reasons including pregnancy. Federal law requires departments that offer this type of insurance to employees with temporary disabilities to also provide them to women "disabled by pregnancy" (National Center for Women and Policing, 2005b). Given some of the challenges discussed above, it is not surprising to see few women working as patrol officers and even fewer in higher level policing positions.

C. American Women in Higher Level Policing Positions

As of 2000, there were less than 200 women leading US police departments and sheriff's offices: 157 were police chiefs and 25 were sheriffs. Yet, it is important to note here that it is difficult to know the exact numbers from the more than 18,000 police agencies operating across the US (Schultz, 2004b). According to Schulz (2004b: 195): "Counting sheriffs was easier than counting chiefs because sheriffs are elected for specified terms, generally two or four years. Chiefs, though, may have short tenures. In policing, a chief is never more than one scandal away from dismissal." The International Association of Chiefs of Police estimated that major city chiefs serve in that capacity for approximately two and a half years. Also, the Police Executive Research Forum reports the average tenure to be below five years for police chiefs whose jurisdictions include more than 500,000 residents (Rainguet and Dodge, 2001). Moreover, "it is difficult to locate women chiefs … in small departments or in departments, such as colleges and universities or airport and transit departments, that rarely are included in statistical compilations of police agencies" (Schulz, 2004b: 195).

Women who became chiefs in the 1970s and afterwards are typically referred to as "modern women chiefs." Schulz (2004b: 51-52) states that "these are women who had chosen careers in policing and who, with only one exception, had worked in police departments in ranks lower than chief. Although many had come into policing as civilians, all had become eligible for sworn officers' positions in the 1970s, and many had been the first or only female officer in their department."

One of these first "modern women chiefs" was Sue Wegner, who became chief of police of Minneloa, Florida, in 1979. By 1988 there were less than 50 women chiefs in office in the US. Almost all were in charge of small departments in small communities. In fact, the largest department consisted of 28 sworn officers, and the largest community had a population of 35,000. Karla Osantowski was the first modern female chief who did not have any prior experience in policing. She served as chief of police of Chicago Heights, a southern suburb of Chicago with a population of about 35,000 residents from 1994 to 1996. She was an assistant state attorney for Cook County for five years when she was offered the position of chief of the police agency that employed 80 officers, all of whom were male (Schulz, 2004b).

D. American Women Leading Large City Police Departments

There are three women who are considered to be the first to lead large American city police departments. The first woman to lead a large police department was Penny Harrington from 1984 to 1985. She became the first female chief of the Portland, Oregon, Police Bureau, which employed 940 officers. The second woman chief of a large police department was Elizabeth Watson, who served as chief of the Houston Police Department from 1990 to 1992, and the Austin Police Department from 1992 to 1997. The third was Beverly Harvard, who served as chief of the Atlanta Police Department from 1994 to 2002.

The US Department of Justice annually lists the 50 largest police departments in the country that are determined by the number of full-time sworn officers. They range from the largest, which is always New York City's police department with 40,000-plus members, to departments of under 1,000 members (US Department of Justice, 2000). As of 2000, only 87 city or county police departments out of approximately 18,000 police departments across the country employed more than 500 officers, and less than 10 women had served as chiefs of the top 50 police agencies (Schulz, 2004b).

This changed in 2004 when four women were hired to lead four of the top 50 departments within a few months of each other. Ella Bully-Cummings became chief of the Detroit Police Department in November of 2003 (as of 2000, it was the nation's sixth largest police department with over 4,000 sworn officers); Nannette Hegerty became chief of the Milwaukee Police Department also in November of 2003 (as of 2000, it was the nation's 18th largest with just under 2,000 sworn officers); Kathleen O'Toole became Boston's police commissioner in February 2004 (as of 2000, it was the nation's 16th largest with over 2,000 sworn officers); and Heather Fong became the chief of the San Francisco Police Department in April 2004 (as of 2000, it was the nation's 14th largest with over 2,225 sworn officers) (US Department of Justice, Bureau of Justice Statistics, 2000).

Picture issued by Penny Harrington.

Penny Harrington: The First Woman Chief of a Large American Police Agency

Penny Harrington was the first woman to become chief of a major metropolitan police agency in the US in 1984—the Portland Police Bureau. After graduating from Michigan State University with a degree in police administration, she and her husband were offered jobs in Portland, Oregon, with the Multnomah County Sheriff's Office. However, since the county had a policy against hiring married couples, her husband took the job and Harrington worked as a legal secretary until a position became available with the Portland Police Bureau. After taking the entrance exam, she was hired by the Portland police in 1964 to work in the Women's Protective Division. At the time, the bureau consisted of 700 officers of which only 18 were women. Their primary assignments were to work with women, girls of all ages, and boys who were eight years of age or younger. However, the Women's Protective Division certainly did not shelter female officers from potentially deadly situations. For example, policewomen responded to shootings in progress and confronted armed persons in police-related assignments at people's homes.

Harrington fought against systemic gender discrimination by filing 22 lawsuits against the police department throughout her policing career. Prior to 1971, women were paid less than men, even though they were required to have a college degree, whereas most of the men had only a GED. Women were not allowed to transfer out of the Women's Protective Division or take promotional exams for positions outside that division. They did not wear uniforms and they did not work in patrol cars, and female and male officers had different titles (i.e., "policewomen" and "policemen/patrolmen"). As a result of Harrington's efforts, the first women police officers (as mentioned previously, a title distinct from "policewomen") were hired at the end of 1973.

. Harrington eventually became the first woman to transfer out of the Women's Protective Division, and the first woman to become a detective, sergeant, lieutenant, captain, precinct commander, and chief of police. In her position as chief, she became the first woman to lead a large metropolitan police department in the US. Additionally, in 1995, she founded the National Center for Women and Policing, a division of the Feminist Majority Foundation (personal communication with Penny Harrington, 2007; Schulz, 2004b; Harrington, 1999).

All of these women started their policing careers in the departments they would eventually serve as chief. This pattern is similar to women serving as chiefs in small police agencies. With the exception of O'Toole, all had moved up the ranks within their department, serving in a wide range of patrol and administrative assignments. O'Toole started off as a patrol officer, but after being laid off, she obtained a number of management positions in various police and civilian agencies and earned a Juris Doctor degree (JD), which is the professional graduate degree in law offered in the US, before returning to the Boston Police Department 17 years later to serve as the police commissioner.

Moreover, all these women were well-educated. They all had a bachelor's degree and either a law degree or a master's degree. Also, two of the four women represented racial minority groups. Fong, for instance, is Asian-American. She is one of a few Asians to ever serve as chief of a US city police department and the first Asian-surnamed woman. Bully-Cummings is multiracial; her father is African-American and her mother is Asian (Schulz, 2004b). Other African-American women who have served as chief include Atlanta, Georgia's Beverly Harvard (1994-2002); Evelyn B. Hicks in Opa-Locka, Florida, in 1995; Ivin B. Lee in Dunbar, West Virginia, in 1996; and interim chiefs Sonya Proctor in Washington, DC, (1997-1998) and Mary Bounds in Cleveland, Ohio (2001-2002). In 2003, in addition to Ella Bully-Cummings in Detroit, Annetta Nunn became chief in Birmingham, Alabama. "The numbers of minority women, particularly African-American women, have been increasing annually in large-city police departments but have remained static—in some cases nonexistent—in small departments, often in communities with few or no minority residents" (Schulz, 2004b: 199).

E. Has There Been a Significant Increase in the Number of American Women
Officers as a Result of Certain Changes in Legislation and Police Policies?
Despite the successes noted above, the number of women in top command positions remains very small. For argument's sake, even if the number had tripled today to approximately 600 from Schulz's recorded number of 200 in 2000, that would still equal poor representation with just over 3 per cent of women chiefs and sheriffs in the country.

By 1998 American women constituted 12 per cent of all police officers. In 1999, 14.3 per cent of all sworn officers in large police agencies (with 100 or more sworn personnel) were women; 16 per cent of municipal officers (operating at the municipal or local level) and only 7 per cent of state police were women (National Center for Women and Policing, 1999). Municipal agencies include city, county, village, and county police departments, sheriff's departments, and a variety of special-purpose agencies such as campus police, transit authority and housing authority police, which are responsible for enforcing the laws, maintaining the peace, and providing service to the local communities. The state police, on the other hand, consist of highway patrols that regulate traffic and maintain order on state and federal highways. Many states also have special investigative agencies that provide statewide law enforcement (Langworthy and Travis III, 2003).

In 2001 women constituted 12.7 per cent of all sworn law enforcement officers in large US police agencies with 100 or more sworn personnel (4.8 per cent were women of colour), and 8.1 per cent of all officers in small and rural agencies (1.2 per cent were women of colour) (National Center for Women and Policing, 2003). Smaller police agencies have been more resistant to hiring women. Policing as a whole has been one of the most resistant fields to accept women (Belknap and Shelley, 1993), but larger police agencies have hired more women in comparison to smaller ones. Interestingly, one exception has been the Madison Police Department. Madison, Wisconsin, has a population of approximately 200,000, but almost 30 per cent of its sworn police officers are women (National Center for Women and Policing, 1999). At the federal level, as of 2001, women constituted 14.4 per cent of all federal agents (Hickman and Reaves, 2001). Most federal police agencies have limited responsibilities and do not provide police services to members of the public. The FBI (Federal Bureau of Investigation), for instance, investigates violations of federal law and provides other specific services that include maintaining national crime data and fingerprint records, and operating the national crime laboratory (Langworthy and Travis III, 2003). As of 2002, women comprised 18 per cent of FBI agents, 28 per cent of the Internal Revenue Service law enforcement agents, 12.1 per cent of agents in the Immigration and Naturalization Service, and 8.6 per cent of agents in the Drug Enforcement Administration (Reaves and Bauer, 2003). Interestingly, in 2000 and 2001, the number of women in policing overall declined from the previous year, from 14.3 per cent in 1999, to 13 per cent in 2000, and then 12.7 per cent in 2001 (National Center for Women and Policing, 2003).

The recorded number of women in higher level positions is even lower. In large police agencies (100 or more sworn personnel), women hold 7.3 per cent of the top command positions (women of colour account for 1.6 per cent of these positions), and 9.6 per cent of supervisory positions (women of colour account for 3.1 per cent). In small and rural police agencies (less than 100 sworn personnel), women account for only 3.4 per cent of all top command positions (women of colour account for 0.3 per cent), and 4.6 per cent of all supervisory positions (women of colour account for 0.4 per cent). Over half (55.9 per cent) of the large police agencies surveyed had no women representing top command positions, and the majority (87.9 per cent) had no women of colour in these positions. The numbers are significantly lower in small and rural police departments. In these agencies, 97.4 per cent had no women in top command positions, and only one out of 235 agencies reported having a woman of colour in their top ranks (National Center for Women and Policing, 2003). It is also important to note that women of colour represent 37.7 per cent of the total number of women in policing (National Center for Women and Policing, 2000).

These numbers are significantly low given the number of American women in the paid work force today. Sixty-three per cent of married women with children under the age of six work for an income. The number of married women with children between six and 17 years of age who work for an income jumps to 77 per cent. The numbers are even higher for divorced, separated, or widowed women with children with comparable figures of 76 per cent of women with younger children and 87 per cent of women with older children between 6 and 17 years of age working for an income (US Census Bureau, 2002). However, from 1972 to 1999, women in policing in the US have gained an average of about half a percentage point per year within large police departments.

The second wave brought about significant changes in US laws and policies that helped "open the doors" for many women in the field of policing, but many challenges remain. Similarly in Canada, change has been slow in various substantive areas relating to gender and policing.

US Timeline

1908   Lola Greene Baldwin is the first woman sworn in to "perform police service" for the city of Portland, Oregon.

1910   Alice Stebbins Wells is appointed to the rank of detective by the Los Angeles Police Department; this officially gives her the classification of "policewoman."

1916   Georgia Robinson is the first African-American woman appointed as a matron to the Los Angeles Police Department; she becomes a "policewoman" in 1919.

1910-1917   There are approximately 125 "policewomen" across the US.

By 1929   There are approximately 600 "policewomen" across the US.

By 1940   The number of "policewomen" in the US decreases to about 500.

By 1950   There are approximately 2,500 "policewomen" in the US.

By 1960   There are approximately 5,600 "policewomen" in the US.

1964   Congress passes the Civil Rights Act.

1965   The Civil Rights Bill becomes law. Title VII of this legislation deals with discrimination in employment on the basis of race, colour, religion, national origin, and sex.

1968   Betty Blankenship and Elizabeth Coffal become the first women to be appointed to regular patrol work as male officers.

1971   The US Supreme Court rules that a policy or practice may be discriminatory if it has a disproportionate effect upon a particular group of people and is not job-related or justified by job necessity (*Griggs v. Duke Power Company*).

1972   Title VII is amended to apply to state and municipal governments.

1970s-1980s   Lawsuits against police departments throughout the US result in court orders or consent decrees that establish affirmative action programs.

| 1987 | More than 50 per cent of police departments serving populations larger than 50,000 have implemented affirmative action programs. |

| 1991 | The Civil Rights Act of 1991 is passed. Title VII prohibits "disparate impact discrimination." |

| 1998 | Twelve per cent of all sworn police officers are women. |

| 2001 | Precisely 12.7 per cent of all sworn officers in large police agencies (with 100 or more sworn personnel) are women (4.8 per cent are women of colour); 8.1 per cent of all officers in small and rural agencies are women (1.2 per cent are women of colour); 14.4 per cent of all federal agents are women. |

Canada and the Second Wave of the Women's Movement

As in the US, the second wave in the women's movement was shaped by both individual women working within different organizations, as well as feminists working at the grassroots level (Freeman, 1984; Adamson, Briskin, and McPhail, 1988). In 1967 the Royal Commission on the Status of Women strengthened the network of women's organizations across Canada as they prepared briefs for the public hearings. The Royal Commission's report, published in 1970, documented several examples of sexual inequalities and proposed 167 recommendations to alleviate them. This ultimately led to the conference on "Strategy for Change" in 1972, which gave birth to the National Action Committee on the Status of Women (NAC). NAC provided a formal network for Canadian women across the country in their pursuit for equality and ultimately gained political clout as it brought together many different women's organizations. It began to serve as an effective lobby group monitoring legislative progress and the impact of particular policy and legislative changes on the lives of women (Wilson, 1996).

In the early 1980s, women's groups in Canada rallied for the inclusion of women's rights in the Charter of Rights and Freedoms. They formed the Ad Hoc Committee of Canadian Women to ensure the inclusion of an equal rights clause (Wilson, 1996), and in November 1981, section 28 of the Charter was reinstated to read, "Notwithstanding anything in this charter, all the rights and freedoms in it are guaranteed equally to male and female persons" (Kome, 1983).

In 1982 the British Parliament ceased its power to legislate for Canada, and the Constitution Act, 1982, was passed, which included the Charter of Rights and Freedoms. The Charter guaranteed individuals' fundamental rights and freedoms, since prior to 1982 there was no guarantee that certain fundamental rights and freedoms could not be taken away from Canadians. The existing Canadian Bill of Rights was an act passed by the Parliament of Canada and thus could be amended or even thrown out by Parliament at anytime. Moreover, even though the provinces had passed laws establishing certain rights, they too, like any provincial laws, could be changed or repealed by legislatures. Writing the Charter into the Constitution made it difficult for any government or legislature, including the Parliament of Canada, to interfere with individual rights and freedoms. The Charter limited the power of both provincial and federal governments in favour of the rights of citizens, and, for the first time in Canadian history, the Constitution recognized women's legal equality. It guaranteed women's full equality under the law, and permitted affirmative action programs, such as equal employment opportunities, in order to achieve equality (Canada, Intergovernmental Affairs, 2008; Human Rights Program, 2007; Greschner, 1985).

Women at the grassroots level also contributed to the second wave movement, but "it is difficult to know how many women have participated in grass-roots feminism in Canada. Some groups and organizations have become 'institutionalized' over time; others come together and disband as needs change" (Wilson, 1996: 149). Grassroots groups avoid traditional organizational structures and typically exist without particular individuals who "speak" for the group as a whole. These groups often provide a voice to women who continue to be marginalized politically and economically. It is evident that grassroots organizing has served as an effective political strategy for social change in Canada. For example, individual women police officers working at the community level have brought attention to issues of sexual harassment in police departments and discrimination in hiring and promotions. As mentioned earlier, issues such as these are often first voiced by women working in their communities at the grassroots level and then later addressed by women's organizations at the national level.

A. Canadian Women Police: From "Policewomen" to "Police Officers"

Once again, the literature on the history of Canadian women in policing during the second wave of the feminist movement is limited, as it is for the earlier period. Two of the first major studies of Canadian female officers were funded by the Solicitor General's department and included Rick Linden's 1984 study and Sandra Walker's 1993 study. Linden studied female police officers at a time when the police had started assigning women to general patrol duties in the Vancouver Police Department and in the RCMP (Royal Canadian Mounted Police). Linden found that women police were as effective as men, which included having similar arrest rates (Linden, 1984; Linden and Fillmore, 1993). Walker, on the other hand, looked at the experiences of women in Canadian policing in the early 1990s. Marcel-Eugene LeBeuf (1996) also attempted to examine the experiences of women in Canadian policing from the 1970s to the 1990s, but noted that the vast majority of sources referred to were either American or European.

What we do know, however, is that by the 1960s, during the second wave of the movement, 0.5 per cent of all police officers were women; that is, fewer than 200 persons (Juristat, 2001), and by the mid-1970s, women constituted only 1 per cent of sworn police officers in Canada (Shankarraman, 2003). In the early and mid-1970s, women began to carry guns, but they carried them in specially designed handbags (Toronto Police Service, 2007). Even in the RCMP, the first class of women hired to serve as regular members in 1974 were expected to carry their guns in their purses, despite the fact that the organization was promoting the idea of equality between women and men.

> We were supposed to report for work with our gun in purses! It didn't take us long to realize that the credibility gap would be almost insurmountable, even before we finished our first shift on the road, if we showed up for our first day at work with a purse. This may seem like a small thing but I think it is evidence of how difficult it was for the institution of policing to accept that women could actually stand side by side with their male partners and get the job done. The purse story has a happy ending in that we were able to convince those responsible that the liabilities, never mind the appearance of a police officer with a loaded weapon in a purse, was not a good idea (Busson, 1997: 145-46).

By the 1970s and 1980s, female officers across Canada were routinely assigned to regular patrol duties and to other positions that were formerly reserved for men. However, legal changes and changes to internal police policies in the 1980s and 1990s had an impact on the number of women hired to work in many large urban police agencies. Nationally, in 1988, 5.1 per cent of all sworn officers were women; over 95 per cent of these were constables, 4 per cent were noncommissioned officers, and 0.01 per cent were command officers (Forcese, 1999). In the province of Ontario, by the mid-1980s, female officers accounted for only 2.7 per cent of police personnel and only a few police agencies had implemented any initiatives to hire more women (Ministry of the Solicitor General, Ontario, 1986).

In 1990 mandated employment equity provisions were implemented in Ontario. This new legislation required police services to carefully review their management practices in areas such as recruiting and make necessary changes to attract applicants from diverse groups. This, in turn, resulted in a significant increase in the number of female police recruits; about 30 per cent of the new recruits trained at the Ontario Police College at that time were women, and by 1994 and early 1995, the percentage of women rose to the high 40s. However, by 1995, employment equity provisions were removed from the Police Services Act and replaced with a voluntary employment opportunity policy. This voluntary approach resulted in an immediate decrease in the number of female, Aboriginal, and visible minority recruits. For instance, by the beginning of 1997, there were only 52 women from the total number of 276 new students at the Ontario Police College. In other words, female recruits represented 18.84 per cent of the total number of recruits (Josiah, 1997). However, the Vancouver Police Department, through a voluntary affirmative action program, recruited a significantly higher number of women in 1996, whereas the number of women recruited by the Toronto Police Department, one year after the employment equity law was revoked throughout the province, was significantly lower.

1996	Total Recruits	Women	Percentage
Metro Toronto Police	293	46	15.7
Vancouver Police	39	15	38

Source: Eng (1997)

Susan Eng (1997: 51-52), the former chair of the Toronto Police Services Board, offered the following as an explanation for the significant disparity between the two departments in 1996:

> The outreach recruiting strategy was not used or was not effective. Intake was only 19% women [658 women and 2,787 men] so it is not surprising that the final representation of women was only 16%. Metro Toronto Police simply sent out ads and made no apparent effort to seek out women or minority groups in universities and schools.

Eng further discussed the differences in physical test results between women and men for each of these two departments. In Toronto 38 per cent of the women passed, whereas 77 per cent of the men passed. In Vancouver, on the other hand, 55 per cent of the men and 45 per cent of the women passed. She asserted that the difference in performance had to do with the fact that all of the applicants in Vancouver were given an information session at the Justice Institute that included a video of the actual physical tests. Moreover, Vancouver worked with the YWCA to provide women with physical training pertaining to the actual physical tests. She added that in the case of Toronto there were no efforts made to challenge the common stereotypes of policing that included the image of policing as being "for men," and being synonymous with crime control and brawn. Alternatively, the Vancouver Police Department had identified four preferred qualifications for the job of police officer that challenged these images. These qualifications included a university degree or college diploma (minimum two years); a second language or culture; voluntary experience, particularly in the area of criminal justice; and an employment history that highlighted individual strengths such as strong interpersonal skills.

By the 1990s, police departments across the country had abolished age and minimum weight standards and many departments had implemented minority recruitment programs that aimed at increasing the number of individuals representing particular minority groups. These included women, Aboriginal people, racial minorities, and the physically disabled. For some departments, this was the result of legislative requirements, and for others, it was due to the efforts of progressive individuals representing human resources management. The OPP (Ontario Provincial Police) started a recruitment drive in 1984, headed by a female officer, resulting in a significant increase in women applicants: The number of female applicants doubled from the previous years (based on the first six months of each year), and over 4,000 females applied (*Ottawa Citizen*, 23 July 1984). Still, 50 per cent of the police agencies contacted by Walker (1993) reported they did not have any women assigned to recruiting duties to reach out to more female applicants.

In 1994 the RCMP established new recruiting priorities in order to become more representative of the large population. As a result, 32 per cent of the cadets in 1995-1996 were women. Also, changes made to recruitment policies, as well as policies relating to harassment and promotions, altered the attrition rate for women between the 1980s and 1990s. In 1989 the attrition rate was 4 per cent, whereas in 1995 it dropped to 1.3 per cent (Villeneuve, 1997).

By the mid 1990s, women comprised approximately 10 per cent (over 5,000 persons) of all sworn police officers across Canada (Juristat, 1996). In Winnipeg, Manitoba, in 1997, targeted recruitment increased the number of women police officers to 123 of the 1,212 sworn officers. By 1997, 11 per cent of the total number of sworn officers in Toronto were women; that is, a total of 550 female officers. In Vancouver women officers totalled 12 per cent. In Saskatoon, of that same year, 38 per cent of new hires for constables were women. Moreover, there were two women chiefs of police — in Calgary, Alberta, and Guelph, Ontario — and there were also two deputy chiefs; one in Toronto, Ontario, and one in the OPP.

B. Gender Discrimination, Policies, and Gender Equity Analysis

Despite recruitment efforts, women continued to experience gender discrimination. Many women in the 1980s were recruited to work with sexual assault and domestic assault victims, since female officers were perceived to be more able to address the needs of female victims of these specific crimes. Interestingly, however, a study conducted in 1988 involving both Canadian and American policewomen revealed that female officers believed they had been fairly assigned to their duties, and, for the most part, that they had the same opportunities as the men. Yet, the opinions of women with more years of service differed, as they were less likely to recommend police work as a career choice to other women (Garrison, Grant, and McCormick, 1988).

A study done in Canada as part of an MA thesis (Jackson, 1997) included women who worked for the RCMP, the military police, and municipal and town police agencies in the Atlantic Canada region. Jackson (1997) found that many female officers believed they had been assigned files because of their gender. In some cases, the perception was that male officers justified these decisions because of the nature of particular crimes. That is, they dealt with a "gender-specific crime or complaint." In other instances, female officers believed they were assigned certain cases when male officers feared that possible false allegations could be made against them by female complainants or offenders. Moreover, 72 per cent of the sample believed they were more likely to be assigned cases that involved "women and children issues" and 41 per cent were uncomfortable with assignments that were directly linked to their gender. Jackson (1997) also found that the officers considered their work schedule to be a source of stress. The constant changing shift schedule is a source of stress for a disproportionate number of female officers because of the fact that most women continue to have more childcare and other family-related responsibilities.

Hyacinthe Josiah, a senior adviser with the Ontario Civilian Commission on Police Services, was a speaker at the Women in Policing in Canada workshop held in Ottawa, Ontario, in 1997 and stated the following with regard to gender discrimination:

> How many times have we heard a police manager say, "Yes, I have female officers, but I wouldn't want *my* daughter to be one." Or, "I look upon all of these girls as if they were my daughters and I treat them the same way." Or, "Police women really don't want to do the same work as policemen." Or, "I'm not sure it is a good investment to train women. They get pregnant and take off for months at a time, you know" (Josiah, 1997: 81).

Thus, policies are crucial in promoting equality between the sexes and recognizing the differences in women's lives. Necessary policies relating to policing and employment equity must address promotion, recruitment and officer selection, parental leave, job-sharing, workplace harassment, and pregnancy.

However, equally important is applying a gender equity analysis (GEA) to the creation of policies and laws, and in making operational decisions. This approach is key to ensuring that the different social realities of both women and men in the workplace are taken into account (Frost, 1997). Frost (1997: 90) states that GEA has two main goals:

- Fairness: to produce fairer laws and a fairer justice system by avoiding systemic discrimination.
- Accuracy: to produce durable policy without unintended negative impact.

The Canadian federal government recognized the importance of GEA in 1995 when the Cabinet adopted the Federal Plan for Gender Equality (1995-2000). It mandated that all federal departments and agencies, including the Department of Justice, conduct gender-based analysis of policies and legislation. With regard to fairness, section 15 of the Canadian Charter of Rights and Freedoms protects individuals from discrimination on the basis of sex, and section 28 guarantees gender equality. According to Frost (1997: 90-91):

> Section 28 is the strongest section in the Charter, taking precedence over all others due to its notwithstanding clause. That is to say, a reasonable limit under s. 1 would not be acceptable if it created conditions of gender inequality. Similarly, a government would not be able to enact certain laws in defiance of s. 2 and 7-15 of the Charter (under the "opting-out" clause in s. 33), if such laws would generate gender inequality.

Employment policies must avoid systemic discrimination and must produce fewer unintended results. For instance, GEA may

> suggest a reconsideration of the physical elements of police work that has been tradition-ally considered "essential," to determine whether these standards (based on male norms) continue to be valid. Particularly in the light of community policing and the move to problem solving and early intervention, it is possible that physical skills may be of rela-tively lesser importance in the modern policing context than communications, interper-sonal skills, and conflict resolution.
>
> Employee benefits policies need to be reviewed to take into account gender realities. For example, since women tend to have the majority of child-rearing responsibilities, work assignments (including shift assignments) will have to take this reality into account if work-ing conditions are to be sensitive to gender equality. However, developing this perspective benefits more than women. A greater number of men are taking active roles in child-raising, and they too can be benefited by policies which respect the importance of commitment to families (Frost, 1997: 96).

Frost makes the following recommendations to police personnel in terms of how to "do" GEA, or gender-based analysis, in policing. She asks police to look at all of their initiatives and to identify the policy or operational issues: goals, purpose, and means.

> 1) Do a factual assessment of the situation of women and men in relation to the proposed policy or operation. A good way to do this is to consult with NGOs who deal in women's issues—what do they say are the implications of current or proposed policies or operations?
> 2) Assess the impact, intended or unintended, of the contemplated policy or operation on both women and men. Ask the following questions:
> How will these policy or operational options impact on women differently than on men?
> How will they impact on women in diverse groups of women (poor, women of colour, aboriginal women, sexual orientation)?
> 3) Assess the real differential impact between women and men by juxtaposing the effects or implications of the policy or operational decision with the social reality of men and women it will affect. Amend the policy, if necessary, in the light of this analysis to ensure the measure does not have a systemically discriminatory effect (1997: 96-97).

In addition, GEA/GBA should be applied to internal police policies relating to members of the public to ensure that police services do not ignore the needs of women as a group and the different needs of women representing different social categories (e.g., race, sexual orientation, ethnicity, class, etc.). The police, for instance, must recognize the unique needs of women in racial and ethnic minority communities in order to fairly address law enforcement issues. For example, the Metropolitan Toronto Police (now the Toronto Police Service) Inter-Community

Relations Unit (ICRU) in the 1990s created rather narrow profiles of many of the city's minority racial and ethnic groups. These "profiles" were intended to assist officers in their handling of people representing these groups.

Unfortunately, the profiles, for the most part, fed into stereotypes and failed to apply a gender-based analysis. Several ethnic minority communities, such as the Greek, Indian, Italian, and Pakistani communities, were described as being "male-dominated" and "traditional," where men were "the head of the family." Therefore, officers responding to these homes were encouraged to speak to the men rather than the women to avoid being perceived as "disrespectful of the culture." These profiles falsely assumed that all families representing these cultures shared a common identity. This served to marginalize women who lived in families that did not fit the profile. Women, on the other hand, who lived in so-called male-dominated families were also silenced by officers who were reluctant to listen to their complaints and/or experiences. This approach also failed to recognize individual agency on the part of these women, since officers often assumed they were "weak," "passive," and/or "unintelligent" (personal communication with officers from the former ICRU, 2007). Applying a gender-based analysis to the creation of policies and laws is an important step in recognizing some of the current gendered realities.

C. Pregnancy and Policing in Canada

Pregnancy/maternity policies have been introduced to police services in Canada to address a wide range of issues, including the choice to work on nonpatrol status, maternity uniforms and appropriate holsters, and maternity leave. Up until the 1970s, women police officers who had a baby had to resign. In Toronto women who became mothers were forced to resign up until 1972 (Toronto Police, 2007). In Ottawa, in 1983, the chief of the Ottawa Police Force refused to transfer a pregnant officer to nonpatrol status and ordered her to take unpaid leave when she was three months pregnant. This officer had been hired in 1979, along with three other women, following a decision made by the Ontario Human Rights Commission ordering that the department change different aspects of its physical requirements as they discriminated against women. The Police Commission, however, overturned the chief's decision and the officer was subsequently placed on "light duties" (*Ottawa Citizen*, 30 November 1983). Other departments placed pregnant officers on "light duties" but at reduced pay, whereas other officers who had injured themselves on or off the job, or, had other medical reasons, were given "light duties" at full pay (*Ottawa Citizen*, 30 November 1983).

There were two landmark cases in Ontario in 1993 relating to pregnancy and police work. Two pregnant first class officers asked to be accommodated early on in their pregnancies with full-time assignments in positions of "minimal risk" in the later stage of their pregnancies.

The board refused the request and placed the women on unpaid leave of absence. The police association took the matter to arbitration. In a related case, a pregnant officer was refused any accommodation neither to hours or condition of work. The test, of course, is "reasonable accommodation" and "undue hardship."

At later hearings in both cases, it was found that the police services had, in the past, accommodated a number of males with "light" duties, including an officer who had broken a leg playing baseball off-duty. The arbitrator found that "no real efforts were made" and ordered the police service to accommodate the pregnant officers. In the second case, the Human Rights Commission found the board erred in not accommodating the pregnant officer and ordered payment of a compensatory award (Josiah, 1997: 86).

By 1996 several police departments, including Toronto, Winnipeg, Vancouver, Saskatoon, and the RCMP, had introduced maternity clauses in their police contracts. With respect to maternity leave, in Saskatoon the maternity clause mandated no loss in seniority or benefits and a "top-up" to 95 per cent of wages while receiving 17 weeks of unemployment insurance benefits from the government. Today, many Canadian police departments' maternity leave clauses provide financial top-ups to unemployment insurance benefits and ensure that a pregnant officer on leave does not lose seniority, sick leave, employer pension contributions, vacation pay, court attendance benefits, and clothes and equipment allowances. Moreover, several departments have job-sharing policies. Job-sharing usually translates to a temporary accommodation for employees with particular difficulties related to childcare, maternity leave, health problems, or other family issues. It can also reduce an officer's level of stress from feeling responsible for leaving their platoon members short-staffed.

D. "Firsts" in Canadian Policing

In addition to some important policies that were introduced during the second wave of the feminist movement, many women became "firsts" in a variety of different policing positions. For instance, throughout the 1980s and 1990s, many "firsts" were witnessed in the RCMP. In 1981, the public witnessed the first woman to be promoted to the rank of corporal. In 1987 the first woman in the RCMP "AIR" Division was hired as a pilot, the first woman was posted to a foreign post (Lyon, France), and two women were posted to the National Recruiting Team. The year 1989 marked the first woman to be in charge of a RCMP operational detachment in a contract province, Arviat Detachment, Northwest Territories, and the first woman to be appointed to a United Nations contingent (Namibia). And the list goes on: In 1991 the first female RCMP sergeant was appointed; in 1992 the first woman was commissioned to the officer rank of inspector; and by 1994, for the first time, approximately 10 per cent of regular members of the RCMP were women, and women started to serve on the Tactical Troop. Beginning in 1995, in the RCMP, women were promoted to staff sergeant (1995), superintendent (1996), chief superintendent (1997), assistant commissioner (1998), commanding officers of their own divisions (1999), division staff relations representative (2000), and deputy commissioner (2002). Moreover, what appears to be quite progressive for police departments was the creation of the Women's Issues Advisor position in the RCMP in 1997, which was established in recognition of earlier discriminatory and isolating practices. Beginning in 2001, the RCMP was the first police agency in North America to offer part-time hours to female regular members who had family needs (Policewomen in the News, 2007). Moreover, in the 1990s, Canada witnessed its first female chiefs of police.

First Women Police Chiefs in Canada

1994-2000   Lenna Bradburn becomes the first female chief of police, serving as chief of the Guelph Police Service.

1995-2000   Christine E. Silverberg becomes the chief of the Calgary Police Service. She becomes Canada's second female chief, but the first to serve a large city police department (over 1,100 police officers).

1998-2000   Gwen Boniface becomes the first woman commissioner of the OPP.

E. Canada's First Woman Chief: Lenna Bradburn

To date, only a handful of women have led Canadian police departments. The first female chief of police in Canada was Lenna Bradburn. She served as the chief of the Guelph Police Service from 1994 to 2000. Bradburn's (1997) policing career began in the early 1980s when she worked as a sworn officer with the Metropolitan Toronto Police Service. There, she encountered several instances of systemic gender discrimination. When she first became a police officer in the early 1980s, she was only one of three female officers in her division (of approximately 180 officers). Since there was no separate locker room or washroom for women officers, the three of them had to share a locker room with the sergeants from the CIB (the Central Investigative Bureau) and with the male parking control officers, and they had to use the public washroom. When she was a probationary officer, in 1982, she was told that she would replace the inspector's secretary while she was on leave. When she asked why she was being given this assignment, she was told that her new role would allow her to gain a better understanding of the administration of the division which would serve her well for future promotions. Bradburn responded by saying that she was still learning to be a front-line officer and that perhaps the inspector should consider officers who were about to be promoted, given their immediate need for administrative experience. Needless to say she did not replace the inspector's secretary, but she discovered at a later date that a letter was placed in her personnel file stating that "this officer should not be given any opportunities to advance herself in the future" (Bradburn, 1997).

Another example of systemic gender discrimination offered by Bradburn (personal communication, 2007; 1997) related to the segregation of the troupe of 50 officers who marched annually in the Police March Past. Each of the Metropolitan

Toronto Police Service's five divisions sent a troupe of 50 officers to participate in the march, but these troupes never included any women. Instead, in 1982, 50 women officers from the entire police department formed a sixth troupe. They were not allowed to march with the male officers because they were told they were too short, their legs were not long enough, and their hats were different from the men. They subsequently ended up marching behind the men, but in front of the horses. This segregated practice did not end until 1991, when both female and male officers marched side by side. With regard to their different hats, women were not allowed to wear the forage cap that is traditionally known and recognized as the police hat. Instead, they wore hats that resembled the ones once worn by female flight attendants, which often resulted in confusion among members of the public as to whom they worked for. On one occasion, Bradburn was mistaken for a post office employee. The segregating practice relating to the hat officially ended in Toronto in 1991.

Bradburn's experiences with systemic gender discrimination also included the design of bulletproof vests. Prior to 1983, officers in Ontario were not required to wear bulletproof vests. However, in 1983, the provincial government offered to pay 50 per cent of the cost to supply all officers with the safety gear. Subsequently, the Toronto police department purchased several vests, but they were the same for men and women. Unlike the importance of the symbol of the forage cap for all of the officers, the vest presented particular problems for many women. The early vests issued by the department were designed for men's bodies. In other words, men were assumed to be "the standard." Management did not account for differences in women's bodies. This obviously concerned many of the women given that bulletproof vests are made of Kevlar, not the most pliable of materials. Bradburn and others shared their concerns with management and requested that the department purchase vests that were designed to accommodate women's bodies. The women did their own research and found the model number for women's vests from the supplier which cost $25.00 more, and, in the end, were successful in obtaining them (personal communication with Bradburn, 2007; 1997).

Systemic gender discrimination was further seen in units that excluded women. One such example was the motorcycle unit. The motorcycle unit prohibited female members because they believed that the "bikes" were too heavy for the women to lift. Ironically, many of the male officers working in this unit could not lift the motorcycle on their own without the assistance of another individual, but this was not perceived as a problem (personal communication with Bradburn, 2007; 1997).

Bradburn, like so many other women in the police organization, had to find ways to challenge systemic barriers. Bradburn was interested in police policy-making and early on in her policing career had applied for a position in one of the department's planning units. She was successful in obtaining an interview, but did not get the position. Even though she had the research skills and other related skills for the position, she was told she did not get the position because she was not a sergeant. Interestingly, the job posting did not list this as a prerequisite. Bradburn realized that she could not rely on the formal police process to obtain a position in policy-making in her near future, and therefore she had to try and find ways to challenge these processes. She did this by becoming involved with her police association. She became the first female officer elected to the board of directors of the Metropolitan Toronto Police Association and as a result of the combined efforts of herself and other association members, policies concerning childcare leave, job-sharing, and flexible work hours were created.

After three years of experience on the board, she was able to become part of the police service's Corporate Planning Unit where she was involved in strategic planning, community policing initiatives, and researched and drafted Metro Toronto's vision document, Beyond 2000. Ironically, while working on Beyond 2000 document, she interviewed several senior officers who said that the police officer of the future "must be able to show compassion, be empathetic, and be able to use their mind not their brawn" (Bradburn, 1997: 137). Yet, almost 10 years earlier, she was criticized by a sergeant for having those very same qualities during an instance when she successfully arrested an offender (she was perceived by the sergeant as not being aggressive enough). Clearly, Bradburn worked hard to challenge many different types of oppression. One of her statements in her presentation given at a policing conference in Canada in 1997 was very telling: "If I had a dollar for every time I was told that I shouldn't rock the boat I would be rich" (1997: 138). Bradburn ultimately left the Metropolitan Toronto Police Service in 1991 to work with the Ministry of the Solicitor General before becoming Canada's first female chief of police in Guelph in 1994.

F. Canadian Women Chiefs

Christine E. Silverberg was Canada's second female chief of police, and the first female to serve as chief of a major city police department. On October 10, 1995, Silverberg began her tenure as chief of the Calgary Police Service. She led Calgary's 1,132 member force until her retirement in 2000. She first became a police officer in 1971 for the city of Mississauga, Ontario, at the age of 22, becoming only the second woman to serve for that department. Since women were not assigned to uniformed patrol duty at that time, she began her work in the youth bureau investigating child abuse cases, juvenile crime, and missing children. In 1974 the Mississauga department merged with four other forces to become the Hamilton-Wentworth Regional Police Service. Silverberg served as deputy chief of the Hamilton-Wentworth Regional Police until 1990 when she left to begin her work with the Ministry of the Solicitor General. She served as chief of the Calgary Police Service from 1995 to 2000. Today, she practices law in Calgary (*The Canadian Encyclopedia: Historica*, 2007).

Another Canadian woman chief, Gwen Boniface, became the first woman commissioner of the OPP in 1998 and the first female president of the Canadian Association of Chiefs of Police. Boniface lead the OPP from 1998 to 2006 and then resigned to join a newly established three-person panel that oversees Ireland's

Picture issued by Lenna Bradburn.

Lenna Bradburn: Canada's First Female Chief of Police

On December 19, 1994, Lenna Bradburn became the first woman to head a city police department in Canada, the Guelph Police Service, at the age of 34. She lead Guelph's 142 officer force until 2000. In order to promote equitable practices for all officers, Chief Bradburn worked to ensure diverse representation on various internal committees. For instance, by including women on the Health and Safety committee, several concerns relating to female officers were identified. For one, the rubber gloves issued to all officers were only one size. They were too large for many of the female officers, who in turn went to hospitals to obtain smaller ones. Also, the holsters that were initially utilized by the officers did not have a secure locking mechanism (they were "cross-draw" holsters) and thus they were replaced by "front load" holsters. This new holster had a spring mechanism that prevented officers' guns from falling out while they ran. However, for many female officers who tended to have shorter torsos in comparison to their male counterparts, this new holster proved to be uncomfortable—it raised the gun grip up into their armpits while they sat in their police cars or at their desks.

Women serving on the Health and Safety committee were instrumental in identifying practices that disadvantaged certain groups and ensuring that the department made the necessary changes. For example, because of their efforts, the department purchased gloves in different sizes and introduced holsters with loops that allowed individual officers to make necessary adjustments. Bradburn also initiated and chaired the Human Resource Management committee for the Ontario Chiefs of Police (OCOP). During this time, the provincial government worked with the Ontario chiefs and the police associations to implement an equitable constable selection system that did not disadvantage particular groups of people. The Human Resource Management committee recognized the continued need for physical tests for applicants, but was committed to establishing measures that reflected the typical everyday physical demands of the job rather than the exceptions. Thus, they introduced a standardized constable selection system that reflected several changes, including the elimination of the one-mile run. This new selection process was endorsed by OCOP in 1998 and most of the police services across the province subscribed to it.

Bradburn's policing career began in 1982 when she served as a sworn police officer for the Metropolitan Toronto Police (now the Toronto Police Service). In 1991, she left the police department to work with the Ministry of the Solicitor General in inspection and operation management positions. More recently, she worked with the Ontario Ombudsman's office as director of complaint services, and as of 2008, she became the Chief Security and Compliance Officer for the Office of Player Protection for the Ontario Lottery and Gaming Corporation. Bradburn completed her bachelor's degree in criminology at the University of Toronto and earned a master's degree in public administration at Queen's University (personal communication with Bradburn, 2007; Bradburn, 1997).

13,000-member National Police Force (CBC News, 28 July 2006). Currently, the province of Ontario has two female chiefs: Chief Wendy Southall leads the Niagara Police Service and Chief Tracy David leads the Hanover Police Service (personal communication with Myra James, president of Ontario Women in Law Enforcement, 2008).

G. Has There Been a Significant Increase in the Number of Canadian Women Officers as a Result of Certain Changes in Legislation and Police Policies?

Despite some of the accomplishments noted earlier, as of 2004, women in Canada accounted for only 17 per cent of the total number of police officers in Canada. In other words, there were almost 9,900 female officers from a total of approximately 59,000 across the country. However, there had been a 6 per cent increase in the number of women since 2003, whereas the number of male officers remained virtually the same (Statistics Canada, 2005).

Also, the number of women representing different ranks has been increasing slowly. As previously mentioned, in 1988, 5.1 per cent of all sworn officers were women; over 95 per cent were constables, 4 per cent were noncommissioned officers, and 0.01 per cent were command officers (Forcese, 1999). In 2004, however, women represented 5 per cent of senior officers, 9 per cent of noncommissioned officers, and 20 per cent of constables. The province with the highest representation of women officers was British Columbia: over one-fifth were women in 2004. The lowest proportion of women was seen in the Atlantic provinces where only one in every eight officers was a woman. Interestingly, Canada has 188 officers per 100,000 people, which is about 20 per cent lower than in the United States (Statistics Canada, 2005).

Furthermore, the number of women representing visible minority groups is small. In 2001 visible minorities (defined by Statistics Canada as "persons, other than Aboriginal persons, who are non-Caucasian in race or non-white in colour [i.e., Chinese, South-Asian, Black, Arab/West Asian, Filipino, South East Asian, Latin American, Japanese, and Korean]") constituted 13 per cent of the Canadian population (15 years of age and older), but only 4 per cent of public police officers were a visible minority. When visible minority status and sex are combined, 4 per cent (385) of all female officers and 5 per cent (2,395) of all male officers represented a visible minority group (Juristat, 2001).

Aboriginal persons (defined by Statistics Canada as persons "who reported identifying with at least one Aboriginal Group, i.e., North American Indian, Métis or Inuit (Eskimo) and/or those who reported being a Treaty Indian or a Registered Indian as defined by the Indian Act of Canada and/or who were members of an Indian Band or First Nation"), constituted 3 per cent of the overall Canadian population (15 years of age and older) and 4 per cent of police officers were Aboriginal. The police officer percentage includes individuals who represent self-administered First Nations police services; that is Aboriginal police officers who police their own communities. When Aboriginal status and sex are combined, 5 per cent (485) of all female officers and 4 per cent (1,955) of all male officers have Aboriginal status (Juristat, 2001).

With respect to education, women continue to have higher levels of education as was the case with early policewomen. According to Statistics Canada, over half of police officers (55 per cent) had completed either a college certificate/diploma or a university degree, but, similar to American women, female public police officers (and private investigators) have higher levels of education than their male counterparts. In 2001, 27 per cent of female police officers had a university degree compared to 17 per cent of male officers (and 17 per cent of female private investigators had a university degree compared to 11 per cent of male private investigators) (Juristat, 2001).

The second wave of the feminist movement brought about several changes relating to gender and policing in both the US and Canada, but different types of challenges remain as will be presented throughout the book.

The Third Wave of the Women's Movement

As previously stated, some have recently referred to the feminist/women's movement from 1980 to the present as the third "wave" of the movement (Denfield, 1996; Heywood and Drake, 1997; Walter, 1999). One of the main arguments made is that the recent wave in the movement has called attention to the many different and multiple experiences of women. Emphasis is placed on the diverse social categories that women represent, including race, sexual orientation, ethnicity, immigrant status, class, disability, religion, etc., and the differences in lived experiences as a result of these categories. Academics have started to write about these differences, which include the experiences of women police officers. Ferree and Hess (2000) point out that the differences in women's experiences have become more apparent in recent years, but the women's movement has always represented interconnected networks of people working at both the bureaucratic and grassroots level and not just one collective voice. Also, equally important at present must remain the recognition of the impact of the various patriarchal social forces, occupational cultures, and organizational structures on human behaviour. For instance, the police occupational culture and paramilitaristic organizational structure produce certain shared gendered experiences for women regardless of race, ethnicity, sexual orientation, etc. (Corsianos, 2004). This does not mean that all women have the exact same experiences, or are oppressed in the same way, but rather that women share experiences of oppression (see Chapter 7).

Canadian Timeline

Early 1800s   Rose Fortune is the first woman recognized for taking on policing duties in Canada, in Annapolis Valley, Nova Scotia.

1887   Mrs. Whiddow (as she was referred to) is the first woman to officially hold the title of "police matron" with the Toronto Police.

1912	Lurancy Harris and Minnie Miller of Vancouver, British Columbia, and Annie Jackson of Edmonton, Alberta, become the first "policewomen" in Canada.
1940s–1960s	There is a slow but gradual increase in female officers.
1950s	Some departments establish women and youth bureaus that are staffed almost entirely by women.
By 1960s	Approximately 0.5 per cent of all officers are women (i.e., fewer than 200 persons).
Mid-1970s	One per cent of all sworn officers are women.
Until 1970s	Women continue to be seen as auxiliary personnel.
1982	The Constitution Act is passed; the act includes the Charter of Rights and Freedoms.
Mid-1990s	Approximately 10 per cent of all sworn officers are women (i.e., over 5,000 persons).
2004	Approximately 17 per cent of all sworn officers are women (i.e., almost 9,900 persons).

Questions

1. What impact did the first wave of the women's/feminist movement have on female officers in both the US and Canada?
2. What impact did the second wave of the women's/feminist movement have on female officers in both the US and Canada?
3. What forms of discrimination did women in policing experience prior to the 1970s, and what forms of discrimination do female officers experience today?
4. Could the "separate spheres" approach to policing be applied today in particular circumstances? Why or why not and what would be the implications to this?
5. Will a GEA for the creation of police policies always be necessary? Explain.

CHAPTER 2

Gender Analyses in Criminology and Policing

Feminism refers to a variety of theories about gendered experiences and oppressions and a number of strategies for social change. It is not enough to simply describe women's experiences within policing systems. Rather we must attempt to analyze and explain them, assess the relevance of gender in our society generally and in criminology and policing more specifically, and work towards eliminating social barriers. Feminism advocates social equality between women and men and opposes patriarchal ideologies, social systems, and structures.

According to Daly and Chesney-Lind (1988) and Morris (1987), there is no one single feminist perspective in criminology. Academics have offered different definitions of feminism that entail several paradoxes. Some call for an acknowledgement of diversity among women's experiences, while asserting there are collective experiences that all women share. Others call for the elimination of oppressive gender categories, but at the same time encourage people to become conscious of the relevance of gender in their lives, or use gender categories for political praxis. Still others suggest the need for gender-specific legislation that addresses the current different social realities of women, while advocating for the elimination of gender discrimination. Danner (1989: 51) defines feminism as "a women-centered description and explanation of human experience and the social world. It asserts that gender governs every aspect of personal and social life.... Also, feminist theory is activist and seeks social change to end the neglect and subordination of women." According to bell hooks, feminism is "the struggle to end sexist oppression" (1984: 26). She argues that all forms of oppression must be eliminated in order for sexism to end.

There are different feminist theoretical paradigms/perspectives that include liberal, socialist, Marxist, radical, antiracist/multiracial, and postmodern (as discussed in Chapter 3). However, despite their differences, there are specific elements of feminist research in general that distinguish it from nonfeminist schools of thought. For instance, feminist research makes the distinction between sex and gender, explaining that observed behavioural differences between the sexes are not the products of nature/biology, but rather the result of socialization, patriarchal ideologies, and socio-economic factors. Sex differences between women and men refer to the biological differences that include reproductive organs, body size, muscle development, and hormones. Gender differences, on the other hand, are socially constructed; that is, are ascribed by society. Gendered differences can be seen in the use of language, wage disparities, career choices, styles of dress, childcare responsibilities, sexual performances, etc.

These observed differences in behaviour/social performances, ideas, and beliefs between many women and men are not biologically determined, but are determined by society. Gender roles are learned through socialization beginning in infancy. The assumptions many people make and the beliefs many have of individuals appearing to belong to a particular sex are the result of dominant historical, economic, and political social forces. When people say, "he's acting like a girl" or "she's a tomboy," these serve as examples of normative conceptions of sex-appropriate behaviour that many falsely assume to be the product of biology. According to West and Zimmerman (1987: 137), "doing gender means creating differences between girls and boys and women and men, differences that are not natural, essential, or biological. Once the differences have been constructed, they are used to reinforce the 'essentialness' of gender." Sexism and patriarchy are vital components in the distinction between sex and gender. Patriarchy is a form of social organization where men are privileged over women and hold the majority of political, economic, and social power. Sexism is the ideological basis of patriarchy and is the belief that one sex is superior to the other. Central to patriarchal ideologies is the assumption that observed differences between the sexes are the result of biology. For example, patriarchal ideologies promote the idea of women as nurturing, emotional, and passive compared to men and define these as sex differences. Feminists, however, identify them as gender differences and point to the complex and multiple historical social forces that have produced these performed "differences."

In feminist research, gender inequality is viewed as a major cause of the continued oppression and marginalization of women and girls, and gender categories are organized in ways that enable and promote men's social and political-economic dominance. Moreover, feminist research is not limited to topics on or about women, but, rather, questions are framed, results are interpreted, and suggestions for social change are made in ways that recognize the centrality of gender in our social world and how it produces and reproduces differences in experiences between the sexes. For instance, feminist research on paramilitaristic social institutions like policing, where patriarchal ideologies have been central to the current policing systems and structures, are vital even though the majority of the people interacted with and/or interviewed in the field have been men. Unfortunately, "the irony is that feminist scholarship is characterized as being only about women or as hopelessly biased toward women, when in fact the project is to describe and change both men's and women's lives" (Daly and Chesney-Lind, 1988: 501).

What is Feminist Criminology?

Distinctions are made about the origins of patriarchy and sexism and suggestions for social change between the different schools of feminist thought. Thus, according to Morris (1987: 17), a feminist criminology is not possible because neither feminism nor criminology is a "unified set of principles and practices." However, feminist theories are an integral part to studying crime, power dynamics, laws, and the criminal justice system. Feminist theories and feminist inquiries into criminological knowledge enable us to critically evaluate past and current studies on criminal offending, victims of crime, and the entire criminal justice system, including the police.

Prior to the 1970s, feminist perspectives in studies on crime, deviance, and social control were virtually nonexistent. As noted by various academics (Naffine, 1996; Messerschmidt, 1993; Leonard, 1982), most criminological studies failed to study women. They either ignored women's experiences, or falsely assumed that conclusions from research that solely focused on men could be applied to women. For the most part, biology-caused crime arguments were central in the few studies (Lombroso and Ferrero, 1895; Pollack, 1950; Thomas, 1923) that examined the differences between female and male criminality. These studies assumed that experienced differences between the sexes must be the result of biological differences. Unlike feminist theorists, these early studies failed to look at how society socializes men and women differently; that is, to act and think according to one's gender. As Simone de Beauvoir (1974: 38) said: "One is not born, but rather, becomes a woman."

These early studies failed to make the significant distinction between sex and gender, rather depicting women in sexist and stereotypical ways without the necessary evidence to support their claims. Otto Pollack, similar to the biology theorists before him, used the biology argument to explain female criminal behaviour. He argued that nature causes women to commit crimes as frequently as men, but that women are more likely to be involved in sex crimes or crimes that entail deceit and/or slyness (e.g., prostitution, fraud, forgery, embezzlement). Additionally, he formulated a "chivalry thesis" explaining the causes of reactions to women's crimes. He claimed that women were significantly less likely to be arrested, prosecuted, and/or convicted due to chivalrous attitudes by male criminal justice agents.

Chivalry assumes that males were protective of women who were often perceived as weak and dependent. As several feminist scholars since the 1970s have pointed out, Pollack assumed that all female offenders were given leniency, without exploring differences in experiences between women who represented different social categories (e.g., women of colour versus white women; wealthy women versus poor women, etc.). He did not examine the differences in experiences between women and the types of crimes committed. Several academic writings have since shown that social class, race, and ethnicity play a significant role in the different treatment of women (and men) by criminal justice agents (Reiman, 2007; Comack, 2006; Balfour and Comack, 2006; Corsianos, 2005; 2003; 2001; Faith, 1994; Chesney-Lind and Shelden, 2004; Barak, 2003; Koons-Witt and Schram, 2003; Barak, Flavin, and Leighton, 2001; Neugebauer, 1999; Logan, 1999; Russell, 1998; Visano, 1998; Maher and Daly, 1996; Nagel and Johnson, 1994; Harding, 1991; Steffensmeier and Allan, 1988; Naffine, 1987; Leonard, 1982; Steffensmeier and Cobb, 1981). Alternatively, others have found that women who are seen as "fallen women" or "morally loose" (e.g., women convicted of prostitution) and women who violate their gender roles by committing more violent crimes that have been traditionally associated with men tend to be treated much more harshly by the criminal justice system (Eaton, 1986; Dell, 1999).

By the 1960s, a few criminologists (Reckless, 1961; Heidensohn, 1968; Bertrand, 1969) began to discuss the limitations of many of the widely accepted theories of crime for neglecting to include female offenders, for falsely assuming that these theories could be applied to women and girls, and for neglecting to explain the significant differences in the number of crimes committed by women versus men.

Early Feminist Critiques in Criminology

Early feminist criminological research in the 1970s and 1980s was primarily focused on female offenders and began to identify many problems in the previous nonfeminist work. Feminists were critical of research that focused solely on men, where the findings/conclusions were applied to female populations, resulting in criminological theories excluding women. They further identified several limitations to the limited nonfeminist writings that attempted to explain female criminal behaviour.

For instance, nonfeminist research failed to see the social constructions of gender that led to the differences in the experienced realities of women versus men. This is despite the fact that gender was and continues to be the strongest indicator of one's likelihood to commit a criminal offense. Furthermore, it was feminist criminologists who pointed out that certain types of behaviour on the part of women and/or girls, such as prostitution and engaging in sexual relations while under the legal age, and noncriminal status offenses such as running away from home and curfew violations, were perceived as immoral and largely comprised the "criminal" acts of women and girls that mainstream criminologists studied (Klein, 1973; Chesney-Lind, 1973; Temin, 1973; Millman, 1975; Smart, 1976; Heidensohn, 1985; Morris, 1987). Interestingly, the earlier work done by predominantly middle-class white male researchers (Lombroso and Ferrero, 1895; Thomas, 1923; Pollack, 1950; Shaw and McKay, 1969) neglected to see gendered differences in the policing of such behaviours. In other words, the police often applied a "double standard" when it came to policing particular crimes. Female prostitutes, for instance, were more likely to be policed in comparison to their male customers, or even males working as prostitutes. Also, girls were more likely to be policed for various status offenses, such as "running away," in comparison to boys (Chesney-Lind, 1974).

Early feminist research began to make profound contributions to our understanding of gender and criminology, focusing initially on female offenders and female victims of crime, and subsequently on women working as criminal justice agents. A few examples of these early studies by Chesney-Lind and Rodriguez (1983), James and Meyerding (1977), and Silbert and Pines (1981) found that women and girls who committed crimes had high rates of victimizations, such as physical abuse, sexual assault, and incest. Others found that women representing different racial categories experienced differences in incarceration rates and treatment (Freedman, 1981; Rafter, 1985). Also, despite early "liberation theories" linking female criminal activity to the women's movement (Adler, 1975; Simon, 1975), many early feminist studies concluded that the rate of female offenders remained steady with the exception of less serious property crimes (Leonard, 1982; Naffine, 1987; Steffensmeier and Allan, 1988; Steffensmeier and Cobb, 1981).

Feminist Criminological Research Today

Feminist criminology was founded on the principle that women were not represented fairly in criminological theories and research. In the early years of second wave feminism, there tended to be commonality in feminist theorizing. However, some of the theories and writings were criticized for focusing primarily on white, middle-class, and heterosexual women's experiences. Today, however, different feminist perspectives have presented us with multiple feminist voices (Burgess-Proctor, 2006; McDermott, 2002; Brush, 1997; Frug, 1995; Austin, 1995; Engle, 1995; Spelman and Minow, 1995; Crenshaw, 1995; Ackoff, 1988; Flax 1987; Harding, 1986a; 1986b; 1986c). Feminist research today has given voice to different groups of people including, but not limited to, persons of colour, lesbians, and the poor. This has led to what is referred to by some as the third "wave" of feminism, which includes multiracial feminist research, as well as masculinities research.

Multiracial feminism looks at multiple identity categories that create and sustain inequalities. Many feminist writings today strive to demonstrate the interconnectedness of gender, culture, politics, sexuality, economics, and history. According to Burgess-Proctor (2006: 37), "the intersectional approach recognizes that race, class, gender, sexuality, and other locations of inequality are dynamic, historically grounded, socially constructed power relationships that simultaneously operate at both the micro-structural and macro-structural levels."

However, equally important has been the research on masculinities. Messerschmidt, for instance (1993; 1997), addresses the impact of gender not only on women's criminal behaviour but also on the criminality of men. He asserts that masculinity is central to explaining criminal behaviour and identifies three gendered social structures relevant in our understanding of differences in that behaviour. They include the gender division of labour, gender relations of power, and sexuality.

He further asserts that race, class, and gender in relation to these social structures produce different types of behaviour in establishing masculinity. For example, young poor males who represent minority groups are not able to prove their masculinity in more conventional ways and thus may use violence and crime to confirm their masculinity. Bottcher (2001: 896), on the other hand, points to some limitations in Messerschmidt's approach because he does not "fully reveal the process by which crime becomes a resource for doing masculinity." Moreover, few studies have attempted to understand women's and girl's involvement in criminal activity if crime is used in ways to establish masculinity.

According to Connell (1995: 77), "hegemonic masculinity" is defined as "the configuration of gender practice which embodies the currently accepted answer to the problem of legitimacy of patriarchy, which guarantees (or is taken to guarantee) the dominant position of men and the subordination of women." In other words, "hegemonic masculinity" is the cultural demonstration of men's domination over women. Also, Totten (2000) and Gilligan (1996) point to how crimes such as violent crimes often revolve around gender identity, male sexuality, and proving "hegemonic masculinity." According to Totten (2000), adolescent boys who cannot openly discuss their sexuality (for example, "coming out" as gay) may act out violently against other persons. Moreover, there are heterosexual men who perceive violent acts against gays as commendable because they serve to reinforce their own sexual identity, and these acts are condoned by mainstream social institutions such as the family, the military, the media, and the educational system (Comstock, 1991; Kinsman, 1987). All of these multiple feminist voices have contributed, in different ways, to the criminological research. Also, the number of feminist criminological studies to date cannot be ignored.

Feminists today are addressing different social identities and attempting to decode the dynamics and impact of various social forces on people's lived experiences. Moreover, some universities are producing feminist scholars, and some criminology, criminal justice, and sociology departments have hired scholars who specialize in feminist criminology. Undoubtedly, feminists have made an impact on criminology as a discipline by presenting new concepts and ideologies and by debunking "common sense" assumptions and conclusions made regarding women in crime and criminal justice. According to Brush (1997), women cannot expect equal treatment if they do not seek to redress the issues that gave them second-class status in the first place. "Only by decoding the dynamics that make feminists seem moralistic and pointing to the links among violence, sexuality, culture, and economics, can feminists begin to bring the full promise of democratic politics to bear on women's progress" (Brush, 1997: 253). According to Comack (2006), because of feminist work over the past 40 years, we know so much more about the lives of criminalized women, but feminist criminological research is by no means complete.

McDermott (2002) examines the impact pragmatism and feminism have had on feminist criminology. Feminist criminology, in addition to feminism and pragmatism, focuses on the human potential for change as a crucial element in ending inequalities. Brush (1997) cites three ways in which feminist thought has influenced criminology.

- Criminology has been influenced by the critiquing and evaluation of mainstream criminology concepts, theories, and methods and by specifically examining the misrepresentation of women in crime and criminal justice.
- Feminists have presented new concepts and ideologies that have made major impacts on how victimization is defined in terms of domestic violence, rape, and sexual harassment.
- The development of feminist thought as an interdisciplinary effort has had a significant impact on the discipline of criminology.

For all of the reasons discussed above, feminist theories, despite their differences in identifying the causes of gender oppression and inequalities and their strategies for social change, enable us to ask different questions and identify areas that mainstream criminology has ignored.

Yet, despite these successes, Renzetti (1993: 219) points out that feminist criminology appears to remain at the margins of the "malestream" (i.e., the "mainstream"). Also, Comack (2006: 55) asserts that during "these neo-liberal times, meeting the challenge of containing—and especially countering—dominant understandings about women and crime is all the more necessary."

Indeed, there has been an increase in the number of feminist journals that frequently feature articles on gender and crime, including topics such as female and male offenders, gendered differences in arrest and incarceration rates, treatment of offenders in the criminal justice system, violence against women, and experienced gendered differences by victims of crime, as well as by criminal justice agents. However, mainstream criminology journals, particularly in the US, do not typically publish feminist research unless the information is presented in ways that satisfy the status quo.

Mainstream criminology continues to be nonfeminist on many levels, as demonstrated in the areas studied, methodological approaches taken, questions that are asked, and in its neglect to critically reflect and analyze human behaviour relating to social constructions of gender, race, ethnicity, class, sexual orientation, and age. Not surprisingly, research studies that include male-only participants often do not identify this in the title, however, studies focusing solely on females, or both males and females, are frequently made apparent in their titles. Criminology as a discipline is limited, as it is overwhelmingly the result of white economically privileged men's experiences. MacKinnon (1989) argues that the state and the legal system operate from men's perspectives and, therefore, criminology reflects patriarchal ideologies and experiences. Smart (1989) believes the legal system is so inherently patriarchal that it is impossible to make any meaningful changes within the current system.

Moreover, most policing research continues to ignore the impact of gender on human behaviour and theories relating to crime and the criminal justice system.

Gender Analyses in Research on Policing

Unfortunately, the research on gender and policing has not experienced a significant increase in the academic world. Only a handful of academic books have focused on the relationship between gender and policing globally, let alone within a North American context (Schulz, 2004b; Gerber, 2001; Westmarland, 2001; Heidensohn and Brown, 2000; Miller, 1999; Appier, 1998; Schulz, 1995; Heidensohn, 1992; Martin, 1990).

More recently, several descriptive and/or critical books on gender and crime and the criminal justice system have been published; however, the area of policing is often reduced to a chapter or two, or a few paragraphs (Martin and Jurik, 2007; Belknap, 2007; 2001; Schram and Koons-Witt, 2004; Grana, 2002; Pollock, 2002; Barak, Flavin, and Leighton, 2001; Van Wormer and Bartollas, 2000; Baskin and Sommers, 1998; Price and Sokoloff, 1995). Only a handful of academic books have been published recently in the area of gender and policing in North America (Schulz, 2004b; 1995; Gerber, 2001; Miller, 1999; Appier, 1998). Schulz (2004b) offers a descriptive account of the personal histories of American female officers who gained access to upper management positions within American police organizations. In addition, Schulz (1995) details the changing role of women in policing from matrons to police officers; Gerber (2001) offers a psychological analysis of American women in policing; Miller (1999) studies the impact of gender on community policing (CP) in a midwestern city in the US; and Appier (1998) examines the origins and struggles of pioneer policewomen in big city police departments such as the Los Angeles Police Department.

Most policing research has continued to ignore gender from its analysis and has not bothered to evaluate its relationship to police organizations and police culture. Some policing scholars have noted that the reason for excluding gender is because women continue to make up a small number of sworn officers in both Canada and the US. This is astonishing, but not surprising. One would think that more policing scholars would want to include gender in order to pinpoint why the number of women working in this particular area of "criminal justice" is small, despite the significant increases in women in other traditionally male-dominated fields such as law, engineering, and medicine, or why the "macho image" continues to remain synonymous with policing.

A. Early Studies in Gender and Policing

The 1970s sparked some policing studies in the US to evaluate if women could perform patrol duties as effectively as men. Studies of American cities included New York City; Washington, DC; Denver, Colorado; Philadelphia, Pennsylvania; St. Louis

County, Missouri; Newton, Massachusetts; and the California State Highway Patrol (Lord, 1995). The studies concluded that women demonstrated successful performance comparable to their male counterparts. Yet all of these early studies assumed that males were somehow superior to females, and the methods and approaches used in policing implied that they were somehow the correct or best ways of "doing police work" (Bloch and Anderson, 1974; Sherman, 1975; Bartell and Associates, 1978; Bartlett and Rosenblum, 1977; Sichel et al., 1978; Grennan, 1987).

Additional early studies (Kanter, 1976; Martin, 1979) focused on the issue of women as "tokens" in policing. In other words, many police departments initially hired a few women to show that they were somehow committed to diversity, but, in actuality, no real efforts were made to attract and recruit women, as well as other under-represented groups. In Kanter's research (1976), token women worked in police departments where they constituted less than 15 per cent of the total police personnel; their low numbers made them highly visible as "policewomen." In turn, this led to dysfunctional performance pressures and resulted in a higher level of attrition in comparison to their male counterparts.

B. Recent Research on Gender and Policing

A recent study by Belknap and Shelley (1993: 47) supported earlier claims by concluding that "the most consistent characteristic significantly related to policewomen's perceptions and experiences was the percentage of women in the department." Also, a number of studies have critically evaluated the relationship between gender and the paramilitaristic police model; the continued emphasis on policing as being synonymous with brawn versus specialized knowledge, skills, and training, and the continued use by some US police departments of the "in-your-face" training model (similar to some military boot camps) that often involves screaming, and the use of profanity and demeaning acts against police recruits (Charles, 1981; Bell, 1982; Morash and Greene, 1986; Martin, 1990; Heidensohn, 1992; Martin, 1999; Miller, 1999; Martin and Jurik, 1996; Heidensohn and Brown, 2000; Birzer and Tannehill, 2001; Gerber, 2001; Prokos and Pedavic, 2002; O'Connor, 2003; Sims, Scarborough, and Ahmad, 2003; Garcia, 2003; Corsianos, 2004; 2005; 2007a).

The idea that police work is primarily based on fighting and the need for physical aggression is misleading. Contrary to what officers are taught in the police academy (in the US), or the police college (in Canada), approximately 80 per cent of police work involves activities typically associated with social work. Hence, it is believed that the majority of police work reflects issues in which women have been largely socialized to be more efficient at resolving (Garcia, 2003). However, given the emphasis on physical aggression, it is not surprising to see that higher turnover rates are more prevalent for female officers (Doerner, 1995), and that women are less likely to pursue a career in this field. For instance, in the US, women comprise only 13 per cent of the total number of sworn police personnel (National Center for

Women and Policing, 2003), and in Canada, the national average of female officers is slightly higher at 17 per cent (Statistics Canada, 2005c).

The police occupational culture continues to preserve and promote patriarchal ideologies, as do police academies and colleges. In a recent study on training and the police academy (Prokos and Padavic, 2002), researchers focused on the domination of characteristics associated with "masculinity" and gender stereotypes in training that served to ostracize and marginalize women. Prokos enrolled in a police academy in a rural county in the southeast US to conduct participant observation. She did not reveal her research intention to the administrator or students in order to avoid obtaining biased data. The study found that the written curriculum was promoted as being gender-neutral, however, there was a hidden curriculum that promoted the idea that police work was for men and not women. Numerous methods were used by male students and instructors to exclude female students; gendered language served as one example, where students were referred to as "guys" or "gentlemen." Men would engage in activities that encouraged male bonding (e.g., bragging about their sex lives, etc.), but they would stop their discussions when a female entered the conversation, preventing female students from bonding with male students. Some males commented that these topics were not appropriate for "ladies," which served as a way to keep women as "outsiders."

Moreover, women were excluded from classroom examples. In one demonstration, instructors taught male officers how to ensure female sexual privacy during a search, whereas female officers were not given instruction on how to conduct a proper search on men. Interestingly, even the female instructors geared their teaching towards a male audience, which included a discussion on appropriate clothing attire for men during job interviews — a comparable discussion on appropriate attire for women was not presented. Moreover, gender differences were often exaggerated. The fact that most women tend not to have the same physical strength (defined in narrow terms) as most men was stressed frequently. The idea of women as "weak" and men as "strong" was promoted. Male officers were rarely paired with female officers in physical combat training. Additionally, males were frequently disrespectful to female instructors (approximately 12 per cent of the instructors were female) by questioning their authority or disregarding their instructions. Male students often treated class material on issues regarding domestic violence and rape as insignificant and chose to focus on the physical appearances of the women actors portrayed in classroom training videos. Also, derogatory language was used to refer to men who were perceived as acting in a "nonmasculine" manner. Overall, Prokos and Padavic concluded police training was treated in a very sexist gender-specific fashion that served to promote gender stereotypes and masculine traits as the norm in the field of policing.

Not surprisingly, the policing research confirms that male officers' negative attitudes towards women signal stronger support for traditional policing styles. In a recent study (Sims, Scarborough, and Ahmad, 2003), American researchers set out to evaluate if attitudes towards women could be used to predict the attitudes officers have about CP versus traditional reactive policing. A sample of 560 officers from the Little Rock Police Department in Arkansas were selected and mailed surveys. The survey included questions regarding attitudes towards women and female police officers, as well as attitudes relating to community and traditional policing methods. Three hundred and fifteen surveys were completed. The mean age of respondents was 36 years and the sample consisted of 80 per cent males, of which 69 per cent were Caucasian. Female officers were more likely to view women more favourably than their male counterparts. They were more likely to view women as being just as competent as men, and take women seriously when discussing issues such as sexism in the workplace. Similarly, minorities were more likely to agree that women continued to experience discrimination in the US. Also, male officers who were married or lived with a female significant other were more likely to have a positive image of women and their police-related abilities, and the more favourable officers were towards women, the more supportive they were of CP.

For the most part, the research shows that female officers continue to be criticized for not possessing the perceived necessary "masculine" traits of aggressiveness, rationality, bravery, objectivity, and brutality, which are, in turn, perceived to be required for so-called effective crime-fighting police officers (Charles, 1981; Miller, 1999; Corsianos, 2007a; 2005; 2004). Interestingly, others have commented on how policing is often viewed as "masculine" work that focuses on crime-fighting, but note that police work frequently involves activities that are defined as "feminine" (Martin, 1999; Martin and Jurik, 1996).

Martin (1999), on the other hand, examined the varieties of emotional labour involved in police work and the dilemmas that norms related to emotional labour presented to women officers. These criticisms often lead to sexist claims that women are inherently not competent to perform traditional police work, and that they are better suited in police roles that deal with social-service-type functions (e.g., in community-oriented police capacities, working with domestic assault victims, youth, etc.) (Heidensohn and Brown, 2000; Heidensohn, 1992; Bell, 1982; Drummond, 1976). These attitudes serve to marginalize women and place them in the periphery of policing; that is, outside of mainstream, or "malestream," policing.

A limited number of studies have attempted to evaluate female police officers' work performance in ways that do not emphasize situations and characteristics associated with definitions of "masculinity" (Corsianos 2007a; 2005; 2004; Gerber, 2001; Morash and Greene, 1986). Most of the research continues to assume that male police officers are somehow the standard to which female officers should be compared. Alternatively, some research has indicated that female police officers (and female prison workers) have a less aggressive style than male officers and are better at de-escalating potentially violent situations (Belknap, 1991; Belknap and Shelley, 1993; Grennan, 1987; Bell, 1982) and that female officers may be more likely to have traits associated with positive forms of policing, such as providing different forms of support to female victims of violence (Feinman, 1986; Homant and Kennedy, 1985; Kennedy and Homant, 1983; Price, 1974).

C. Research on Hiring and Promoting More Women Officers

The National Center for Women and Policing is a strong advocate of more female police representation in the US. They assert that higher numbers of women in policing will bring positive changes by helping to reduce deviant behaviour and brutality, promote the use of conflict resolution and effective communication over the use of force, and improve police response to certain crimes such as domestic violence. However, research is divided in terms of the extent that the police culture can change by increasing the number of female officers (Martin, 1990; Belknap, 1991; Fletcher, 1995). Some findings have shown that women who are hired as tokens in traditionally male-dominated fields like policing are at a disadvantage as their token status limits how much change they can bring to these jobs (Belknap and Shelley, 1993). More recently, according to Belknap (2007), hiring, firing, and promotional decisions should not be made solely on the basis of sex; however, women must be actively recruited in fields like policing, and administrators must implement methods to keep existing women employees and promote them in rank. Female representation remains low at all levels within policing. According to the National Center for Women and Policing (2001), in both large and small American police agencies, women hold few policing positions (see tables below).

American Female Police Officers in Large Police Agencies (100 or More Sworn Personnel)

Top Command Positions	7.3 per cent occupied by women (1.6 per cent occupied by women of colour)
Supervisory Positions	9.6 per cent occupied by women (3.1 per cent occupied by women of colour)
Line Operation Positions	13.5 per cent occupied by women (5.3 per cent occupied by women of colour)

American Female Officers in Small and Rural Police Agencies (Less Than 100 Sworn Personnel)

Top Command Positions	3.4 per cent occupied by women (0.3 per cent occupied by women of colour)
Supervisory Positions	4.6 per cent occupied by women (0.4 per cent occupied by women of colour)

Line Operation Positions   9.7 per cent occupied by women
                                (1.5 per cent occupied by women of colour)

Over half (55.9 per cent) of the large American police agencies surveyed had no women in top command positions, and the majority (87.9 per cent) had no women of colour in these positions. The number of women in top command positions in small and rural police departments is significantly lower. In these agencies, 97.4 per cent had no women in top command positions, and only one of 235 agencies reported having a woman of colour in their top ranks. Similarly, according to Statistics Canada (2005), the number of Canadian women in policing is low at all levels within police organizations (see table below).

Canadian Female Officers

Senior Officers   5 per cent women

Noncommissioned Officers   9 per cent women

Police Constables   20 per cent women

A study done by the International Association of Chiefs of Police (IACP) in 1998 aimed to collect information on a number of issues relating to women in policing, including recruitment/hiring, promotion, attrition, and resignation. A random sample of 800 of IACP's 14,000 members was selected to be surveyed by telephone. The survey respondents consisted of 97 per cent males and 3 per cent females, and 94 per cent were chiefs of police and 6 per cent held other positions. Respondents were employed in agencies of all sizes: 277 of the agencies had fewer than 21 officers; 311 had 21 to 50 officers; and 210 had more than 51 officers.

The survey revealed a number of different findings. With respect to recruitment, retention, and promotion the following was reported: The survey found that 26 per cent of the agencies had policies/strategies in place to recruit women, and that larger agencies were about three times more likely to actively recruit women than smaller agencies. The details of these policies/strategies were not discussed. Also, 86 per cent of the agencies had a written gender discrimination policy. However, the larger agencies, those that actively recruited women, and those that had mentoring programs for women were more likely to have such a policy in place (93-95 per cent).

Moreover, 28 per cent of the respondents reported that their departments had somewhat more trouble retaining female officers, but faced retention issues with both women and men. Respondents were also asked for the reasons given by women officers for resigning. Family, children, and/or the birth of a child was the number one reason given by respondents (12 per cent). Other responses included better job/career (10 per cent), better pay/money (6 per cent), career change (4 per cent), and advancement opportunities (3 per cent). Twenty-three per cent of respondents listed these reasons. Also, when asked why they thought it was difficult to promote women, 18 per cent said there were too few women in the ranks to move up, 13 per cent reported a lack of promotional opportunities, 9 per cent cited gender bias in limiting promotions for women, and 6 per cent said that a lack of acceptance hindered women from being promoted. Also, respondents were asked whether they had mentoring programs that aimed to create a supportive work environment for newly hired women officers by pairing them up with senior female or male officers. Only 13 per cent of respondents reported having such programs in their agencies (IACP, 1998).

Another study that looked at the Los Angeles Police Department between 1990 and 1999 also found that it had more trouble retaining female officers than males. Women were twice as likely as men to leave the academy due to resignation or termination; 19 per cent of the women versus 9 per cent of the men (Los Angeles Police Commission, 2000).

With regard to promotions specifically, a lot of consideration is given to officers' performance evaluations. Most police agencies evaluate officers' performance on an annual or semi-annual basis. These evaluations become part of an officer's permanent personnel file and can be used to determine promotions and transfers to various units/assignments and special training. However, many female officers believe they are subjected to unfair evaluations due to their gender. They are frequently viewed as "weak," or as token hires and this results in unfair performance evaluations by their supervisors, which serve as barriers when seeking promotion (Schulz, 2004a).

Also, highly valued assignments and specialized training are heavily weighted when seeking promotion. These assignments are often perceived to be dangerous and/or emphasize a particular definition of physical strength and include units such as Special Weapons and Tactics (SWAT), homicide, undercover narcotics, and gang investigations. Women are least likely to be awarded these assignments, and men are more likely to have mentors who support them during the application for transfer stage. That is, their mentors are likely to "push for them" in various circles and make the arrangements. Women are more likely to be awarded the assignments that are less valued by the police community, such as working in domestic violence and sexual assault units, community relations, etc., which, in turn, negatively affects them when applying for promotions. Officers with experience in the "valued areas" are more likely to receive higher scores during the oral interview stage (Harrington and Lonsway, 2004).

Another reason for the low number of women in top command positions is that most choose not to apply for promotion. According to research done by the former Portland Police Chief Penny Harrington and her co-author Kimberly Lonsway (2004: 504), reasons for this include the following:

- Women view the promotion systems as biased against them and do not wish to expend the effort it takes to prepare for the process — especially when they believe that they will not succeed.

- Women know that if they do succeed in the promotion process and receive a promotion, they will once again be under intense scrutiny — more than their male counterparts. Female officers know that promotion means that they would once again have to prove themselves, and the "proving" would never end. As a supervisor or command-level person, a woman would be more highly visible within her organization and thus more intensely watched.
- Usually, a promotion requires an officer to relocate to a new unit and drop to the bottom of the seniority list. Because many aspects of an officer's work life (such as shift assignments, days off, and vacation days) are regulated by seniority, promotion may therefore mean assignment to a shift that makes it extremely difficult to find child care. The promotion may even mean that the officer can no longer have weekends available to spend with family; these issues can be especially difficult for single mothers.
- Especially at the command level, women often find themselves being promoted back into the "women's jobs" that they had previously left behind. For example, women commanders are frequently given assignments to head the records division, planning division, youth division, domestic violence and sexual assault divisions, or community relations. In contrast, men who are promoted to the level of commander are typically given prestigious assignments to head patrol divisions, detective divisions, vice and narcotics divisions, or other tactical units.

Some Canadian police departments, however, have recognized that many women have experienced difficulties in gaining access to these coveted positions that can provide them with the necessary management experience and hands-on experience in specialized areas needed for promotions. Thus, "in many police services, collective agreements specify how temporary assignments, deployment to special projects and acting rank must be done" (Josiah, 1997: 84). Many Canadian departments today have implemented new promotional policies and procedures that attempt to deal with past discriminatory promotion practices. However, as Josiah (1997: 84) notes, "There may be unintentional barriers to women's increased participation; these should be examined closely by police services boards, labor and management, with adequate representation of women on the working group."

It used to be that promotions were the purview of the "old boy's network — not what you knew as much as who you knew and how long you had been around. Police services are now implementing gender-neutral promotional policies based on a combination of examination marks, assessment of potential for effectiveness, seniority, review of past performance and interview results for part of a comprehensive promotional process. Behavioral interview techniques, training for interviewers, gender-balanced interview panels and structured reference checking are also elements of these new processes intended to eliminate bias and ensure objective assessment of all candidates (Josiah, 1997: 84).

Challenges, however, remain. According to Corsianos (2005), officers are typically given the opportunity to serve in different detective units in temporary training positions. Yet, permanent detective positions are difficult to secure. Often decisions for these positions are made before "the call" is ever put out to the entire division. In the few rare instances where there is no one person in mind for the position, the detective and detective sergeant carefully screen applicants, paying close attention to an officer's ability and willingness to be a "team player." The criteria believed to be crucial for a "team player" present several gender challenges for female officers (see Chapter 6).

To date, little research has been undertaken on female law enforcement agents who have been successful in achieving and/or maintaining high-rank positions such as police chiefs, sheriffs, and special agents (Schulz, 2004b). In addition, although less overt than in previous decades, women who are hired to work as police officers continue to face discrimination, harassment, and intimidation, leading some to leave the field of policing altogether (Schulz, 2004a; 1995; Martin, 1999; 1994; 1980; Miller, 1999; Haar, 1997; Orban, 1998; Martin and Jurik, 2007).

D. Research on Gender, Race, and Policing

Some recent analyses of gender and policing have also explored the intersectionality of race and gender. Women of African descent tend to report different experiences in comparison to white female and male police officers, and also male police officers of African descent. African-American female police officers and other women of colour experience multiple levels of discrimination due to both their gender and race (Dodge and Pogrebin, 2001; Martin, 1994; Felkenes and Schroeder, 1993). For instance, Dodge and Pogrebin (2001) examined the perceptions of African-American female police officers of their professional peer relationships and their relationships with the communities they served. White female officers were not viewed as being supportive and were described as being more focused on gaining approval from white male offices than supporting female officers. Black male officers also seemed more concerned with gaining acceptance from white male officers than being supportive of their black female peers. Some women in the sample believed that African-American male officers gained advantages from the black females within the agency, because they were no longer perceived as being at the bottom of the police hierarchy. Also, African-American female officers perceived white officers in general as not knowing how to relate to black women.

Furthermore, white males were perceived as being more concerned with the physical appearance of white female officers than their job performance. They also felt that white officers were disrespectful of minorities and frequently used racial insults. Perceptions of their relationships with the communities they served were mixed. All of the officers expressed the importance of being sensitive towards minority community members. They asserted that their status as black women made them more accessible to African-American community members and that they were more understanding of the multiple issues relating to black communities. Interaction with members of these race-specific communities enabled them to improve police-community relationships in ways that could positively influence those neighbourhoods. Most of the women in the sample also believed that black community members were more likely to trust black police officers. On the other hand, some felt that African-American citizens had a very negative feeling towards them, including viewing them as traitors to the community, or lesbians.

Canadian research on the police and racial minority groups, including African-Canadian, First Nations/Native, and Asians (Burtch, 2000; Monture-Angus, 2000; Neugebauer, 1999; Commission on Systemic Racism, 1995; Harding, 1991), conclude that these groups continue to experience marginalization and forms of oppression by criminal justice agents such as the police. For instance, Neugebauer (1999) conducted interviews and focus groups with 35 members and representatives of community-based organizations in a Native community in a large Canadian city. Her study found that First Nations people were often mistreated by the police by being subjected to rude and cruel verbal exchanges, aggressive acts, and an overall hostile demeanour. With regard to First Nations women in particular, the police dealt with them in cases involving spousal violence. However, these women experienced further victimization due to both their race and gender status. Neugebauer asserts that these women are victims of multiple oppression and that the violence against them is further perpetuated by institutions such as the police who are mandated to respond to violence. Typically, First Nations people refused to report their crimes to the police. They believed that their reports would not be taken seriously and they feared reprisals (Neugebauer, 1999).

According to Harding (1991), there has been increased support for tribal policing as an alternative to traditional crime control policing. Female and male tribal officers can work with community members to address particular community problems in a preventive manner rather than through the use of arrests. Harding (1991: 369) states that "what is needed in most Aboriginal communities is more help to local people, and not criminalization of the underlying social, economic and political problems. Mediation is much more crucial than prosecution." However, further research is needed in both Canada and the US to more fully assess officers' perceptions of race within policing circles, as well as any improvements in police-community relations in minority racial and ethnic neighbourhoods that are policed by officers who self-identify as members of those groups.

Feminist Methods in Criminological Research

There is no one particular research method that is innately feminist, but rather feminists use a variety of means to collect data. Interviews, surveys, participant observation, secondary analysis, and experiments can all be feminist approaches depending on how they are conducted. Firstly, feminist method refers to the inclusion of previously marginalized voices in research. A feminist approach can often be distinguished from mainstream methodologies by its choice of social problems and feminist objectives; that is, by focusing on areas and/or people that have been ignored by scholars in the past and bringing them to the forefront. Secondly, feminist methods can often be identified by the kinds of questions asked, by the careful intellectual scrutiny of various assumed "truths" in the social structures, systems, ideologies, and social relations studied, and thirdly, in the sensitivity of the treatment of human subjects.

For example, many of the studies on domestic violence in the past focused exclusively on the police response, which disproportionately reflected male police officers' perceptions given the very small number of female officers employed in the 1970s and 1980s. Many researchers failed to interview actual victims of domestic violence in order to learn about the victims' perceptions of their experiences. Rather, they relied heavily on police records and/or individual police accounts. Feminist methodological approaches seek to gather information/knowledge from previous marginalized groups and consider the relevance of gendered experiences. These approaches have provided detailed accounts of the "victims," or, as more recently identified, as the "survivors" of domestic violence. These previously unheard and marginalized voices have been given attention and have provided us with vital knowledge to aid our understanding of their violent experiences and treatment at the hands of criminal justice agents.

Moreover, the kinds of questions asked can determine whether a study is feminist. To use the above example of victims/survivors of domestic violence, a feminist approach would ensure that the research questions put to respondents were stated in a clear nonelitist fashion and that assumptions of "common sense" understandings were suspended. For instance, a feminist scholar studying heterosexual female survivors of domestic violence would not ask questions such as, "Have you ever been assaulted?". This question assumes that the participants have the same or similar definitions of "assault" as the researcher. More appropriate questions would include, "Have you ever been intentionally hit by your boyfriend/husband/partner/lover?", "Have you ever been intentionally slapped by your boyfriend/husband/partner/-lover?", or "Have you ever been forced to have sexual intercourse by your boyfriend/-husband/partner/lover?". Depending on the particular method used in the research, participants could be empowered to answer questions in a manner most suited to them. Open-ended questions used on surveys, in interviews, and during field research could enable participants to answer questions using their own language. The open-ended approach could also lead to a number of new questions from the researcher that had not been considered before.

Feminist Methods in Researching the Police

A. First Criteria: Inclusion of Previously Ignored Areas in Policing

Feminist methodological approaches to studies on the police can ask vital questions relating to experienced gendered differences between female and male police officers that have been ignored in the past. For example, studies to determine sexist practices often question officers' ability to "choose" particular units they wish to work in. Others examine the decisions made by police supervisors relating to the pairing of officers (e.g., are women as likely to be paired with other women in patrol cars, or while working on foot patrol?), and the likelihood for promotions and/or awards given to officers for exceptional performance in areas least likely to be associated with traditional styles of policing (e.g., making the "big arrests") (Corsianos, 2007a; 2005).

B. Second Criteria: Intellectual Scrutiny of Assumed "Truths" in Policing

The second criteria in feminist methodological approaches, as mentioned above, is the intellectual scrutiny of various assumed "truths" in the social structures, systems, ideologies, and social relations studied. A feminist study examining the advancement of female police officers in both numbers and rank is critical of existing patriarchal social structures, such as policing, that pose several challenges for women. Therefore, rather than simply looking at the disproportionate number of women officers leaving the field of policing within a certain number of years, feminist scholars ask questions relating to the structure and operations that tend to present unique challenges to women specifically. Areas of concern identified by Corsianos (2007a) include the lack of choice in choosing to work a particular shift, or work part-time; the lack of on-site daycare facilities; and sexist ideologies and practices (e.g., physical qualifications, gender-specific assignments, etc). Given the fact that a disproportionate number of women in Canada and the US take on the bulk of child-rearing responsibilities, it would be beneficial to many female officers to have the choice to work a particular shift if they had children of school age and had to be home after school hours. The option to work part-time for a particular period would also be more beneficial for women officers. Women with newborn babies could choose not to participate in the paid workforce full-time, but rather opt to work part-time, generate some income, and not lose their seniority. On-site daycare facilities could also help increase the number of women becoming police officers. It could enable mothers, especially officers who are single moms, to bring their children to work with them and free them from the emotional and financial stress experienced by so many mothers in the paid workforce today (Corsianos, 2007a).

Feminist scrutiny of common perceptions of police work could also include the overwhelming emphasis on a particular definition of physical strength as part of the qualifications of becoming a police officer. Many of these physical requirements reflect patriarchal ideologies. It is obvious to many feminist scholars who study the police that the number of "push-ups" or "chin-ups," and the time it takes to run a certain distance are irrelevant to the everyday tasks of police officers. Typically, officers are not involved in physical confrontations with members of the public (Corsianos, 2007a; 2005; Manning, 1997; Garner et al., 1996; Bayley and Garafalo, 1989; Sykes and Brent, 1980) but spend most of their time patrolling the streets, speaking with citizens, and completing reports (Corsianos, 2007a; Manning, 1997).

Having officers that can communicate effectively with citizens and de-escalate potentially violent situations is important for the safety of both the officers and the public (Corsianos, 2005). However, in situations where physical force is required, officers are equipped with a range of devices to subdue an individual. They range from batons, to pepper spray/mace, to tazers, to guns. Officers receive extensive training on how and when to use these devices (dictated by "continuum use of force" regulations). Adequate and effective training is intended to provide officers with the skills to do their work properly.

With respect to running, once again, for those familiar with the realities of police work, officers will usually chase a suspect for no more than a couple of hundred feet. If the suspect is not caught within that distance, then the chances of him/her being apprehended at that moment in time are very slim. The reason for this is the sheer weight the officer is carrying. This typically includes the police boots, bulletproof vest, and the gun belt around the waist, which, in addition to the gun and ammunition, holds handcuffs, a flashlight, a baton/nightstick, hand-held radio, and mace. These add up to approximately 35 pounds in weight. Yet, despite these facts, female officers who tend to be disproportionately smaller than many of their male counterparts continue to remain targets of sexist comments and assumptions relating to their physical strength and ability to perform policing duties.

Feminist scholars are critical of the emphasis on "physical strength" (especially upper body strength) in policing and the patriarchal ideologies that continue to promote the idea of particular forms of physical strength as being synonymous with superiority. The question a feminist methodological approach would raise is how does being able to do X number of push-ups or chin-ups, and run X amount of miles/kilometres in X amount of time determine one's ability to be an effective officer? These particular physical exercises are not linked to particular police duties. Rather, they are treated as "common sense" performances. That is, it is assumed that if you can pass these tests, you are somehow going to be a better officer. Interestingly, the concept of physical strength takes many forms, but when these "forms" are disproportionately associated with women they are typically not used as examples of strength.

Many of the police physical tests that are believed to measure "ability" and "competence" among police applicants are arbitrary, are not linked to particular police activities, and reflect patriarchal sexist ideologies. Yet, they have been in place for a long time and many people accept them as "common sense" without critical reflection as to their relevance. However, some police departments today have made some changes to their physical tests.

In the province of Ontario, for instance, a standardized Constable Selection System (CSS) was endorsed by the Ontario Chiefs of Police in 1998. Subsequently, most police services across the province subscribed to this new process (Ministry of Community Safety and Correctional Services, 2004). The new physical tests for applicants are believed to reflect the typical everyday physical demands of police work rather than the exceptions. Thus, particular tests used in the past, such as bench-pressing and the 1-1.5-mile run were eliminated by most police departments. This was a first step to admitting that "physical strength" as traditionally defined is not central to police work and that various aspects of some of the service's earlier tests did not determine one's ability to perform effectively as a police officer. Even the Peel Regional Police (Ontario) recently decided to change its physical testing component and adopt CSS. Up until June 2008, they continued to use physical tests that placed a lot of emphasis on upper body strength. For instance, their tests included push-ups, chin-ups, the bench press, curl-ups, as well as others, such as a 1.5-mile run (2.4 kilometres), a 100-yard sprint (91.4 metres), and a body fat test (Peel Regional Police, 2007). In July 2008, however, they announced they would be replacing their "fitness test" with the Physical Readiness Evaluation for Police (PREP), which is the same test used by CSS (although it is the only portion of CSS they will be adopting) (Peel Regional Police, 2008).

Moreover, some agencies continue to set different physical standards for female versus male applicants. Maintaining these different standards promotes the sexist idea that women are "weaker" and therefore less competent and less capable officers. Also, what do the different standards mean in relation to officers' ability to perform police activities? In other words, if the minimum time requirement for completion of the 1.5-mile run for male applicants is one minute faster than the minimum required time for female applicants, then this means that a male officer who completes the run one minute over the minimum set for men fails the test, but a female who completes the run in the same time as him passes. Yet, what does this mean in relation to officers' ability to perform police activities? Men and women are hired to do the same work, but the example above suggests that one would be qualified and one would not, even though their performance results were the same.

These physical agility tests present further problems. Assuming that controlled tests will determine one's ability to effectively carry out various physical aspects of the job is limiting, because these tests do not take into consideration the strength of an officer, or her/his ability to perform effectively in a dangerous situation when adrenaline is "running high." An officer's physical and emotional state cannot be replicated by these standardized tests.

Moreover, contrary to popular belief, officers are trained to call for assistance or backup when in dangerous situations. Improvements in training and officer safety

(Birzer and Tannehill, 2001; Hoover, 1995; Lundman, 1980), along with lawsuits filed by police officers against police departments, have led to the creation of rules and regulations dictating when and how officers should call for backup. These challenge the common perception that officers must handle dangerous calls alone or else risk being viewed as "weak" or "cowardly" for calling for backup.

Feminist scrutiny can also be applied to the overwhelming emphasis on gender-specific assignments. Feminist methodological approaches raise questions such as how to encourage both male and female officers into nongender-specific assignments. For example, how can we encourage more male officers into CP, domestic violence and sexual assault units, and youth bureaus? Alternatively, how can we encourage more women into homicide units and tactical units such as Special Weapons and Tactics (SWAT) in the US, or the Emergency Response Unit (ERU), Emergency Response Team (ERT), Tactical and Rescue Unit (TRU), or the Emergency Task Force (ETF) in Canada? Feminists typically question the structure and gendered expectations of many of these specialized areas that attempt to exclude various officers. For instance, are male officers prevented or discouraged from working in domestic violence units through the use of deliberate tactics such as sexist comments and ridicule? Or, are women discouraged from applying to work in areas such as in tactical units through the use of sexist exclusionary practices such as particular physical tests?

C. Third Criteria: Sensitivity towards Treatment of Human Subjects
The third feminist methodological criteria entails sensitivity towards the treatment of human subjects. This includes a whole host of actions and discourse on the part of the researcher. For one, when working with human subjects, feminist approaches can attempt to ensure that those participating in the study are made to feel comfortable, valued, and respected. Also, using everyday language versus academic rhetoric discourages confusion and helps create a nonthreatening nonelitist environment. When conducting face-to-face interviews, it is important to be sensitive to the particular group being studied. Ensuring tolerance and/or respect for particular practices, cultures, and expressions is vital to a feminist approach. According to Naffine (1996: 31):

> The reason that feminist scientific work represents an improvement on the older methods is that feminists have generally been more self-reflective than orthodox criminologists. They have been conscious of the political goals of their inquiry, and they have explored the methods which are more sensitive to the effects of the relationship between investigator and investigated.

Knowledge and Action in Feminist Research
It is equally important to note that feminists have pushed for the realization that science is not objective and that human emotion and power dynamics play significant roles in the social construction of knowledge. Sociological and criminological knowl-

edge is subjective and political. No researcher gathers data uncritically or without her/his own personal biases reflected in the research at some level. Furthermore, feminist criminologists have been critical of the heavy reliance on statistics in criminology, and note it is naive to view this particular method as being somehow "objective." Through application of feminist strategies, we are encouraged to see the limitations in this methodology, as well as the enhancements that can be made through it.

It was feminist criminologists who first outlined the problems with the use of statistics collected using the Conflict Tactics Scale (CTS) (Straus and Gelles, 1986) that showed both men and women were just as likely to be abused in intimate relationships. The CTS was designed to measure battering among cohabitating and married couples. However, as many feminist researchers pointed out, the scale did not include all forms of violence. It did not take into account that women often hit in self-defense; that women are more likely to be injured than men, and that women are less likely to have the resources to leave an abusive relationship. In other words, the CTS data misrepresented the social reality of domestic violence (Comack, Chopyk, and Wood, 2002; 2000; Dekeseredy and Schwartz, 1998; Comack, 1996; Dobash and Dobash, 1992; Dobash et al., 1992; Dekeseredy and Hinch, 1991; Breines and Gordon, 1983).

Furthermore, some feminists have worked tirelessly to transform their work into action-research. They assert that feminist issues are central to any search for social justice. According to Bologh (1984), the goal of feminist action is the process of continuous change that can be accomplished by utilizing research methods and theoretical frameworks that are antipositivist and antipatriarchal. Bristow and Esper argue that feminist action-research must be tied to specific implementation goals. For instance, in their work on rape, they outline how research must be converted into action (1988: 80):

> We believe that we must utilize our privilege as researchers to go beyond the vacuum of professional dissemination qua professional advancement and bring the voices of raped women into public awareness. This means deliberate attempts to introduce our research findings into arenas where access to professional literature is least likely to be available (e.g., lower class women). This can be done through popular media and community presentations. Furthermore, we introduce our research to people in social policy areas ... by educating judges and attorneys, as well as jurors, through expert testimony regarding rape myths.... In addition, we hope to raise the consciousness of mental health workers to both the prevalence and long-term effects of rape.

Feminist action-research should first strive to evaluate individual and organizational behaviour to look for biases within. Kamens (1981) argues that evaluation in mainstream research often involves using the stated goals or purposes as the criteria for evaluation and does not typically question them (i.e., the goals and purposes). She further asserts that in order for the work to be feminist, the evaluator must articulate his/her justice values and apply them to the process, not only to the content, of the evaluated program.

Historically, feminist researchers such as Stuart Campbell (1892; 1890; 1883) used specific methodologies (e.g., interviews) for social reform purposes, and sociologist Komarovsky (1988; 1985) has been a long-time advocate of interview research for feminist purposes. Reiter (1975) and Epstein (1986; 1973; 1970), on the other hand, maintain that feminist research is inherently linked to action. In fact, many feminist researchers and methodologists believe research is feminist *only* if it is linked to action (Lather, 1988; Krieger, 1985; Paget, 1990a; 1990b; 1983).

Feminist action-research means deliberate attempts are made to introduce research findings into arenas where access to professional literature is least likely to be available (Bristow and Esper, 1988), such as in policing. However, in order to promote social action-research, as previously mentioned, the evaluator must articulate her/his justice values and apply them to the overall research process and not only to the content (Kames, 1981). Other scholars have asserted that by offering a different form of understanding to those within various arenas (such as policing), we can reshape our possibilities for change. For instance, Ferguson's (1984: x) work on bureaucracies discusses knowledge-creation as praxis. She asserts that:

> By exposing the contradictions and manipulations contained within a bureaucratic society, one can demystify the theory and practice of that society. Since the organizational society is maintained in part by creating and perpetuating the appropriate ideology, one that both reflects and distorts the reality it describes, a different form of understanding is in some ways also a form of action.... I do believe that political theory can be transformative, can help us to live well, if it is used to rethink our lives, reshape our possibilities, and resist the official definition of reality.

The goal in feminist action-research is to not only to interpret the world but to change it by changing people's consciousness (Fetterley, 1978). Feminist action-research is political because it demystifies; that is, it raises consciousness and it can change consciousness when people consider situations and new "realities" in a new light. For instance, one of the questions that is important to me is how to utilize my studies to inform the public of the origins and operations of policing as linked to many of the current police-societal problems. By documenting the activities and experiences of individuals, we work to conceptualize people's behaviour, social systems, and structures as an expression of power, and utilize feminist research to help participants understand and change their situations. Social justice theories help us challenge the status quo and should be linked to action (Paget, 1990a; 1990b; 1983; Epstein, 1986; 1981; 1973; 1970; Lather, 1988; Krieger, 1985; Reiter, 1975).

The emergence of a gender analysis in policing raises alternative explanations for some of the current problems in policing. In the demystification framework, by obtaining knowledge of various social forces as a first step, we can create the potential for change. For some, the personal experience is the cornerstone of knowledge and the process by which social change can occur. This foundation is often expressed in feminist action-research, which uses a more critical viewpoint centred on the question of whose personal experiences are actually influencing knowledge and social change. Feminist action-researchers believe that the human potential for change is a crucial element in ending inequalities. Furthermore, individuals must take steps to empower others to strive for positive change. This act becomes a "moral enterprise" (McDermott, 2002), and this ideology reflects feminist criminology's commitment to social action.

Questions

1. What contributions have feminist scholars made to criminology?
2. What contributions have feminist scholars made to the study of policing?
3. What types of feminist methods are used to study the police and why are they important?
4. What are the differences between feminist and nonfeminist research?

CHAPTER 3

Responding to Gendered Aspects of Policing Using Different Feminist Perspectives/Paradigms

The purpose of this chapter is to introduce the six main feminist theories (liberal, socialist, Marxist, radical, antiracist/multiracial, and postmodern), along with a few suggestions to address and change the current problems relating to gender and policing. The point of this exercise is to offer readers some concrete examples of the possibilities for change presented by the different feminist theoretical paradigms, and to encourage readers to think through some of their implications. These should serve as a guide for upcoming chapters. Whether one is reading about the police culture, community policing (CP), the paramilitaristic police organization, or detective work, readers are encouraged to relate the information back to these feminist perspectives/paradigms in order to assess their application to today's society, policing systems, and to the promotion of equitable changes.

Feminist Schools of Thought: Liberal Feminism

The goal of liberal feminists is to create a society where equality of opportunity is guaranteed. The origins of this feminism stem from the late eighteenth century with Mary Wollstonecraft's publication, *A Vindication of the Rights of Woman* and later John Stuart Mill's article, "The Subjection of Women." This theory is rooted in the classic liberal thinking that individuals should be free to pursue their own goals and interests. Yet, according to liberal feminists, in order to enable people to move in this direction, we must expand the rights and opportunities of women, in part by passing equal rights legislation, affirmative action, and other opportunity laws or policies.

Women's access to the public sector, which includes equal access to education and employment, has historically and up to the present-day been restricted by traditional and/or legal constraints. The belief is, that by removing legal and cultural barriers, women and men can improve their lives through their individual efforts.

Liberal feminists contend that equality in opportunity can be made possible when gender roles become blurred and discriminatory policies are eliminated (Simpson, 1989). For instance, some point to the problems with the traditional nuclear family that continue to promote gender-specific identities along sex lines (Beirne and Messerschmidt, 1991) and are critical of policies that fail to recognize the rights of homemakers. Liberal feminists have fought to introduce legislation that provides women with equal access to employment, equal pay for equal work, reproductive freedom, and equal treatment of the sexes at all levels, and have sought to bring about change in lesbian and gay rights and homemakers' rights to name but a few.

What Suggestions for Social Change Can Be Made by Liberal Feminists to Address the Current Problems Relating to Gender and Policing?

A. Policies Promoting a More Family-Friendly Work Environment

Firstly, feminists working from this perspective can point to the low number of women who currently are employed as sworn police officers. In the US today, women constitute approximately 13 per cent of all police officers, and in Canada, 17 per cent. Why is this number so low given the significant increase in the number of women in other traditionally male-centred occupations? Some liberal feminists would contend that not enough has been done in police departments to create rules and policies that promote a more family-friendly work environment. The fact that most police officers work rotating shifts without having the chance to choose any one particular shift presents several challenges to police officers who are mothers and, more specifically, single mothers. The choice to work part-time, at least temporarily, would provide more options to female officers with children under five. Structural changes such as these would encourage more women to consider policing as a profession, ultimately increasing female representation.

B. Recruiting/Hiring and Performance Evaluation Policies

Liberal feminists would also suggest more aggressive advertising to encourage more women to apply for jobs in policing. Unfortunately, most of the advertising is geared towards men. A stronger effort should be made to attract women by placing recruitment literature in places frequented by women, and by sending female recruiters to those locations. Advertising should also be geared towards moving away from the mainstream image of the police as being paramilitaristic and the mainstream media's overglamourized portrayal of police confrontations with members of the public and the potential dangers associated with the job.

Moreover, the oral interview process utilized in hiring can also discriminate against women seeking careers in policing. In many police departments, oral interview boards consist mainly of current male officers who are not screened for personal biases and therefore bring their own prejudices into the interview to determine whether applicants possess the qualities of a "good police officer." Thus, it is not uncommon for women to receive lower scores from these boards because their work experiences, which may include backgrounds in social services, childcare, and education, are not as valued as those of individuals (mostly males) who have backgrounds in the military or security services (Harrington and Lonsway, 2004).

With regard to performance evaluation criteria, they may appear on the surface to be gender-neutral but may end up being based on men's performance standards. According to liberal feminists, this will have an impact on the number of women who ultimately stay in policing and thus a gender equity analysis (GEA) is essential. For example, Martin (1990) found that performance evaluation criteria used in assessing "quantity of work" in the Chicago Police Department only included number of arrests, court attendance, traffic enforcement, and award history. In Corsianos's research (2007a; 2005), women's successes in crime prevention and proactive policing were not valued as much as were the types of activities that produced arrests. Also, women were at a disadvantage when evaluated for promotion. On the surface, the promotional process appeared to be objective. However, in actuality, decisions relating to who would be promoted were often made before the formal interview process commenced. This put many women with childcare responsibilities at a disadvantage, since they could not regularly "hang out" and socialize with other officers after work. It was believed that this form of networking made the difference in who was ultimately promoted. Moreover, officers seeking entrance into detective units were evaluated on their ability to be a "team player." They were evaluated on their ability to work in a "team environment," which included being able to "take a joke" and "not be offended racially, ethnically, sexually, religiously, politically, and so forth" (see Chapter 6) (Corsianos, 1999b).

C. Policies Relating to Equal Access to Specialized Units

Specialized police units continue to be gendered. A disproportionate number of women are employed in domestic violence units, sexual assault units, youth bureaus/units, and CP units; alternatively, a disproportionate number of male officers are often found in homicide units, vice, and fraud. According to liberal feminists, the creation of internal policies are needed to allow all officers the opportunity to serve in all of the specialized units equally, rather than encouraging people to pursue more gender-specific postings.

D. Sexual Harassment Policies

Liberal feminists would also advocate for the strict enforcement of sexual harassment policies. All police officers who come forward with sexual harassment complaints should be taken seriously and not be dismissed for not being able to "take a joke" or be perceived as someone who is "rocking the boat" and betraying the "brotherhood of policing." One suggestion that is supported by some liberal feminists, as a means to increase police accountability in this area, is to introduce legislation and police policies that would require the police to aggressively monitor possible acts of gender discrimination and other inequitable and/or illegal police practices. For example, legislation could mandate the police to place surveillance cameras in all police cars and throughout police stations to monitor all police activities at all times. This is viewed as one practical solution to inequality that can serve to resocialize officers.

E. Policies Relating to the Use of Physical Tests for Hiring

Liberal feminists also support the application of a GEA in all police policies and programs to ensure that they do not disproportionately discriminate against categories of people. For instance, as discussed in Chapter 2, many agencies continue to have standards that place a strong emphasis on upper body strength. These tests do not measure police competency in day-to-day police activities, and they disproportionately discriminate against many women. Many departments do have written policies that prohibit some of these physical tests, such as jumping over solid walls, or indicate that they are inadvisable. Ironically, however, some agencies continue to perceive these tests as appropriate and/or effective measures of police officer performance (Harrington and Lonsway, 2004).

Moreover, officers "on the job" in both Canada and the US are no longer subject to routine physical agility testing and therefore there is no way of knowing whether they can still meet these "standards." Interestingly, the absence of routine physical testing is not used to question officers' abilities to perform police work. In a 2001 US study, 89 per cent of 62 large police agencies used some form of physical agility testing as a condition for hiring, but there was little standardization with regard to the actual physical tests and the measurements used to receive a pass. The departments that did not indicate the use of any physical tests as a condition for employment had 45 per cent more women serving as sworn police officers (National Center for Women and Policing, 2003).

F. Pregnancy/Maternity Policies

Liberal feminists assert that all police agencies must introduce clearly defined pregnancy/maternity policies to ensure that pregnant officers can be accommodated when requesting police maternity uniforms, suitable police equipment (e.g., bulletproof vests, gun belts), and "light duty" assignments. At the same time, departments must be aware of the rights of pregnant officers and ensure that there are no discriminatory policies in place, such as requiring officers to requalify on the shooting range during their pregnancies without the necessary safety precautions. Many officers have refused to qualify on the range due to their concerns relating to the possible harm to the fetus resulting from the consequent high noise level and lead pollution (see Chapter 1).

G. Policies Relating to Firearms

Applicants are trained to use firearms while at the academy. However, a disproportionate number of women have no previous experience in firing guns, which places them at a disadvantage given the services' heavy reliance on weapons. Many of the male applicants, on the other hand, have some familiarity with guns since many have a background in the military or private security. According to liberal feminists, training can and should be offered to officers with no prior gun experience to prepare them for academy training (as was seen in Vancouver, British Columbia, when the police department worked with the YWCA to provide physical training to applicants in preparation for the actual physical tests [See Chapter 1]).

Also, police management should take into consideration any differences between males and females when making decisions on police equipment rather than continuing to treat males as the "standard." For instance, many of the weapons that are issued to officers do not account for differences in grip strength and hand size between women and men. Not surprisingly, a study of recruits with no prior firearms experience found that women's marksmanship scores and grip strength were significantly lower than that of the men. With training, scores improved but remained lower compared to men's due to women's lower grip strength (Charles and Copay, 2001). However, introducing policies that allow officers to have weapons with different gun grips in order to accommodate different hand sizes would help promote gender neutrality by ceasing to assume that males are the standard. Being able to achieve a firm grip is crucial to ensuring accuracy when shooting. An officer's finger should rest comfortably around the gun trigger in order to be able to gently squeeze it. When the officer does not have a firm grip on the pistol grip, due to a smaller hand size, then more leverage is needed to pull the trigger. Subsequently, this results in an officer "jerking the trigger," which causes the gun to move, affecting his/her accuracy.

Liberal feminists assert that by creating policies that promote equality along gender lines, more women will pursue careers in policing, more will be hired, and more will start to occupy positions up the chain of command.

Socialist Feminism

This group of feminists advocates a collective means to gain equality between the sexes. Socialist feminists view class and gender as being equally important social categories in shaping and affecting social realities, but, unlike liberal feminists, they do not accept the assertion that equality under the law will promote equality in access and outcome. They contend that extreme aspects of capitalism must be eliminated and replaced by a more state-centred economy in order to achieve equality between the sexes. Both class and patriarchy must be examined as dual systems of domination. Capitalism strengthens patriarchy. The pursuit of profit is the goal under capitalism that undermines nonincome-generating types of work such as child rearing and housework. Since women continue to take on the majority of these responsibilities in many households, women ultimately have the most to lose. Under a patriarchal capitalist socio-economic order, mothers in the paid workforce often have to settle for unstable poorly paid work that can provide them with the flexibility to be home after school hours to care for their children. Alternatively, mothers who take time off to be with their preschool children must give up their paid positions. For reasons such as these, socialist feminists are critical of the argument that equality under the law is enough to produce equality in access and outcome. They are critical of liberal feminists for failing to recognize the gendered differences in women's experiences that must be taken into consideration when attempting to work towards equality between the sexes.

Socialist feminists support a more state-centred economy. Through higher taxes, government programs can be established to address the needs of every citizen more equally. This way, everyone collectively contributes to the betterment of the society. Programs such as subsidized daycare, paid maternity and paternity leave, protection of one's job when on maternity/paternity leave, subsidized school busing, universal health care, and a universal education system can contribute to a collective society and, in the end, present choices that make a significant difference in the quality of people's lives.

Socialist feminists point to the fact that women who live in socialist countries, most often concentrated in Northern Europe, are afforded the highest standard of living in the world. Sweden ranks first in the world with regard to women's standard of living. As a result of Sweden's higher tax system, a wide variety of social programs are offered to support its citizens. Sweden offers one and a half years of paid maternity/paternity leave (approximately 90 per cent of the new parent's income is covered by the government). It offers subsidized daycare, subsidized school busing, universal health care, and universal education. The Swedish government will even pay for a citizen's funeral (Macionis, 2007). These services are intended to promote a collective society and promote stability by lessening huge disparities in wealth and access to resources between different people. These programs relieve citizens of many of the pressures experienced by a disproportionate number of women in more capitalist societies such as the US, where few socialist programs are offered.

Unlike the US, Canada offers some key socialist programs such as universal health care and one-year paid maternity/paternity leave, but in other areas individuals must find the means to accomplish various tasks on their own. For these reasons, when looking at women's standard of living, Canada ranks seventh in the world, while the US ranks eighth (Macionis, 2007). A more state-centred economy promotes equality for women, as well as other oppressed groups (e.g., people of colour, ethnic minorities, etc.) (Fine et al., 1997). Also, by making changes to basic structural arrangements in society, social categories such as gender, sexual orientation, class, and race will no longer serve as barriers to equal access and distribution of resources (Elliot and Mandell, 1998).

What Suggestions for Social Change Can Be Made by Socialist Feminists to Address the Current Problems Relating to Gender and Policing?

Firstly, socialist feminists point to the need for more socialist universal programs to increase the number of women choosing a career in law enforcement. Programs such as a one-year paid maternity/paternity leave, as seen in Canada, and subsidized daycare for all would give women (and men) more choices. A new mother, whether single, married, or living with her partner, can take time off for a year, recuperate, and spend time with her infant before returning to police work without the financial pressures encountered by citizens in societies such as the US that are without such programs. Couples could also choose to divide the leave in such a way where one parent would be off for the first few months, and then the other parent would be home for the remainder of the period. One-year paid parental leave would equally serve single fathers and men in same-sex relationships raising children.

Subsidized daycare would also make life easier by offering options that would encourage more women to apply for jobs in policing. Female police officers could continue their work without the financial pressure of trying to find affordable child-care. In addition, childcare facilities that catered to the shift work of occupations such as policing would enable female officers to arrange for the care of their children without being forced to give up their job. Policies and programs such as these would benefit both women and men, but since women continue to take on most of the child-rearing responsibilities in society and given the increase in the number of single mothers, such policies and programs would benefit a disproportionate number of women. Undoubtedly, they would serve many men as well, given some of their increased family responsibilities in recent years. In one Canadian study that included four major police agencies, sources of stress among both female and male officers were examined. When looking at stress related to family obligations, it seemed that male officers were beginning to experience increased pressure due to their increased responsibilities in family-related matters (Seagram and Stark-Adamec, 1992).

Policies and programs such as subsidized daycare for all and subsidized maternity/paternity leave would increase the number of women seeking careers in policing. Also, police departments could offer choices in work schedules to police officers with young children. For instance, giving officers the choice to work a particular shift would help parents with young children. By choosing to work the day shift (i.e., the shift that ends by 4 or 5 PM), the officer could be home to greet her/his young children after school. This option could be made available until the children were of an age where they could care for themselves without the supervision of an adult. In cases where an officer's spouse or common-law partner was also employed as a police officer for the same police department, this option could be offered to only one of the two. Moreover, on-site childcare facilities during the day shift could be set up to accommodate officers with preschool children throughout the year, as well as young school-age children during the summer months. Another option would be for police departments to offer officers the choice to work part-time for a particular period (i.e., until their children were in school or until the children were of an age where they could care for themselves at home without an adult present).

Dick and Jankowicz (2001) challenge the "common sense" perception that policing requires and depends on continuous rotating shifts. They assert that by maintaining this system, women continue to be marginalized as many of them are parents with young children. As noted above, most women continue to be the primary caretakers of their children, which presents many difficulties when working rotating shifts. Furthermore, almost all police departments in Canada and the US do not provide on-site childcare facilities. Departments such as the Portland Police Bureau in Oregon are a notable exception. In addition to the above noted problems, live-in police academies present particular problems for female applicants with young children (Harrington and Lonsway, 2004).

According to socialist feminists, the changes discussed above would ensure that women were not being financially penalized for choosing to have children. In fact, choice would become possible under socialist systems as seen in countries such as Sweden, Denmark, Norway, and Finland (Macionis, 2007). More women would be in the financial position to have children when they wanted to rather than postponing their decision for several years until they were more financially stable. It is important to note that more women are remaining childless by choice today compared to previous decades, but more women are also postponing having children because of financial reasons. The number of women postponing having children for financial reasons, however, has also meant an increase in the number of women experiencing infertility associated with age. For many of these women, this has led to a number of stressful, invasive, and expensive treatments and/or procedures in their attempts to conceive (Macionis, 2007).

Marxist Feminism

This group of feminists advocates a one-class society to gain equality between the sexes. Marxist feminists view class and gender as being equally important social categories in shaping and affecting social realities. Therefore, capitalism must be eliminated in order to achieve equality between the sexes. For this group, capitalism invokes an inherent division of labour according to sex. The work performed in the home, largely by women, has no exchange value. Since the work in the home does not generate a paycheque, it is not recognized as "real work." According to Elliot and Mandell (1998: 7-8):

> The family under capitalism becomes a microcosm of society's larger class relation. Wives resemble the proletariat; monogamous marriage develops as part of the formation of private property; and the division of private and public labour becomes gendered. All wives, regardless of their paid labour commitments, are responsible for household management,

child care, the emotional nurturing of dependents, and the general well-being of the family. The work of housewives — their domestic slavery — represents both a private service to the male head of the household and an unpaid economic service to society as a whole.

Capitalism strengthens patriarchy as property relations and the capitalist mode of production increase gender and class inequalities (Beirne and Messerschmidt, 1991). The goal of Marxist feminists is to change the socio-economic order to one where everyone equally shares in the earth's resources, equally owns property, and has equal access to education, health care, etc. By creating a system where everyone equally shares in the means of production, all women will become liberated because they will not be economically dependent on men. Equality in outcome is the only way to quantitatively measure equality between the sexes. The pursuit of profit is the goal under capitalism and the traditional family is preserved in order to pass on private property to offspring. Child-rearing responsibilities and housework are undermined because they do not produce an income. Therefore, it is no surprise that often people in societies with strong capitalistic economies do not refer to these types of activities as "work." Also, women often have to settle for paid work that can provide them with flexibility in their work schedule. These women may be unable or unwilling to take on jobs where they are required to work evenings or weekends. As a result, they take on jobs that have shorter commuting distances in order to be closer to their children, or may search for jobs that offer employer-provided childcare services on-site. Frequently, these jobs do not offer security and adequate benefits and income.

Under patriarchal social systems and structures, work becomes gendered. It does not surprise Marxist feminists that women continue to be disproportionately represented in "pink-collar" jobs such as clerical work and low-level service work. These contribute to the disparity in income between women and men. The median yearly income of American women working full-time in 2004 was $31,223, and for men, it was $40,798. Among full-time workers of all ages, in 2004, 34 per cent of women earned less than $25,000 compared with 23 per cent of men. Looking at those in the higher income group, men were two-and-one-half times more likely than women (18.5 per cent versus 7.2 per cent) to earn more than $75,000 a year (US Census Bureau, 2005). The average yearly income of Canadian women working full-time in 2005 was $26,800, and for men, it was $41,900 (Statistics Canada, 2005a).

Given the lack of supportive social programs in countries such as the US, and to a lesser extent in Canada, coupled with dominant patriarchal ideologies and the gendered responsibilities of parenting, some women who have preschool children choose not to participate in the labour force (if they can afford not to) until their children begin school. During this time, their male peers begin to move ahead through career advancements and by the time many of the women return to the paid workforce, they enjoy less job seniority and are earning less pay than their male counterparts (Stier, 1996; Waldfogel, 1997). Fifty-nine per cent of American married women with children under the age of six are in the paid workforce, as are 76 per cent of married women with children between the ages of six and 17. On the other hand, 71 per cent of American never-married, widowed, divorced, or separated women with children under the age of six are in the paid work force, as are 82 per cent of women with older children (US Department of Labor, 2005). American women represent almost half of the paid labour force, and half of American married couples depend on two incomes (Macionis, 2007).

In countries such as Canada, women tend to have more options as compared to the US. Socialist programs such as one-year paid maternity/paternity leave, job and seniority protection while on leave, and universal health care provide women with a somewhat higher standard of living in relation to women in the US, but they still encounter many of the same challenges and sources of stress experienced by their American counterparts. As noted above, the wage disparity between Canadian men and women is greater in comparison to Americans. Women continue to earn, on average, less than their male counterparts; they are disproportionately represented in the "pink-collar" jobs that provide less job security, less pay, and little, if any, upward mobility; and they are without supportive programs such as subsidized day-care and subsidized school busing for their children. Gender disparities and patriarchal ideologies continue to exist, convincing Marxist feminists that equality in outcome is the only way to produce true equality between the sexes.

Under a one-class system, according to the Marxist feminists, everyone would be equally valued. Hierarchical systems that privilege certain people and certain jobs over others would be replaced by a flat power structure. Therefore, the police officer, the physician, the garbage collector, and the stay-at-home parent would all be equally valued. Their work would be considered necessary for the function of society — society could not function without them and therefore they would all be afforded comparable worth for their skills and responsibilities. In recent decades, countries such as Australia and Great Britain have created "comparable worth policies" that pay people according to the level of skill and responsibility involved in their work, rather than according to the historical gendered double standard. Yet, the question that is still raised here is, who decides? For the Marxist feminists, equality in outcome for everyone removes any bias on the part of individuals to determine what qualifies as "comparable worth."

What Suggestions for Social Change Can Be Made by Marxist Feminists to Address the Current Problems Relating to Gender and Policing?

Marxist-feminists contend that a one-class society would produce the most freedoms for most people. Firstly, the one-class system would significantly decrease the crime rate. People who commit crimes for monetary reasons represent a large percentage of arrested persons. This type of "criminal" would be eliminated in the one-class system, freeing up more time for the police to concentrate on other areas of policing, which would include working on building bridges with the community and creating safe living environments. In addition, it is believed that a one-class society would provide people with more choices. For instance, women who had a passion for policing could join the profession free from the financial worries of daycare or from having to choose between their career and family life. They could hire someone to care for their child at home, their spouse or significant other could choose to stay home with the children, or they could take their children to a childcare facility. Any one of these individuals taking on the role of child caretaker would be equally valued as any other "professional." Women would not be financially penalized for choosing to have children. Individuals would have more options. Women wanting to become mothers would be able to choose to have children when they wanted to rather than the current pattern of postponing their decision for several years to achieve more financial stability. And similar to socialist feminists, Marxist feminists claim that this would prevent some of the increasing problems many women face trying to conceive in their later child-bearing years.

Some Marxist feminists believe the one-class system would most likely encourage more women to become police officers. The paramilitaristic hierarchical police structure would be replaced by a more collectivist flat power structure. This means that the police organizational structure would still have different police roles, which would typically consist of today's "ranks," such as the front-line officer, sergeant, detective, lieutenant, captain, deputy chief, and chief as seen in some US police departments, or the front-line officer, sergeant/staff sergeant, inspector/staff inspector, superintendent, deputy chief, and chief as seen in some Canadian police services. However, in a flat power structure, the titles would be different in order to separate police roles from the current patriarchal paramilitaristic images and systems. The responsibilities of these different police roles would vary, but at the end, every officer would be treated as an integral part in the success of policing and promotion of police-community relations.

Each officer, regardless of title (currently referred to as "rank") could be paid equally and could have an equal voice in identifying problems or concerns in the areas they police and in offering suggestions for social change. It is believed that this egalitarian system would encourage more women to apply. The current paramilitaristic system often deters women from applying. The image of the police operating in a similar way to the military, with an emphasis on weapons training, tactical moves, defense training, etc., does an injustice to our communities by not recognizing some of the problems with this current system.

Policing must equally emphasize and train officers in areas such as conflict resolution, race relations, gender relations, police-community relations, sexuality issues, human sensitivity training, and CP initiatives. Moreover, every citizen would have equal access to education, and a college education could be required for all police officers. This could improve police service and ensure integrity. Some studies show that police officers who hold a college degree are less likely to participate in acts of police corruption and are more likely to be fair and honest (Hoover, 1995; Lynch, 1976). They are also less likely to receive citizen complaints and are more likely to have fewer disciplinary problems (Carter, Sapp, and Stephens, 1988). According to Marxist feminists, in a one-class society, policing as we know it today would cease to exist, giving way to a more progressive educated accountable police "service" rather than "force."

Furthermore, by recognizing every police role as an integral part to the overall police system, we would move away from the gendered division of labour we often see within police departments today. The feminist/flat power structure model would ensure that everyone had an equal chance of serving in all areas within policing and would recognize officers' good work in all aspects of policing through awards, appreciation ceremonies, and internal newsletter announcements. This would produce the needed ideological shift within policing that currently discriminates against certain types of police activities. For instance, police officers today are more likely to receive awards and/or promotions for making a "good arrest" or for the number of arrests made within a particular period, rather than for their successes in areas such as CP. Thus, under a feminist/flat power structure, more male officers would be encouraged to work in areas that have become associated with female officers, and vice versa. For the Marxist feminists, this would free all police officers from the current gendered societal and departmental expectations. Every interested police officer would have an equal chance of serving not only in specialized areas such as detective offices but in areas comparable (or not) to today's sergeants, captains/inspectors, chiefs, etc. This would eliminate the current patriarchal system where a disproportionate number of female officers continue to occupy the lower ranks (i.e., the front-line officer/patrol officer position).

Radical Feminism
Radical feminists believe that patriarchal ideologies, structures, and social systems are so deeply embedded in society that equality between the sexes cannot be accomplished by simply changing the laws to create gender equality as the liberal feminists propose, or through a Marxist revolution to create a one-class society as the Marxist feminists propose, or even by creating more socialist universal programs for all citizens through a higher tax system as the socialist feminists propose. Radical feminists first organized in the 1960s and 1970s as a result of women being treated as second-class citizens in civil rights and antiwar movements. They were also critical of other feminists who focused solely on work-related issues and failed to address other feminist issues such as violence against women and reproductive freedom.

For radical feminists, the only way to achieve equality between the sexes is to eliminate the concept of gender itself and to eliminate patriarchy, which together are central to women's oppression. For these feminists, women's oppression is the first form of oppression. It is widespread, international, and is the hardest form to eradicate (Jaggar and Rothenberg, 1984). What oppresses women is not what oppresses men. Radical feminists are committed to understanding the formation of patriarchy and eradicating it on all levels; this includes eliminating all patriarchal social institutions, such as policing, religion, politics, the traditional nuclear family, and male control over female sexuality. They advocate the formation of feminist culture, systems, and women-only spaces. Cultural separation involves creating alternative feminist ideas, structures, and systems (e.g., feminist sexuality, art, reproduction, mothering, spirituality, etc.). Lesbian feminism is another form of feminist separation that promotes the creation of a woman-identified reality. Some contend that the institution of heterosexuality be eliminated, since many heterosexual relations are hierarchical and do not promote equality between the sexes (Rich, 1980). The elimination of heterosexuality as the societal norm would create the freedom to choose relationships with people without fear of violence, stigma, and exclusion from family, friends, and peers.

Some radical feminists have proposed the use of reproductive technology (e.g., contraception, sterilization, abortion) to prevent pregnancy, or the use of reproduction-aiding technologies (e.g., intra-uterine insemination) to become pregnant. This group asserts that technology can free women and eliminate the traditional family model by providing women with options (Dworkin, 1987). Others, on the other hand, view technology as serving to oppress women rather than free them (Petchesky, 1980). For instance, artificial insemination and in vitro fertilization have become invasive expensive procedures that some women feel they have to be subjected to given the societal pressure to become "mothers."

For radical feminists, women must move away from ideas, systems, and structures that are defined by men, because they serve to maintain male privilege, and subordinate and devalue women.

What Suggestions for Social Change Can Be Made by Radical Feminists to Address the Current Problems Relating to Gender and Policing?

For radical feminists, gender categories oppress female police officers. Feminist criminological research shows that female officers continue to be criticized for not possessing the perceived necessary "masculine" traits of aggressiveness, rationality, bravery, objectivity, and brutality perceived to be required for "effective" crime-fighting, and that these attitudes impact female officers on many different levels (Charles, 1981; Miller, 1999). Others have also commented on how policing is predominantly viewed as "masculine" work that focuses on fighting crime, but note that police work often involves activities viewed as "feminine" (Martin, 1999; Martin and Jurik, 2007). Radical feminists can refer to these studies to support their position to eliminate all male-defined institutions.

Studies show how criticisms of female officers frequently lead to claims that women are inherently not competent to participate in the traditional crime-fighting police model, and that women are better suited in police roles that deal with social-service-type functions (e.g., in community-oriented police capacities, working with domestic assault victims, youth, etc.) (Heidensohn and Brown, 2000; Heidensohn, 1992; Bell, 1982; Drummond, 1976). Also, the units that become "feminized" are not seen as "real police work." The recent feminization of particular policing areas (e.g., CP units), coupled with the fact that they typically do not produce high-speed chases or "big arrests," perpetuates the belief that the work of officers in these units is somehow less important, serving to further ostracize female officers.

Therefore, for many radical feminists, the current policing system and structure must be eliminated because it was defined by men and it continues to serve and benefit males. The patriarchal ideologies and organizational structure of policing undermine and devalue all women; that is, female officers working within the system, as well as female citizens who are policed by the system. According to radical feminists, women-centred institutions must be created in order to develop alternate approaches to caring for communities and responding to individuals who threaten the peace and safety of people. Traditional male approaches to policing communities and aggressive crime control must be eliminated. Cultural separation involves creating an alternative system to service the public and this new "police system" would be determined by women to ensure they were no longer oppressed; that is, women who serve as "police" and women who come into contact with the police. Presumably, the word "police" would not be utilized because it connotes aggressive crime control images and practices. Women could create a collectivist system that focuses on perhaps preserving the peace, helping women to secure jobs, empowering women, and ensuring that women achieve agency in all aspects of their lives.

Radical feminists can also point to the fact that even though studies on female police officers' performance have been conducted since 1972 and most report that female officers are as capable as male officers (Bartol et al., 1992; Grennan, 1987; Sichel et al., 1978; Bartlett and Rosenblum, 1977; Sherman, 1975; Bloch and Anderson, 1974), few studies have attempted to evaluate female police officers' performance in ways that do not emphasize situations and characteristics associated with definitions of "masculinity" (Corsianos, 2007a; 2005; 2004; Gerber, 2001; Morash and Greene, 1986). This further strengthens radical feminists' argument that gender categories must be eradicated. Alternatively, some research has indicated that female police officers (and female prison workers) have a less aggressive style than male officers and are better at de-escalating potentially violent situations (Belknap, 1991; Belknap and Shelley, 1993; Grennan, 1987; Bell, 1982), and that female officers may be more likely to have traits associated with "good policing," such as expressing empathy for female victims of rape and domestic abuse (Belknap, 2007; Corsianos, 2005; 1999b; Feinman, 1986; Homant and Kennedy, 1985; Kennedy and Homant, 1983; Price, 1974). Once again, these studies provide further evidence on how gender defines, influences, and limits our choices as "women" in policing, as well as in other social arenas. All of these studies confirm to radical feminists that there are continuing dangers and oppressions related to the use of gender categories, and therefore both gender and patriarchy must be eliminated. For this group of feminists, only through the formation of feminist systems, cultures, and women-only spaces can equality for women be achieved.

Antiracist/Multiracial Feminism

Women of colour were among the first to criticize liberal, socialist, Marxist, and radical feminists for ignoring race as a category of oppression and not giving voice to the diversity and multiplicity of women's experiences (Brand, 1993; Das Gupta, 1995). Early feminist theorizing, for the most part, treated the experiences of white middle-class heterosexual women as the norm (Spelman, 1988), while marginalizing or excluding other groups of women, including Native-American/Aboriginal-Canadian, Asian-American/Canadian, African-American/Canadian, minority ethnic, poor, lesbian, and immigrant women. The second wave of feminism, for instance, was criticized for its emphasis on theories and practices that were largely based on the experiences of privileged white women. Many women of colour, poor women, and lesbians objected to the idea that all women's experiences are the same. This led to, what is referred to by some, as the "third wave" of feminism, which has taken a multiracial approach to studying gender. It focuses on the intersections of gender, race, class, sexuality, age, physical ability, and other social categories to explain how social inequalities are socially constructed and sustained and how they produce differences in lived experiences.

Antiracist/multiracial feminists contend that in order to achieve equality between the sexes, we cannot ignore the intersections of gender, race, class, ethnicity, and sexual orientation in people's experiences and oppressions. Barriers of exclusion must be eliminated in order to achieve equality. They advocate coalition-building between oppressed groups and support policies and systems such as affirmative action that promote the hiring of more women of colour, as well as the social welfare system to address the social realities of economic disparities between people.

For antiracist/multiracial feminists, a great deal of focus is given to education. They assert that education is central to working towards changing societal views on race, gender, class, and sexual orientation. According to Thomas (1984), a multicultural education that provides information relating to different cultures is not enough. This will not promote change in society unless there is an acknowledgement and intellectual discussions about the current inequalities, and the dominance of some groups over others. Also, calculated steps must be taken to educate people and eliminate stereotypes associated with particular groups and the conventional belief in meritocracy (Thomas, 1984). The idea that one's accomplishments/successes are the result of personal merit legitimizes the existing social inequalities and places blame on individuals for their perceived failures. Economic failures are assumed to represent a lack of effort, talent, or other personal shortcomings on the part of individuals (Brisken, 1994).

An antiracist feminist pedagogical approach to teaching, programs, and curriculum development are key. Das Gupta (1994) discusses the biased nature of all curricula, despite the popular belief that bias exists, for the most part, in social studies such as history. The language and points of view represented in many textbooks and classrooms are often imposed by members of dominant groups. Scheurich and Young (2002) assert that "knowledge" is based on racially biased assumptions and perspectives. Dominant racist ideologies are so deeply embedded in modernist Western civilization that they are often seen as "natural" rather than as historically evolved social constructions. Thus, institutional racism is endemic. For instance, words such as "defend," "conquest," and "victory" have traditionally been presented from the perspective of the "conqueror." Or, "culturally deprived" has been used often by privileged whites to refer to members of minority groups, implying some sort of deficiency on the part of those individuals. Das Gupta (1994: 23) advocates "going beyond an 'add-on' approach to an 'infusion' approach, where different experiences and perspectives are integrated into the 'core' curricula." Therefore, reading material, class lectures, and classroom structure should represent all students. The experiences of one particular group should not be privileged over others.

The "hidden curriculum" must also be addressed. According to Das Gupta (1994), the person who does the teaching is a critical part of the curriculum. All voices must be represented in curriculum development. "Anti-racist and feminist teaching involves a process of empowerment, i.e., giving voice to and listening to, women and people of colour. This principle can (and should) be included in the process of curricula development" (Das Gupta, 1994: 25).

A diversity of voices will, over time, put an end to some of the current experiences of members of minority groups. For instance, Bannerji et al. (1991: 14) states: "Women of colour in academia are constantly having to prove their credibility in a world where knowledge is defined by upper- and middle-class white English speaking males and where we are socially organized as the historical 'other.'"

The effort to end sexism, racism, and other forms of inequalities must become the responsibility of all members in society and not just those representing marginalized groups (Dei, 1994). This struggle must be a collective movement. "Participation in collective action moves women (and other groups of minorities) from the position of victim to that of agent" (Brisken, 1994: 458).

Antiracist/multiracial feminists similarly discuss the necessity in recognizing the experiences and needs of Third World people living in the Western world. As members of oppressed nationalities (i.e., underdeveloped and overexploited geopolitical regions), their experiences living in developed First World countries must be equally recognized. It is believed that only by becoming conscious of social inequalities across multiple lines can we begin to challenge dominant ideologies and practices such as systemic racism and sexism.

Systemic racism has been identified in many areas within the criminal justice system. For instance, feminist research has found that an offender's status as "woman" does not necessarily mean a lighter sentence. In fact, the rate of incarceration for female offenders has skyrocketed over the years. However, a disproportionate number of women who are imprisoned represent minority groups (Freedman, 1981; Rafter, 1985; Neugebauer, 1999; Barak, Flavin, and Leighton, 2001; Websdale, 2001).

Also, some antiracist/multiracial feminists tend to be critical of the gender-neutral approach to criminal justice because it fails to recognize the differences between lived experiences of women and men. Applying a gender-neutral approach to the treatment of female offenders, for instance, does a gross disservice to women, since the criminal justice system's response is structured around males' experiences. Most female offenders are single parents with dependent children and survivors of physical and/or sexual abuse (Chesney-Lind and Rodriguez, 1983; James and Meyerding, 1977; Silbert and Pines, 1981). Therefore, a gender-specific response to female offenders could be structured in ways that responded and dealt more effectively with such "truths," rather than viewing males' experiences as the norm. However, at the same time, these feminists discuss the differences in the treatment between women representing different social categories (e.g., race, class, sexual orientation, etc.), as well as between men representing these different social categories. For instance, males who are poor and represent minority groups are more likely to receive harsher sentences compared to middle-class whites who commit similar crimes (Reiman, 2007; Russell, 1998). Therefore, antiracist/multiracial feminists are committed to recognizing oppression across many different lines and promoting change through education.

What Suggestions for Social Change Can Be Made by Antiracist/Multiracial Feminists to Address the Current Problems Relating to Gender and Policing?

Antiracist/multiracial feminists often support programs such as affirmative action policies in policing, or the use of quotas as a means to hire officers representing marginalized and under-represented groups within such organizations. The use of consent decrees in the US has proven to be effective to some extent. Consent decrees attempt to remedy the discrimination in hiring and employment practices experienced by women and other minority groups by establishing affirmative action programs. According to the National Center for Women and Policing (2000), US police agencies without a consent decree had fewer sworn female officers in comparison to police agencies that had a consent decree (see tables below).

US Police Agencies without a Consent Decree

Percentage of Female Sworn Personnel	9.7 per cent
Percentage of Sworn Personnel Who Are Women of Colour	6.3 per cent

US Police Agencies with a Consent Decree

Percentage of Female Sworn Personnel	14 per cent
Percentage of Sworn Personnel Who Are Women of Colour	11.7 per cent

According to this group of feminists, the failure to renew consent decrees within police agencies will undoubtedly contribute to a decrease in the number of women and persons of colour being hired and promoted. An example of this is seen in the Pittsburgh Police Department. As reported by the National Center for Women and Policing (2003), beginning in 1975 to 1991, the Pittsburgh Police Department was ordered by the courts to hire one white woman, one African-American man, and one African-American woman for every white man it hired. In 1975 the number of sworn women in the department accounted for only 1 per cent, but by 1991, that number had increased to 27.2 per cent (the highest in the country). However, failure to renew the court order since 1990 has led to only 8.5 per cent of women being hired from the 50 per cent rate mandated earlier. As a result, the number of sworn women in the department dropped to 22 per cent as of 2001.

By 1987 more than half of the US police agencies serving communities larger than 50,000 had implemented affirmative action programs as a result of court orders or consent decrees (National Center for Women and Policing, 2003). However, over the last few years, many consent decrees have expired and are not being renewed at comparable rates. Among surveyed agencies in the 2001 annual survey of women in policing conducted by the National Center for Women and Policing, eight consent decrees had expired during the period between 1999 and 2002, yet only two consent decrees were implemented since 1995, and only six were implemented during the entire decade of the 1990s. Also, from the 247 agencies with more than 100 officers, 40 had been under a consent decree at some point in time, but only 22 of those remained in effect (National Center for Women and Policing, 2003).

Moreover, seeing that education is central to consciousness raising and ensuring change, restructuring courses taught at police colleges/academies would be an important step according to antiracist/multiracial feminists. Different experiences and perspectives should be integrated into the core curricula. Reading material, class lectures, and classroom structure should represent all students, and diverse voices must be integrated into police training. "Knowledge" of policing must be the product of combined diverse perspectives, rather than the voice of a few white males as is currently the case. In other words, the perspectives and experiences of one particular group should not be privileged over others. Also, "special topics" training that includes race relations, gender relations, LGBT relations (lesbian, gay, bisexual, transgender), etc., must not be treated as an "add-on" to general training, or as being less serious or insignificant. These subject areas must become integrated into all aspects of police training, rather than being allotted only a few hours as classroom presentations. Moreover, for many antiracist/multiracial feminists, police officers should be formally educated beyond a high school diploma. Requiring an associate or bachelor's degree, particularly in areas such as sociology, criminology, interdisciplinary studies, gender and sexuality studies, race and ethnic relations, and social stratification, could lead to hiring police officers who are more critically oriented and willing to move beyond the stereotypes that often plague a number of different groups/categories of people.

Postmodern Feminism

Postmodern feminists challenge modernism's ethnocentric domination of "others." Postmodernism can be understood as a philosophy or critical method that challenges the values, ideals, and beliefs that have dominated modernity and have represented a specific period in the history of the Western world. Modernist views perceive the individual as a rational being, and purport that reason provides an objective universal basis for knowledge (Flax, 1990). Postmodernists, on the other hand, view the individual as contradictory and socially constructed. In other words, knowledge is the result of multiple social forces and has varied meanings and interpretations. There is no one "truth," no universal essence. History is nonlinear and not necessarily progressive and is read, or understood, through the limited perspective of the present (Lather, 1991).

Postmodern feminists attempt to apply nonuniversalizing, nonessentialist theories of women. They assert that there are multiple experiences among women and that not all women share the same experiences just because they belong to, or represent, the category "women." Experiences among women often vary depending on their social class, race, ethnicity, sexual orientation, age, disability, religious beliefs, etc., and differences among women who share certain social categories also exist. All social categories, including "women," must be questioned and redefined (Butler, 1992). According to postmodern feminists, modernist conceptions of "gender," "patriarchy," "truth," and "women" have been as oppressive to women as they have been beneficial to men. Socially constructed categories such as "women" oppress women because of the historical baggage associated with these terms. The category "women" serves to pigeonhole many females in terms of their choices in wardrobe, use of language, careers, political beliefs, having children, relationships, as well as their attitudes towards sex and sexuality. Feminist postmodernism is often discussed as a theoretical perspective, but it also reflects an epistemological position because it raises questions about the nature of knowledge (i.e., how it is we know what we know).

However, other feminists, while celebrating several significant contributions made by postmodernists, argue that postmodern feminists have failed to recognize the current gendered social realities throughout the world, both generally and in specific social arenas such as policing. This has disempowered people from coming together to advocate for social change and engage in political praxis. Gendered social realities include the following: A disproportionate number of women live below the poverty line; women continue to earn less money in comparison to men; the majority of victims of domestic violence and sexual assault are women; women are more likely to be killed by men who they have been intimately involved with, whereas men are more likely to be killed by nonintimates; and female police officers are disproportionately represented in policing and in gender-specific assignments. Unlike in the early years of the second wave of the women's movement, postmodern thought has addressed multiple identities and concerns with identity politics, but it has, in the process, in many ways disempowered feminism according to some feminists (Ackoff, 1988; Flax, 1987; Harding, 1986a; 1986b; 1986c).

The critics of postmodern feminism assert that the identity categories "women/men" do not correspond to any unified and unifying essence, but that in a patriarchal society they have been socially constructed to imply various relatively fixed qualities by many people. "Women" and "men" have been constructed to represent various "truths" and regardless of how different their personal experiences as individuals have been, there are overwhelming similarities in certain experiences that impact their lives (Corsianos, 2004). Given the existence of historical patriarchal social forces, it is no surprise that "masculine" traits, which are often defined in positive terms, become associated with males, and "feminine" characteristics, which are often defined in negative terms, often become synonymous with females.

What Suggestions for Social Change Can Be Made by Postmodern Feminists to Address the Current Problems Relating to Gender and Policing?

Postmodern feminists argue that we must look at the multiple experiences of female police officers. For instance, looking at experiences according to race, ethnicity, sexual orientation, and age, etc., would illuminate the differences that exist rather than presenting the experiences of all female officers as being identical or similar. In addition, postmodernists want to make every effort to move away from thinking in terms of "women" and "men" within the social world more generally, and within policing more specifically. The social category "women" hinders and oppresses female officers. It often serves to pigeonhole people in ways that do a disservice to them, and can promote very different identities for the individual officer than the ones with which she/he self-identifies.

Individuals often categorize people based on stereotypes of sex (or perceived sex) and physical appearance. Some assume they "know" or "understand" various "women" based on what they are wearing, how they speak, or how they act. For reasons such as these, it is important to continuously question modernist constructions such as gender and deconstruct them in order to learn more about the processes by which they are formed. Then we can move in the direction of presenting multiple definitions and interpretations of current social categories. This constant critical exercise can begin to challenge many of the assumptions, beliefs, attitudes, and values that many officers and citizens have of female, as well as male, police officers. It also allows us to question whether "new," more feminist initiatives, such as CP and increases in female representation, can actually change policing systems. Do these perceived changes offer alternative forms to traditional male approaches to social control, or do they simply present a feminized social control discourse and image that hide the fact that policing still promotes and is committed to preserving "masculine" characteristics such as aggressive crime control, discipline, and punishment?

For the "skeptical" postmodernists, there is no basis for determining "truth" or objectivity and thus they invest their energies in deconstructing "truths" and revealing the nature of knowledge by showing biases in societal constructions. They do not propose alternatives because that would suggest that there are particular realities. Yet, "affirmative" postmodernists, on the other hand, examine the conditional "truths" that people rely on to actively build their social world in ways that can attempt to benefit all diverse groups (Henry and Milovanovic, 1999).

As noted, the current police literature reports that female officers continue to be criticized for not possessing particular "masculine" traits often believed to be required for officers to conduct their work (Heidensohn and Brown, 2000; Martin, 1999; Miller, 1999; Martin and Jurik, 1996; Heidensohn, 1992; Bell, 1982; Charles, 1981; Drummond, 1976). However, through continued critical reflection of police ideologies and practices, we can begin to see the relationship between the hierarchical paramilitaristic police model and all its accompanying constructed "truths," including the "brotherhood of policing." According to many postmodern feminists, we would be able to move away from the oppressions and limitations of our gendered categories that continue to be used against human beings to silence, control, and/or define them. We would ultimately, over time, no longer need research that examines the differences in police performance and in people's expectations of the police according to gender, or research on the gendered experiences of police officers.

For postmodern feminists, gendered findings, assumptions, and expectations must cease to exist in order for both women and men to gain certain freedoms. They assert that their insistence on continuous questioning will free us from oppressive socially constructed categories.

Questions

1. Can a feminist criminology exist given the existence of different feminist theories and methodological approaches?
2. Which feminist approach discussed above do you think best identifies the causes of inequalities between women and men in policing?
3. Which feminist theory discussed above do you think can promote the most positive change for female and male officers?
4. Discuss some of the current media representations of women in policing. Are these representations gendered? How so?

CHAPTER 4

The Police Culture: Gender, Ideology, and the "Brotherhood of Policing"

The Police Culture

The police occupational culture is often referred to as the complex system of attitudes that defines the normative and behavioural social world of police officers. To date, several academics have written on different aspects of this occupational culture (Crank, 1998; Manning, 1997; 1992; 1977; Scripture, 1997; Westley, 1953; McNulty, 1994; Fyfe, 1991). Academics have identified occupational themes that determine police culture. They include conformity and/or solidarity, loyalty, secrecy, autonomy, authority, uncertainty, danger, suspicion, "us versus them mentality" (i.e., the police versus the public), administration, and being distinct from other occupational cultures (Birzer and Tannehill, 2001; Crank, 1998; Manning, 1997; 1990; Farkas and Manning, 1997; Scripture, 1997; Storch and Panzarella, 1996; Brandl, 1996; McNulty, 1994; Dixon, 1992; Fyfe, 1991; Goldsmith, 1990; Hale, 1989; Van-Maanen, 1984; Doig, 1978; Skolnick, 1966; Westley, 1953). According to Crank (1998), police officers are socialized to have a distinct way of understanding the world and their roles as police officers; they relate to one another because they share a common culture. Similarly, Lundman (1980) asserts that police recruits are relatively homogeneous in terms of their class, gender, education level, and race. However, the socialization they experience throughout their police training is what ultimately produces uniformity in officers' perceptions of police work and their roles as officers.

Others highlight the importance of police autonomy in order for officers to deal with the various ambiguous situations in their day-to-day interactions. Additionally, the combination of work in the field and the organizational structure produces specific organizational knowledge (McNulty, 1994). For instance, secrecy is highly valued.

[The police officer] regards the public as his enemy, feels his occupation to be in conflict with the community, and regards himself to be a pariah. The experience and the feeling give rise to a collective emphasis on secrecy, an attempt to coerce respect from the public, and a belief that almost any means are legitimate in completing an important arrest. These are for the policeman basic occupational values. They arise from his experience, take precedence over his legal responsibilities, [and] are central to an understanding of his conduct (Westley, 1953: 35).

Police culture affects the social and political environment and is simultaneously affected by these environments (Fyfe, 1991). For others, police culture is shaped by the authority that their job provides them, the code of silence, as well as the danger that is associated with their work (Skolnick, 1966; Hale, 1989). The common police practice of making uncertain and risky decisions, as well as the level of danger that is associated with their work, shapes and defines police attitudes and hence the police culture. According to Manning (1990), autonomy, authority, and uncertainty are the main occupational themes for the police and these determine their social world. Doig (1978) asserts that police culture affects the new recruits as they learn the rules of police work "on the street" that challenge the administrative rules, and that individual personalities, levels of education, and cultural pressures shape and guide the police culture.

Unfortunately, in most criminological research, feminist inquiries into the area of policing are absent. Missing is the exploration of patriarchal aspects of the police occupational culture. Research has not traditionally shown these effects on police officers' sense of understanding of their police roles, the policing system, and the communities they serve, as well as the effects of experienced gendered differences on officers. According to Corsianos (2001: 114), police culture

reflects the normative and behavioral social world of police officers and is shaped by both 1. the organizational police structure that consists of administrative rules, a crime control model, a paramilitaristic hierarchical structure (that demands respect/loyalty to the rank and file, and shapes the power relations within the department), and the restructuring of departments as a result of "community policing" initiatives, and 2. the wider social economic order that shapes policing as a whole (e.g. police expected to appear as they operate "fairly" while serving dominant economic interests).

The occupational culture serves those in privileged positions and excludes the marginalized "others." This includes satisfying the paramilitaristic organizational structure that shapes the power dynamics within, and operates to legitimize, the police department to the public by promoting a positive police image. For instance, in Corsianos's study (2003) of a large Canadian police department, insight into the police occupational culture was gained by examining the investigations that become prioritized by the police. Decision-making in the social construction of "high-profile" cases was influenced by variables such as the "status" of the accused, the "status" of the victim, the role of the media, the desire by the police to conceal any questionable and/or illegal police conduct from the public, the possible political "bomb-shells" at stake, and the public's reaction to a case and/or their expectation of the police. For example, the mainstream media often created a sense of accountability on the part of the police department. Officers believed their actions would be scruti-nized more carefully under the "watchful eye" of news reporters and thus wanted to ensure that mistakes were not made. As a result, the police level of accountability increased; more time, energy, and police resources were utilized in these investiga-tions; and, at times, decision-making moved up the hierarchy involving final inves-tigative decisions being made by members of the management.

In addition, officers' decisions leading to an arrest or not directly affected the laws that essentially were or were not enforced. Criminal laws define certain actions/behaviours as illegal and hence, criminal. However, criminal behaviour that officers are expected to police and ultimately apply their discretionary powers to, in terms of which laws to enforce and when, challenge a particular historically and socially con-structed social order, and therefore "criminal" conduct and the policing of such behaviour is an inquiry into expressions of patriarchal power and cultural controls. As noted by Chesney-Lind and Shelden (2004), police in the past have often used their power to arrest women and girls for acts that were perceived as violating con-ventional moral standards. For example, girls were typically arrested for noncrimi-nal status offenses such as being out past curfew. Males, on the other hand, were not arrested for these types of violations.

The police culture operates in a manner that encourages the policing of the less privileged (Ericson, 1982), the protection of the economically powerful (Gordon, 1987; Visano, 1998), and operates to protect police interests by maintaining a posi-tive police image to the public (Manning, 1997; Corsianos, 2003). Any theory that tries to explain police culture by neglecting to recognize the centrality of patriarchal ideologies, politics, and power is limited.

Ideology, Power, and Police Culture

Dominant ideological social forces of the wider culture affect/influence, and to a large extent, define police culture. For instance, how police officers and members of the public perceive the roles of the police, the types of policing styles that should be recognized and awarded (e.g., making arrests versus fulfilling certain community policing [CP] initiatives), identifying who the "criminals" are (i.e., what constitutes criminality), and appropriate responses to suspects/accused persons (e.g., the con-tinued emphasis on the use of force versus effective communication) are largely shaped by the dominant culture. The sociology of police culture cannot be separated from an analysis of the dominant ideologies that produce and reproduce gender inequalities, as well as other inequalities including race/ethnicity, class, and sexual orientation. Also, different aspects of the police organizational structure, such as the paramilitaristic hierarchical structure, shape the occupational culture, including the gendered power relations within departments. Therefore, police officers' perceptions of policing are shaped by patriarchal ideologies within the police occupational culture, the organizational structure, and the wider social economic order (Corsianos, 2001). Shearing (1981) notes that police work is presented as incorporating egalitarian ideals (for instance, through certain changes in employment practices), but, in reality, police culture reflects and maintains structures of dominance.

For these reasons, when analyzing the police culture, the complex concept of power must be deconstructed and examined. Power is a complex abstract concept that has explanatory value only when attached to a theory of a historically specific relationship. In order to understand the power dynamics within police agencies, one must critically examine the history of policing. Poulantzas (1980: 147) states that power is not "attached to a 'class-in-itself,' understood as a collection of agents, but depends upon, and springs from, a relational system of material places occupied by particular agents." In addition, one must analyze the kinds of powers that are distributed within social relations and how and why these powers become distributed by looking at the nature of those social relations. There are a multiplicity of power relations in society, and hence within police departments, that cannot be reduced to a single underlying antagonism, nor can they be understood by looking at existential explanations. By closely examining police power relations, more light can be shed on the patriarchal ideologies that are constructed and sustained within policing systems.

Language, Power, and Police Culture

The paramilitaristic hierarchical structure enables particular systems that create specific power relations within police departments. Language is utilized to contribute to the creation of these power relations. Officers occupying high-ranking positions such as chief, deputy chief, captain, and lieutenant (as seen in some US police departments), or chief, deputy chief, superintendents, and inspectors (as seen in some Canadian police services), produce a number of illusions through the use of language in order to legitimize their position of control (Corsianos, 2001). For Gadamer (1976: 3), "language is the fundamental mode of operation of our being-in-the-world, and the all-embracing form of the constitution of the world."

There are several common expressions that are often used by police personnel. These expressions are utilized as a form of advice within police departments, which, at the manifest level, would indicate a partnership among officers relating to one another within a "collectivist equitable police culture," and hence suggest "friendly advice." However, at the latent level, they affirm respect for, and obedience to, the chain of command and to traditional patriarchal police operations. Common expressions utilized within police departments are "the brotherhood of policing," "the blue wall," "you may win the battle but you won't win the war," "bite the bullet," "don't rock the boat," and "the old boy's club is alive and well." All of these clichés serve to protect and promote the paramilitaristic police structure and its traditional operations and maintain particular power relations (Corsianos, 2001). The people who utilize these expressions as a form of advice are viewed as good-natured and trust-worthy, speaking only with the best interest of the listener in mind (Itwaru, 1989: 12).

> Their utterance is not seen as an attempt to persuade the listener to accept being a power-less subject. It is not seen as the very condition of the absence of freedom. It is not seen as the reinforcement of inequality. But rather in a political economy which daily promises authenticity of the subject and daily denies this, this supposedly good advice takes on the persiflage of personal acceptance and concern (Itwaru, 1989: 13).

Itwaru (1989: 15) adds, "these 'advisors' are the legitimators of highly formalized strategies for the imprisonment of the subject. That they may not be aware of these implications in their action does not detract from the agencing role they are playing."

The hegemonizing procedures of domination are operationalized through language; people consenting to this praxis while coercive actions are hidden. Hegemony is a force of rule that exists within a set of ideologies that is secured through consent of the people and promoted by "common sense" (Gramsci, 1957). Therefore, language (e.g., through the use of police rhetoric), serves as a powerful "tool," as it is used to create the illusion that police agencies today are somehow gender-neutral. Particular rhetoric is introduced and used to indicate equal concern and protection for both male and female officers, while simultaneously operating to preserve dominant patriarchal ideologies.

Moreover, expressions used by the police relating to members of the public are also utilized to present police departments as serving every citizen equally. Rhetoric such as "justice for all," "community policing," and "to serve and protect" are promoted to suggest that every person has equal access to police service and to a good quality of service, and thus also equal police protection, equal rights, and an equal voice. At the manifest level, these common expressions indicate "justice" for all people in officers' dealings with members of the public, but at the latent level, they affirm confirmation to the social, economic and political order, which includes exploitation, discrimination, and police self-legitimization (Corsianos, 2001). As Manning (1997: 109) states, "The police organization functions in a political arena where specific interests are protected even though, in theory, the police are expected to be apolitical."

Accepting and/or Challenging the Police Culture

Officers learn to accept the current police culture as is, or choose to challenge positions of power at different levels. Looking at female officers specifically, they either accept the patriarchal social order or various aspects of it consciously or not, or challenge the various tenets of patriarchal positions of power. Some women are able to realize that, at times, they are being silenced and/or marginalized in their work as police officers. They recognize the power of patriarchal social conditioning, however, they learn to tolerate or accept a degree of disempowerment for survival and acceptance. They choose to perform (i.e., physically, verbally, emotionally, and/or ideologically) in specific ways in order to be accepted and rewarded in various dominant social circles (e.g., to be promoted, attain positive work evaluations, attend specific training courses, go to various units, develop certain relationships, etc.). They conform to various degrees because there is an investment to be made in conforming and the investment can be financial, emotional, and/or socio-psychological. Yet, some women police officers have accepted certain levels of disempowerment for survival and/or social acceptance while still challenging other aspects of patriarchal conditioning where resistance does not necessarily have negative consequences to their overall lives within policing (Corsianos, 2004).

Other female officers, on the other hand, do not view themselves as being oppressed as "women." Some, for instance, believe that certain gender differences are innate, or that there are no gender differences today because women have gained equality with men and have moved into a post-feminist era where the politics of feminism are no longer needed. These women neglect to see the manipulation of power, and accept the patriarchal social order as genuine. Indeed, changes have been made to various departmental rules, social structures, and systems to create the image of a progressive egalitarian police department and create the illusion of equality between the sexes, but, despite these, gender inequalities continue to exist.

Alternatively, there are the female officers, admittedly fewer in number, who will often challenge positions of patriarchal power. They are the ones who, for instance, will not tolerate sexist acts or comments, will question and critically evaluate various policies and practices, and/or challenge decisions that exclude their insight or that of other women (Corsianos, 2004).

Masculinity versus Femininity

Female officers experience pressure to conform to the patriarchal culture that encourages machismo and masculine traits. They continue to be criticized for not possessing particular masculine traits such as courage, aggression, rationality, objectivity, and brutality believed to be required of competent crime-fighting police officers (Miller, 1999; Haar, 1997; Charles, 1981). Other studies have discussed the perceived importance between the so-called masculine characteristics and one's ability to participate in aggressive crime control duties, but note that police work often involves activities that are considered feminine (Martin, 1999; Martin and Jurik, 2007).

Martin (1999), for instance, examines the types of emotional labour that are a part of police work and the challenges that norms related to emotional labour pose specifically for female officers. Within the culture of policing, women continue to be criticized by their male counterparts, who assume that women do not have the physical abilities to carry out crime-fighting responsibilities and that they are better suited in policing roles that deal with social-service-type functions (e.g., in community-oriented police capacities, working with domestic assault victims, youth, etc.) (Heidensohn and Brown, 2000; Heidensohn, 1992; Bell, 1982; Drummond, 1976).

Other research shows that even many female officers "buy into" the idea of a "maternal nature" that makes female officers better at some areas of policing, while placing most men at a disadvantage (Corsianos, 2004). Lonsway (2000) found that women police possessed better communication skills than male officers and were more competent in using the necessary tools to instigate CP initiatives. Also, females tend to be able to adapt better to change, deal better with fatigue, and be more open-minded in instances relating to displaying one's emotions (Bass, 1982). According to Orban (1998), female police officers adopted a code of behaviour that "proved" their loyalty to the patriarchal police culture while minimizing their own gender identity. Women fought for acceptance by the "brotherhood of policing" by trying to gain the trust of male coworkers and "prove themselves" to the police organization and to male peers by demonstrating capability, competency, and loyalty. Women officers felt the pressure to "become one of the boys," keep personal problems such as child-care quiet, and never discuss their personal sexual lives for fear of cruel rumours being spread by their male peers. Similarly, McLean (1997a) asserts that many female officers adopt the language, the mannerisms, and/or the roles of male colleagues in order to become integrated into the organization and culture and be accepted; in other words, for many women it is a "survival tactic."

Martin and Jurik (2007: 68), on the other hand, contend that within the culture of policing, female officers threaten many male officers primarily for four reasons:

> In one of the few remaining occupations in which strength and physical ability occasionally are useful, women's presence implies either that the men's unique asset — physical strength — is irrelevant, or that a man who works with a woman will be at a disadvantage in a confrontation. Three other less frequently articulated concerns also support men's resistance to women: the belief that women are "mentally weaker," the view that women are unable to command public respect as officers, and the concern that "moral" women will break the code of silence and expose the men's illicit activities.

Feminization of Policing

Areas where more women are likely to serve (e.g., CP units) are typically perceived to be less important within the police culture (Miller, 1999). In other words, "feminized units," where a disproportionate number of women officers work, are often less valued. Men, on the other hand, are more likely to serve in units that are perceived to be central to the law enforcement field; that is, units that primarily focus on aggressive crime control and arrests. Competition for the "big arrest" becomes prioritized and necessary for career advancement. In Corsianos's studies (2007a; 2005; 1999b), women were more likely to work in units such as the youth bureau, CP, and domestic violence units. Their work in these areas did not receive the recognition comparable to the ones that produced "high-profile" arrests.

Male officers were more likely to work in detective offices that included the major crime unit, homicide, and the intelligence unit where there was competition to make the "big arrest" or a "good pinch." These units were considered prestigious and were very cliquish. Their work in these areas often meant dealing with "large-scale" criminal activity which included narcotics, weapons, and wanted persons. Moreover, such large-scale activities frequently demanded complex, highly sophisticated investigations where special undercover cars and various forms of technology, such as surveillance equipment, were utilized, requiring coordination with other agencies. Also, arrests made in these types of investigations often led to media publicity. The police were eager to promote their "good work" as "crime controllers" to members of the public, and individual officers' efforts were recognized through district awards, promotions, transfers to other detective offices, positive evaluations from supervisors, and acceptance into specialized training courses.

Similarly, the work of detectives in the district drug squads was more valued. These officers were expected to investigate drug-related problems of all levels in their specified area. If they came across what was referred to as "a big player," where the stakes were much higher and the investigation much more complex, requiring more resources, time, and greater detective experience, then it was essential for the case to be turned over to officers in the intelligence unit. This unit was located at police headquarters and was responsible for all high-level drug investigations. Usually the two detectives at the district level, who were involved in the initial investigation, would be relocated to the intelligence unit to assist in the investigation, resulting in an incentive to work on investigating the "big players" and make the "big arrests" which would contribute to one's career advancement (Corsianos, 2007a; 1999b). Clearly, the areas in policing that became "feminized" by the increase in the number of women police officers were less valued, whereas units that were perceived to be masculine were highly respected within the police culture.

Gendered Expectations in the Perceived Masculine Units

Moreover, Corsianos (2005; 1999b) found during her studies of police services that supervisors working in the various perceived masculine detective offices sought particular characteristics in individuals seeking detective assignments. These units are very cliquish and, even though they are lateral movements, they are viewed on many levels as promotions by front-line officers seeking to become detective constables. The gained experience, the ability to work in plain clothes, and the opportunity to make extra money in overtime and court appearances are highly valued. Careful consideration is given to applicants to ensure they meet certain criteria. Ultimately, individuals who have demonstrated they are "team players" and can be trusted are selected. Being a team player includes being able to "take a joke" without becoming offended. Candidates are expected to be able to conform to the dominant patriarchal Anglo-Saxon ideologies. "PWs" (i.e., "policewomen"), "Blacks," "Asians," and "Ethnics" (as they were referred to) were expected to not be offended by racial/ethnic slurs and sexist comments, and were expected to accept the stereotypes regarding race/cultures/gender/sexual orientation and see the "humour" in it all. To some extent, women's participation in detective offices was seen as important, but access to permanent positions was limited and their roles were gendered. They were expected "to be women," but also become "one of the boys."

In one example of the dynamics between gender status and the "team player," a male detective in the drug unit discussed undercover female detectives' success over men in being able to more readily "make a buy" with known drug dealers. This detective maintained that it was much easier for women to buy drugs because "all they have to do is put a little paint on, show a little cleavage, a little leg or something like that, and the old story is these guys are thinking with their dick so it was much easier to sell to the women." The same detective claimed that women had to stop complaining about sexual harassment on the job and not be offended by comments, rumours, or jokes relating to their personal sexuality. He added that he would never have a woman work in his unit who could not "take a joke." Being a "team player" was defined in very narrow ways and was an essential characteristic for those wanting to work in detective offices (Corsianos, 2005; 1999b).

Majority versus Minority Group Status

Feminist research has also shown that male officers, because of their majority group status, experience less pressure to prove to others that they are competent and effective at their jobs. If a male officer makes a mistake then the individual alone is held responsible. However, women, because of their minority group status, experience a great deal of pressure to prove themselves and gain acceptance by their peers (Orban, 1998). Many experience increased pressure and stress to demonstrate capability and competency (Wexler and Logan, 1983). If a female officer makes a mistake then it reflects negatively on the entire group of female officers rather than the individual.

Women officers tend to be subjected to more job-related pressures due to their gender and experience these both on and off the job (Bass, 1982). In fact, research shows that female officers list the negative attitude of male officers as being the most significant problem for them (Independent Commission on the Los Angeles Police Department, 1991). In Jackson's study (1997) of female officers in the Atlantic Canada region, 72 per cent of the officers felt the pressure to prove themselves in their roles as police officers because of their gender. Interestingly, 44 per cent believed that as more women are hired to work as police officers, acceptance by male officers will increase. Also, Corsianos (2007a) found that when there was an obvious visible presence of female officers resulting in several female partnerships "on the road" and/or "on the beat," women were less likely to experience the kind of pressure to prove themselves and be accepted into the "brotherhood of policing" as some women in other agencies have experienced.

Gender, Race, Sexual Orientation, and Police Culture

The pressure experienced by female officers who represent visible minorities has been discussed by some academics, including Pogrebin, Dodge, and Chatman, 2000; McLean, 1997; Martin, 1994; Washington, 1981; and Townsey, 1980. Women of colour experience both sexism and racism in the occupational culture of policing. They experience a "double marginality" and are subject to both internal and external sources of stress. They are subject to "special stressors such as exclusion from the informal channels of support and information, as well as, ostracism and overt racial or sexist comments by white officers" (Pogrebin, Dodge, and Chatman, 2000: 314).

Forms of exclusion include poor instruction communication, peer hostility and ostracism through the silent treatment, oversupervision, exposure to dangerous situations, and inadequate backup by male officers. They are also subjected to degrading stereotypes (Pogrebin, Dodge, and Chatman, 2000). White women, on the other hand, have frequent contact with white males and thus the potential to form alliances, gain power, and move up the ranks. To the contrary, black women are afforded less protection and higher levels of hostility, physical separation, and intimidation. Differences in class and occupational status intersect with those of race and gender in separating black and white women. African-American female officers have less support and less opportunities in comparison to white female officers within police organizations, which are structured by racial divisions, stereotypes, and patterns of dominance that intersect with gender discrimination. They also face several uncertainties that include the unpredictable responses of citizens when confronted by an authority figure who is a woman of colour, and whether they will receive adequate backup from fellow officers (Martin, 1994). Collins (1990) identifies four stereotypes of "controlling images." Whereas virtues of piety, purity, submissiveness, and domesticity are attached to "white women," "black women" have been portrayed by mainstream society as mammies, matriarchs, welfare recipients, and hot mammas.

Moreover, males who represent visible minority groups and white women protect their own interests at the expense of black female officers. This further separates black women from all other officers, positing them as the "outsider within" (Martin, 1994). Caucasian women choose to align themselves with the higher status white male officers in the organization. African-American women often experience subordination and exclusion as a result of both their race and gender (Hurtado, 1989). Alternatively, males who are visible minorities do not challenge the masculine image of the police and align themselves with the dominant majority of white male officers (Martin, 1994). Both black male officers and white female officers are viewed as trading on their racial and gender solidarity with the higher status white male officers (Martin, 1992; 1994). Women of colour are further subjected to minority community resentment by citizens who perceive the police as suspicious and not trustworthy. Given these experiences, it is not surprising to see that women of African descent leave the field of policing much more frequently in comparison to all other officers; on average, they leave by their fourth year of service (Dodge and Pogrebin, 2001).

There is overwhelming evidence that female and minority officers continue to experience discrimination and marginalization. Morash and Haar (1995) report that interaction in patrol units between female and ethnic minority officers and white male officers continues to remain somewhat segregated. With respect to Aboriginal policing, Native female officers utilized distinct policing approaches in their communities compared to other members of Canadian police agencies, but as McLean (1997b: 199) points out, "native female officers share many of the same obstacles and constraints as those female officers working in Canadian police settings and organizations. They face promotional limitations, isolation, and lack of policies specific to female members."

The culture of policing is gendered, racialized, and sexualized. Lesbians and gay men, too, have experienced exclusion, harassment, and limited advancement within police organizations. The image of the police officer that emerged in the early twentieth century was that of a strong, tall, fearless, crime-fighting male. Women ("straight" or lesbian) and gay men threaten this constructed "masculine" and "heterosexualized" police image. Miller, Forest, and Jurik (2004) found that lesbian and gay officers expressed loyalty to the police organization and were committed to many of the traditional policing goals. Like other officers, they wanted to be recognized for their hard work and achievements. However, lesbian officers were more likely than heterosexual females to "downplay" their sexual orientation and take on various "masculine" traits (e.g., aggressiveness) in order to gain respect from fellow officers.

"Hegemonic heterosexuality" (Messerschmidt, 1997; 1993; Connell, 1995) is challenged by the presence of more women because "real men" are prohibited from openly talking about sex and women's bodies. Homosexuality is perceived as a threat to group solidarity and to the overall police culture. Gay men who hide their sexual orientation often experience the pressure to "act straight" and to exaggerate normative verbal and physical heterosexual performances in order to be seen as "team players" and foster relations with other male officers. In comparison to heterosexual women police, lesbian officers who do not hide their sexual orientation are perceived as being more competent because they are assumed to be "masculine," but are still subject to harassment and hostility (Miller, Forest, and Jurik, 2004).

Despite the fact that officers work in an environment that is gendered, racialized, and sexualized, research consistently shows that women can handle the crime-fighting and rescue aspects of policing as well as men, regardless of differences in biology and socialization (Horne, 1980). Also, despite some gender differences, male and female officers are equally effective in patrol work (Sherman, 1975; Anderson, 1976; Martin and Jurik, 2007) and it is easier for female officers to conduct surveillance operations because they are not as conspicuous (Crites, 1973). Feinman (1986: 95) notes that research suggests "men are in no more danger with women as partners than with men as partners." Moreover, the public perceives both male and female officers as being effective, but overall they have sex-stereotypic views that include the belief that women are better at various gender-specific roles such as working with female victims of crime, as well as children (Breci, 1997). According to Susini (1977) and Hilton (1976), women officers started to improve the image of police work by giving it a more human appearance.

The Police Culture and Sexual Harassment

Sexual harassment, from a legal stance, can include quid pro quo harassment and hostile environment harassment. Quid pro quo harassment refers to the use of sexual threats/bribery as a condition of employment and/or employment decisions. Hostile environment harassment includes sexual behaviours, such as sexual comments, touching, etc., that interfere with an employee's ability to do her/his work (Dansky and Kilpatrick, 1997). According to a US National Women's Study conducted by the Crime Victims and Treatment Center, 12 per cent of women experienced or will experience some form of harassment in their lifetime. Canadian studies reveal that lifetime sexual harassment rates for women vary from 23 per cent (Welsh and Nierobisz, 1997) to 51 per cent (Gruber, 1998; 1992). The numbers are likely higher than reported, since many women who experience unwanted sexual behaviours choose not to politicize their personal experiences and/or are reluctant to define them as sexual harassment.

The research suggests women's responses to sexual harassment fall along a continuum of avoidance, negotiation, diffusion, and confrontation (Gruber, 1989). According to Cochran, Frazier, and Olson (1997), many women tend to ignore the harassment. Others attempt to "deal" with it by joking or going along with it (Gutek, 1985; USMSPB, 1981; 1987), while others avoid the person who is harassing them (Cochran, Frazier, and Olson, 1997; Culbertson et al., 1992). A study of the US Navy found that only 12 per cent of enlisted women and 5 per cent of women officers actually filed complaints when they experienced sexual harassment (Culbertson et al., 1992). Sexual harassment contributes to decreased job satisfaction (Gruber, 1992), decreased perception of equal opportunity (Newell, Rosenfeld, Culbertson, 1995), damaged interpersonal work relationships (Culbertson et al., 1992), low morale and high absenteeism (USMSPB, 1981), and sometimes results in quitting the place of employment or being fired (USMSPB, 1987; Coles, 1986). Research also consistently shows there is a connection between sexual harassment and stress and health issues, including anxiety, depression, headaches, and problems sleeping (Fitzgerald, 1993; Gutek and Koss, 1993).

Sexual harassment within policing has been identified, but, unfortunately, continues to be practiced (Martin, 1980; Hunt, 1984; *Arnold v. City of Seminole*,

Oklahoma, 614F. Supp. 853 (1985); *Watts v. New York City Police Department*, 724F. Supp 99 (S.D.N.Y. 1989); *Andrews v. City of Philadelphia*, 895 F.2d 1469 (3d Cir. 1990); Harrington and Lonsway, 2004). In Martin's study (1990), 63 per cent of women officers in her sample said they had experienced sexual harassment on the job. Similarly, Robinson (1993) reported that 61 per cent of the female officers surveyed experienced sexual harassment at work, and Nichols (1995) found that 68 per cent of policewomen reported such behaviour. In 1994 there was a sexual harassment inquiry into the Los Angeles Police Department's (LAPD's) West Los Angeles Division. "The inquiry reported sexist and racist remarks, male police officers who failed to back up female officers needing help, and so deeply ingrained mistreatment that police-women had come to accept it as a part of life" (Van Wormer and Bartollas, 2000: 164). Bartol et al.'s (1992) study found that 53 per cent of female officers had been sexually harassed, mostly by male supervisors. In addition, two women reported being sexu-ally assaulted by their male supervisors. Sexual harassment can create a hostile envi-ronment and become a condition of employment. It is clear that sexual harassment continues to be a source of stress for women (Haar and Morash, 2005; Texeira, 2002).

Police culture does not promote a supportive climate for complainants. Women who file sexual harassment complaints within their departments are typically seen as "rocking the boat" and untrustworthy. Many of these women also become subject to retaliation; the most serious being when fellow officers refuse to respond to their emergency calls. Women who experience this often resign (National Center for Women and Policing, 2000) as this puts their lives and the lives of other citizens in danger. Harrington and Lonsway (2004: 505-06) list some of the most common types of retal-iation that women filing sexual harassment complaints experience. They are as follows:

- shunning or ostracizing, in which other officers refuse to talk to the woman who is being victimized or prevent the woman from receiving information that is important to her job performance or personal safety;
- stalking or harassing, in which the victim is subjected to obscene telephone calls, during which the caller says nothing; hang-up calls at all hours of the day and night; threatening or harassing letters or notes; damage to her automobile; articles left on her desk or in her work area; and other actions that are intended to intimidate or harass;
- spreading rumours about the woman's sexual activity or other demeaning information;
- holding the woman to a higher standard of performance than her colleagues, so her evaluation reports become more critical and limit her opportunities for advancement within the organization;
- filing baseless and harassing internal affairs complaints; this action is done either by other members of the organization or by citizens who have been enlisted to help the harasser;
- denying access to training opportunities;

- denying requests for transfer to specialty jobs;
- denying applications for promotion;
- failing to provide backup in emergency situations; this action is the ultimate form of retaliation.

Welsh (1999) asserts that much more research in the area of sexual harassment is needed, particularly in areas that include the organizational response to sexual harassment, the experienced consequences to filing complaints, as well as sexual harassment against other minority groups. She further notes that there is a need for more advanced survey data collection techniques, as well as qualitative research in this area.

Additionally, even though many police policy manuals have eliminated gendered language, gendered stereotypes continue to be used throughout police academies in the US and police colleges in Canada. According to Pike (1992), women often appear as sex objects in training films. This is a form of sexual harassment. Women are also often teased as a rite of passage from being a recruit to becoming an officer in ways that promote the image of women as sex objects (Pike, 1992), and this, too, constitutes sexual harassment.

Police Culture, Use of Force, and Police Corruption: Are There Gender Differences?

Some acts of police behaviour are universally condemned while others generate disagreement and debate. Moreover, some police actions clearly violate laws while others violate internal departmental policies. Goldstein (1977: 30) defines police corruption as "the misuse of authority by a police officer in a manner designed to produce personal gain for the officer or others." Similarly, Sherman (1974: 30) defines police corruption as "an illegal use of organizational power for personal gain." Langworthy and Travis III (2003: 414), on the other hand, define police corruption as "the intentional misuse of police power." In other words, in order for an act to qualify as "police corruption," it must first be shown that police powers were misused, and second, that the officer(s) misusing police power intended to misuse it. The motive (whether it is for money, personal gain, etc.) is important only in establishing the intentional misuse of power.

It is difficult to know the extent of police corruption beyond the reported cases. Known cases are often the result of reports made by the victims of police corruption to police authorities. Police officers who participate in such illegal acts have no incentives to report their own corrupt activities and risk losing their job and/or face prosecution in criminal courts. Similarly, officers who witness acts of police corruption are deterred from reporting this behaviour. They are expected to respect the police occupational culture and code of silence. Moreover, citizens who willingly engage in acts of corruption with the police have no motive to report their own involvement or that of the officer. Citizens who are less willing participants in corruption (e.g., if the police tell them to pay a fee in exchange for not receiving a citation and they do so), or citizens who observe different forms of corruption may decide not to report these incidents because they believe the police will either not investigate, or they are fearful of retribution (Corsianos, 2007c). According to Cao, Deng, and Barton (2000), both the organizational characteristics of police agencies and the communities in which they operate are important correlates of the rate of citizen complaints relating specifically to the police use of excessive force.

Different levels of police corruption may be found within police organizations, and different types of police corruption have been identified by scholars (Withrow, 2006; Walker, 2005; 1977; Corsianos, 2003; Burris and Whitney, 1999; Inciardi, 1987; Stoddard, 1979; Sherman, 1974; Maas, 1973). Types of police corruption include, but are not limited to, the following (Corsianos, 2007c):

- lying as a witness to cover up the actions of oneself or another officer;
- taking cash or expensive items for personal use from "a call" or crime scene;
- using race as a key factor in deciding to stop and interrogate citizens (referred to as racial profiling, race-based policing, or race-biased policing);
- using excessive force on citizens (e.g., aggravated assault, deadly force);
- accepting cash or gifts in exchange for ignoring some violation on the part of a citizen.

Numerous studies have shown that female officers are less likely to participate in acts of police corruption in comparison to male officers. They are less likely to use legitimate physical force in the performance of their duties, but they are also less likely to use excessive force or police brutality (The Bureau of Justice Assistance, 2001; Lord, 1995; Abernathy and Cox, 1994). According to the Independent Commission on the Los Angeles Police Department (i.e., the Christopher Commission), following the Rodney King case in Los Angeles, "female officers utilized a style of policing that minimized the use of excessive force" (Independent Commission on the Los Angeles Police Department, 1991). The commission also concluded that female LAPD officers were significantly less likely to use excessive force. Similarly, the Bureau of Justice Assistance (2001: 2) reported that "research conducted both in the U.S. and internationally clearly demonstrates that women police officers use a style of policing that relies less on physical force. They are better at defusing and deescalating potentially violent confrontations with citizens and are less likely to become involved in incidents of excessive force."

Gendered Differences in Officers' Involvement in Questionable, Unethical, and/or Corrupt Acts

Corsianos (1999b) conducted field research to study the occupational culture and organizational structure of detective offices in a large Canadian police department.

Methodological approaches used to collect data included interviews, participant observation, and document analysis of various internal police literature. Formal interviews were conducted with 50 current or former detectives (i.e., detective constables, detectives, and detective sergeants). Thirty-seven males and 13 females were interviewed. All of the women were present or former detective constables; and 31 of the males were present or former detective constables, four were detectives, and two were detective sergeants. A variety of detective units were represented, which included the detective office, the youth bureau, the major crime unit, the street crime unit, the sexual assault squad, the fraud office, and the warrants office. In addition, dozens of informal interviews were conducted at various police social settings (e.g., barbecues, popular police bars, and seasonal parties) with detective constables, detectives, and detective sergeants representing a variety of units including homicide, intelligence, and district drug units.

Additionally, participant observation was utilized at two different divisions. This meant access to the detectives as they worked the sally ports and booking rooms where suspects were initially brought, as well as the interview rooms, the jails, the detective offices, and the computer software utilized by the detectives. Data was also collected by participating in "ride-alongs" with five officers who had previous detective experience. Through the use of participant observation, a number of research exercises were utilized. These included direct observation and participation, informal or conversational interviewing (Becker and Geer, 1957), and informal observations (Downes, 1966). These methodological approaches produced rich data on male and female detectives' perceptions on different aspects of the occupational culture and organizational structure of detective offices, including officers' involvement in questionable, unethical, and/or corrupt acts (Corsianos, 1999b).

For most male officers, loyalty to one another within the detective office was the expected norm, even if it meant being unethical, displaying "questionable" conduct, and/or sometimes acting illegally in order to protect a fellow officer. The female detectives, on the other hand, believed that being ethical in the execution of their police duties (i.e., following the administrative rules and obeying the laws) was crucial, even if it meant being "disloyal" to another officer for refusing to lie or "cover" for him/her. Male detectives who claimed they made a conscious effort to ensure that their sense of loyalty to other officers did not interfere with being ethical in their work constituted the minority and there had been instances in their careers where they went against their personal convictions. These same detectives claimed that if officers followed the rules and proceeded in a lawful manner in the execution of police duties, then they never had to fear being "discovered" and/or appearing incompetent in court as one lie had to be created to cover another. Also, time and energy would not be wasted in taking the extra steps to shelter any lies or fabrications on their part (e.g., collectively working with one's partner on the information they record in their memorandum books to ensure their "stories" did not contradict in any way).

Ironically, these same detectives had admitted to doing things "against their better judgment" for the sake of "loyalty." In one account, a detective had assisted an officer in charging a man with "possession of narcotics." However, the detective later discovered that this allegation was completely false; the man never swallowed any illegal drugs nor was he in possession of any narcotic. The detective, in turn, did not reveal this in court when the man was being tried. The detective believed that if he had, his actions would have automatically led to criminal charges being laid against the arresting officer and that would have had several ripple effects within the police culture for showing disloyalty to the "brotherhood." He maintained that the only factor that protected the other officer was that the accused man, who was mistrustful of the police, refused to let them transport him to a hospital for treatment. Had he agreed to be examined by doctors in an emergency room, they would have discovered that drugs had not been consumed. Needless to say, the man was convicted of the crime and received a jail sentence since he had prior criminal convictions. The detective expressed guilt for not coming forward with this information, but noted that he did not have a choice given the internal occupational expectations. The irony is that he perceived his job as being compromised through the illegal actions of the other officer, yet simultaneously felt his job would have been compromised had he revealed what really happened (Corsianos, 1999b).

Similarly, there were several instances where male officers spoke of having to "teach him/her a lesson" (i.e., referring to a suspect). These cases typically involved situations where the suspect either showed no remorse for his/her actions and/or disrespected the police by being uncooperative, arrogant, or using obscene language. In the words of one officer: "I will take him to the wall if he's got attitude." Another officer noted, "I'll be more heavy-handed paper-wise because the pen is mightier than the sword" (Corsianos, 1999b). Detectives possess a great deal of discretionary power in their day-to-day case decision-making, with the exception of "high-profile" cases (Corsianos, 2003). In some instances, officers can decide whether accused persons are released until their court date or whether they will be brought to the station and placed in jail until the bail hearing the next morning.

Sometimes their roles as "disciplinarians" meant officers would falsify charges against the accused for the sake of "teaching him/her a lesson." These cases involved individuals who were deemed "career criminals." "Trumped-up" charges did not seem to be the norm; however, detectives had the power to falsify evidence for the sake of charging if the need arose, and these cases involved only male detectives. In one example (Corsianos, 1999b), two men who each had over 30 prior criminal convictions were arrested for stealing a cash box. During the course of their investigation, the detectives assigned to the case realized these two men were not the ones who had stolen the cash box but rather had come across it in a back alley. However, according to one of the detectives, the "suspects" chose to be uncooperative; that is, "they decided to play hard ball and tell us to screw ourselves rather than just tell us the truth that they had found it. So, they had to be taught a lesson." As a result, the suspects were both wrongfully charged with "possession of property obtained by crime."

Both accused persons pleaded guilty and subsequently served a few months in jail. The detective maintained that they pleaded guilty as a result of their lengthy criminal records. Due to their criminal history, they would not have been released subsequent to their bail hearing and would have spent anywhere from six months to a year behind bars awaiting trial. By pleading guilty, they would be released from jail in a significantly shorter time. Disciplining or "teaching people a lesson" was a common theme relating to the police occupational culture and officers' case decision-making, and this appeared to be gender-specific (Corsianos, 2005; 1999b).

Some male officers admitted to conducting illegal searches of cars. If they suspected criminal activity, they used a number of "tactics" to search cars. Some would claim they smelled alcohol on the driver's breath, or they would toss a beer cap in the car, which suggested a possibility of open liquor in the vehicle. These constituted provincial statute offenses and afforded the officers the right to search the vehicle. If the search led to the discovery of drugs, weapons, or other contraband, they would call to get a search warrant to search the entire car (e.g., trunk, glove box, etc.) (Corsianos, 1999b).

Other violations of individual rights included refusing to read suspects their rights. These particular officers made it a habit to always note in their memorandum book that the individual's rights had been read, even if they had not done so. Canada's Charter of Rights and Freedoms was perceived at times to "interfere" with "good police work" and to "tie the hands of good cops." Alternatively, sampled female officers stated they always ensured they read suspects their rights, because they felt it was a good habit to follow procedures and never place themselves in situations where they had to lie to cover up another lie and so on.

Moreover, male officers who admitted to acting in "questionable," unethical, and/or illegal ways tended to adhere to "three basic rules" to protect themselves. First, "if it's not in your memo book, it did not happen." Second, "act surprised and show concern if questioned by superiors," and third, "always stick to your story; the story you record in your memo book." In one account, where a detective constable engaged in unethical and illegal behaviour by physically assaulting a suspect, he ensured that in his memo book he recorded the injuries had been sustained when the individual tripped and fell down some stairs. This information was corroborated by his partner, and together they falsely constructed a story that they similarly recorded in their memo books to ensure there were no contradictory remarks. At a later date, the victim filed a complaint against this detective constable. The officer was subsequently questioned by the detective and the detective sergeant. He acted surprised and concerned with the allegations, insisted that he never assaulted the man (i.e., "tuned him up" in police jargon), and that, according to his memo book, the individual had injured himself by falling down a flight of stairs (Corsianos, 1999b).

Where men and women were more comparable was in the laying of charges for a minor offense in instances where there were "reasonable and probable grounds" to make an arrest, but, due to the nature of the offense, police action was strongly determined by their perceptions of the suspects' "attitude." This constituted "questionable" police behaviour because officers applied selective law enforcement. In other words, depending on the perceived "attitude" of the suspect, officers would use their discretion to charge or not charge in situations that were usually not deemed "serious." In cases where the suspect had no prior criminal record but was perceived as being uncooperative and/or disrespectful to the officers, the police would frequently make an arrest. For example, if a couple was observed in public engaging in a loud verbal confrontation, attracting the attention of pedestrians, the police would intervene. This typically did not warrant the laying of a charge, especially when the individuals did not have a criminal record. However, if one or both parties responded by being rude, disrespectful, and/or unapologetic, then the officer would arrest them for reasons such as "caused disturbance" or "mischief" (Corsianos, 2005, 1999b).

There were also gender disparities relating to questionable and/or unethical acts in the police response to domestic violence. Studies show that female police officers are more supportive and understanding to victims/survivors of domestic violence. Female officers view domestic violence situations as more serious, are more actively involved in these situations, and/or view them as an important part of their roles in policing crimes (Heidensohn and Brown, 2000; Feinman, 1986; Homant and Kennedy, 1985; Kennedy and Homant, 1983; Bell, 1982; Drummond, 1976).

Similar to other studies, Corsianos (2005; 1999b) found that in comparison to male officers, female detectives were more likely to treat domestic violence cases with priority and not perceive them as a waste of time. However, some male detectives engaged in unethical tactics, using these cases to fulfill personal agendas. In 1990 the Solicitor General of Canada sent out a directive to all police departments mandating arrests in domestic assault cases when there were "reasonable and probable grounds" to suggest that an assault had occurred. In other words, no longer would the police have the discretion to determine whether they should arrest or not. If evidence was present (and, of course, this is always the challenge for victims, especially in cases where the evidence translates into his word versus hers), then the police had to make an arrest; the onus was placed on the officers and not the victim(s).

Male officers claimed that the system (i.e., the new directive) forced them to act when very often the arrest and the subsequent charging of the accused person did not lead to a conviction (e.g., the victim did not appear in court on the trial date and therefore the judge dismissed the case, or the victim gave conflicting evidence of the incident leading to a dismissal of the charges). More women officers took the initiative to take certain steps in the hopes of attaining a conviction at the trial level. Victims in these cases were subpoenaed as "witnesses." In other words, they were served with papers that legally required them to appear in court on the specified trial date. Female detectives offered support to the victims by communicating with them prior to trial and explaining the process and the importance of their court appearance and testimony (typically, the victims in these domestic assault cases were women, and even though victims were subpoenaed, some did not show up for the trial).

Most males seemed to be indifferent to these investigations, but some engaged in unethical "bullying tactics" for their own personal agendas. If they believed the victim might not appear in court, they used aggressive tactics to ensure her cooperation, ranging from verbally threatening her, to lying about the possible legal consequences if she did not appear to testify. In the words of one of these detectives, "We try to scare her into coming in; so I'll say something like, if you don't show up we'll come and boot your door in and drag you in if we have to." Another detective stated: "I'll just tell her that the judge would see her as wasting everyone's time, the public's money, and in the end she would have to pay a serious amount of money and face some years in prison." These individuals were interested in attaining a conviction for their own self-promotion, or because they had a personal vendetta against the accused (e.g., had "run-ins" with the accused in the past) (Corsianos, 2005; 1999b).

All of the above narratives demonstrate that understanding social constructions of gender is central to any analysis of police activities and police experiences. The research showed that there were obvious experienced gender differences in relation to the police culture more generally and to officers' perceptions and choices relating to questionable, unethical, and/or corrupt acts more specifically.

Is the Police Culture Starting to Change?

There is disagreement between scholars with regard to whether the occupational culture of policing can change with an increase in the number of women hired to serve as officers. Most seem to think that since the culture continues to be male-dominated, various patriarchal values are embraced, which presents difficulties for many women trying to "fit in" (Orban, 1999; Martin and Jurik, 2007; Belknap, 2007; Fletcher, 1995; Martin, 1990). Also, women often experience a number of conflicts that include trying to assimilate and gain acceptance by their peers and not violate widely accepted gender norms. This translates into a "no win" situation, as women are either seen as not competent; not "aggressive enough;" trying too hard to prove themselves; acting "less feminine;" or acting "too aggressive." Female officers tend to have higher educational achievements and come from higher socio-economic backgrounds in comparison to their male counterparts, but the occupational culture proves to be much more relevant to officers' experiences and acceptance on the job (Van Wormer and Bartollas, 2000).

The homogeneous characteristics of officers as seen in the 1970s and previous decades are not as apparent, but, regardless, a particular homogeneous image of the police continues to exist on many levels. In these earlier decades, the police were mainly comprised of white working-class males, and other groups were excluded through the use of height and weight restrictions, physical agility tests, and written tests. Furthermore, oral interviews and background checks on candidates' families and friends eliminated those who did not display various "masculine traits" such as aggressiveness and "hegemonic heterosexuality" (as referred to by Messerschmidt, 1997; 1993; and Connell, 1995, among others). Despite the increase in diversity among officers in recent years, the effect on the police culture is not entirely clear. For instance, in assessing the relationship between race, ethnicity, and the police culture, the National Research Council (2004) found little evidence that African-American and Hispanic officers interacted differently in their dealings with the public compared to white officers. This may suggest assimilation to the dominant culture. Jackson's study (1997) of female officers in the Atlantic Canada region found that 38 per cent of officers felt it was important to conform and be accepted as "one of the boys."

Corsianos (2007a) found that when there was an obvious visible presence of female officers, where women had the choice to team up with several different women, and often did, then they were less likely to experience the kind of pressure to prove themselves and be accepted into the "brotherhood of policing" as some women in other agencies have experienced. These women seemed to be less interested in worrying about what their male peers thought about them. That is not to say they were not concerned about their job performance and future promotions and/or particular assignments, but they did not empower male officers to serve as "judge and jury." According to one of the interviewed officers (Corsianos, 2007a: 18):

> I'm not interested in getting acceptance from the guys. I mean c'mon, they screw up more than we do (chuckle). I think the women around here feel good about what they're doing; they feel good about their work and are professional. We got nothing to prove to no one. We work together and help each other and I'm very proud to work with these women.

Jackson's Canadian study (1997), found that 62 per cent of female officers in her sample believed that policewomen's negative situations would improve over time as more women were hired and 31 per cent believed that until more women were hired, female officers would continue to be seen as "tokens" in police agencies. This seemed to be the case in Vega and Silverman's earlier study (1982) of policemen's perceptions of female officers in the Southern US. Male officers preferred to be paired with other males because they felt female officers could not adequately handle violent work-related situations. However, the more often male officers were paired up with female officers, the more likely they were to have different attitudes and perceptions of their female colleagues. This, too, suggests that situations for women will improve as more women are hired.

Indeed, the number of male police officers who are supportive of female officers has grown significantly, but these men still rarely challenge the dominant attitudes (Martin and Jurik, 2007). Despite some increased support, the feminization of certain areas in policing (e.g., CP, domestic violence, and sexual assault units) has led to the opinion held by some male officers that these areas are less important and less valued than other areas. However, policing areas where women are either nonexistent or comprise only a handful of members (e.g., in units that rely on traditional definitions of policing and promote narrow definitions of physical strength, such as various tactical units including Special Weapons and Tactics [SWAT], Emergency Task Force [ETF], Emergency Response Team [ERT], and Tactical Rescue Unit [TRU]) are perceived as being more important and more valued. Women officers (lesbian and "straight") continue to threaten the image of the police as "doing masculinity" and promoting "hegemonic heterosexuality." Gender segregation in policing legitimizes the perceived distinction between "women's work" as "feminine" and "men's work" as "masculine" (Williams, 1989). Also, according to Grant (2000), male officers worry about the impact of women officers on the public's image of the police, since many members of the public continue to make generalizations about women as being more emotional and physically weaker than men.

Some women officers, on the other hand, have reached out to other women and formed organizations to provide an arena where women officers can come together, find support, and discuss common experiences and challenges. They have also been instrumental in bringing about policy changes relating to issues such as pregnancy leave, domestic violence, and sexual harassment (Harrington and Lonsway, 2004). Well-recognized American and Canadian organizations include the National Center for Women and Policing (US), Ontario Women in Law Enforcement (Canada), and Atlantic Women in Law Enforcement (Canada). On a global level, there exists the International Association of Women Police whose mission is "to strengthen, unite and raise the profile of women in criminal justice internationally."

Questions
1. How is the police culture different from other occupational cultures?
2. What role has gender played in the different experiences of male and female officers?
3. Will an increase in the number of women in policing change the police culture? Why or why not?

CHAPTER 5

Gender and Community Policing: Can Community Policing Promote Gendered Justice?

The majority of police departments today in the US and Canada claim to "do" community policing (CP) on some level. CP has become central in the ways police agencies define and promote themselves. However, despite "new" CP initiatives and organizational changes in police departments today, policing systems continue to overwhelmingly represent and promote the traditional paramilitaristic crime control model (Zhao, He, and Lovrich, 2003; Ericson and Haggerty, 1997; Manning 1997; Stenson, 1993).

This chapter first introduces readers to the literature on CP, presents arguments made by both its supporters and opponents, and identifies problems with particular CP approaches. The second part of the chapter discusses some of the gendered experiences that officers are confronted with under the current crime control model (despite some organizational attempts at CP) and critically explores the possibility of using CP initiatives as feminist tools to encourage social and structural changes within policing. A key question addressed here is this: Can we encourage emancipatory politics and freedom from sexist ideologies within policing by using the CP model?

What is Community Policing?

It is generally agreed by police specialists that policing achieved professional status by the 1960s and that the police were generally recognized as crime control experts. However, this in no way suggests that policing did not continue to have its problems, especially in the area of public relations. By the 1970s and 1980s, more people began to voice objections against the police, arguing that they served to satisfy the status quo. A stronger collective public voice was questioning the powers of the police, objecting to the violence used by the police, questioning their ability to actually control crime, demanding the improvement of police-community relations, and demanding due process (i.e., protection of citizens from state coercion rather than focusing solely on the crime control model). This movement slowly led to what is referred to by many criminologists as the "community policing era," or, more recently, "community-oriented policing" or "community problem-solving era" (Kelling and Moore, 1988; Bayley, 1988; Trojanowicz, 1983; Spelman and Eck, 1987; Marenin, 1989; Cordner, 1994).

In the 1970s, there were experiments in police effectiveness that found traditional police strategies for crime control did not work and that traditional police responses to crime did not reduce crime rates nor did they make citizens feel safer. In addition, the fear of crime was as important to members of the public as was the actual rate of crime (Langworthy and Travis III, 2003). Police departments responded by promising to redefine police roles. Beginning in the early 1990s, CP programs were developed in some large cities such as Chicago and Toronto. Since then, the concept of CP has received a great deal of attention from police services across North America. Large police departments in both Canada and the US began to present this method/approach as the new central feature in their police operations.

It is important to note that the concept of community-oriented policing (COP) or community problem-solving is not new. This collectivist approach to working together to identify and solve problems and make communities whole and safer reflects the nonaggressive approaches to violence and other types of crime endorsed by different faith communities and cultures, and can be found in Aboriginal healing traditions. Today, the majority of police departments present themselves as operating on some level from a CP model and have embraced various tenets of CP (Greene, 2004; Roth, Roehl, and Johnson, 2004; Skogan, 1996; 1990). In fact, according to Skogan (2004), it is hard to find a police chief that does not claim to have adopted particular "community-friendly programs."

The Community Policing Model
The CP model can be described prescriptively as follows:

1) Police-community relations should be improved by lessening the distance between the police and the public. This could be accomplished by more interaction and exchange of ideas. For instance, officers should meet citizens who live and work in the neighbourhoods they serve in order to begin to "build bridges" between the police and the various communities. They should visit places such as community centres, schools, businesses, places of worship, etc., to introduce themselves, discuss CP goals, and work together with the public to identify and offer solutions to specific problems.

2) More foot patrol units and bicycle units should be introduced in order to help make the police more visible and approachable to members of the public.

3) Proactive policing should be emphasized over reactive policing. In an era of problem-

solving, the police should not rely only on reacting to crimes and problems after they have occurred but should take it upon themselves to identify crimes by doing undercover work and by talking to citizens. Also, the emphasis should be on crime prevention through police efforts to improve social conditions. The police should identify "social problems" (e.g., homelessness, runaways, traffic congestion, noise levels, street litter, etc.) with community members and work together to secure specific services such as employment, housing, sanitation, and health care.

4) Officers should be committed to making members of the public feel safer in the communities in which they work and live. This will encourage law-abiding citizens to become more involved in their communities, which will in turn promote safety.

5) The police should not be viewed as the sole experts in reducing and preventing crime, but, rather, crime control should be a collective effort between the police and the public.

6) Officers should be encouraged to live in the area they police. This will make officers experience a heightened level of accountability and responsibility to the community they serve, since they will have a personal interest in the area (i.e., they own a home in the area, pay property taxes, their children attend school in the area, etc.).

7) Smaller police substations should be created and more officers should be hired to police smaller patrol districts. The parameters of patrol districts in many cities are often too wide, making it very difficult, if not impossible, for officers to get to know people in the areas they police. The presence of more officers patrolling smaller patrol districts would increase the probability of officers and citizens becoming acquainted and working towards "building bridges" together.

8) Police departments should move towards a flatter organizational power structure. By moving away from the traditional paramilitaristic hierarchical structure that demands respect and obedience to the chain of command, every officer would be given an equal voice in the success of CP initiatives. The front-line/patrol officers are the ones who are expected to play the largest role in the success of CP, but, under the current structure, they are also the least likely to challenge the orders given by their immediate "superiors/supervisors." Under the paramilitaristic hierarchical structure, they must respect the chain of command and share their opinions and criticisms only with their immediate supervisors. On the other hand, under the flatter organizational power structure, ranks could be maintained, given the different responsibilities associated with each position, but they would all be viewed as equal partners in the policing system. All officers would play an equal role in voicing their suggestions. This would empower the front-line/patrol officers to share their concerns and suggestions (along with the concerns and suggestions from community members) with "higher" ranking officers (i.e., members of the brass and other levels of management). This would be more effective than hearing only from members of management, who tend to be too removed from "the streets" given the administrative nature of their roles.

Since the 1990s, large police departments throughout the US and Canada have implemented CP rhetoric and organizational restructuring. However, the concept of CP is not well defined. In fact, police departments are quick to advertise their CP initiatives while simultaneously exhibiting difficulty in defining the concept. According to Bayley (1988: 225), "community policing is the new philosophy of professional law enforcement in the world's industrial democracies but the programmatic implementation of it has been uneven ... meaning different things to different people."

The crime control model of policing is based on limited public interaction, motorized random patrol, crime-control-based policing, reactive policing, and a centralized dispatching of radio calls. CP, on the other hand, is intended to shift the emphasis away from an exclusive focus on law enforcement. It has been described as policing organized around perspectives that emphasize crime control and order-maintenance, crime prevention, proactive policing, community problem-solving, and improvement of police-community relations by reducing the social distance between the police and the public and empowering citizens. Both models include crime control, however, under the CP model, crime control is presented as the product of the combined efforts of both the police and the public. The latter is intended to encourage information exchange and support from the public and quick police response to the public's concerns. As already mentioned, CP also advocates a flatter power structure within the police organization where more power is given to front-line officers by encouraging them to engage in critical thinking and problem-solving.

Scholars are divided in terms of the benefits of CP. A great deal of literature on this particular method/approach to policing is based on the assumption that it is a progressive, futuristic idea that will positively transform police departments. Interestingly, there tends to be more support for the concept of CP by criminologists in the US. Their Canadian counterparts seem to be more critical.

Many Canadian criminologists specializing in this area contend that policing has not changed very much since earlier decades (Neugebauer, 1999; Ericson and Haggerty, 1997; Ericson, 1994; Shearing and Stenning, 1987). That is, new rhetoric has been introduced and there has been some organizational restructuring of police departments, but, overall, policing methods/styles have remained the same (Corsianos, 2007a; 2001; 1999a). Many police agencies assign officers to CP functions, but, overall, the majority of them work in a traditional crime control capacity. Zhao, He, and Lovrich (2003) compared survey responses in more than 200 local police departments in 1990 and 2000, concluding that crime control remained a priority for police departments and that CP initiatives were used to fight crime and social disorders. The National Research Council (2004) found that there was not enough evidence to suggest that this "new" model of policing was a success in police departments that utilized various CP approaches. In fact, in 2000, the US government commissioned the National Research Council to review evidence of the effects of CP, and according to Skogan (2004: xiii), who served as the chair, the committee "found precious little to say about the topic."

What Arguments Are Made by Supporters of Community Policing?
Many supporters of the CP model claim that in order to ensure the success of this particular approach to policing, it must consist of:

- community-based crime prevention;
- proactive versus reactive response;
- public participation in police deployment and planning;
- a downward shift of the command structure to empower the front-line officer.

Moreover, there must be constant interaction and cooperation between the police and the public. This, in turn, produces information-sharing leading to procedural changes that focus the officer's attention on solving legal violations, as well as violations of the social order — the idea being that if visible signs of disorder are reduced, so, too, are crimes and the fear of crime.

Some scholars have focused on the CP tactic of reclaiming neighbourhoods through foot patrols (Trojanowicz 1983) and bicycle patrols. This makes the police more visible and more approachable/accessible to the public and encourages public participation in defining and solving problems in their own neighbourhoods. Others have called for greater autonomy for front-line officers and the establishment of a new breed of patrol officers known as CPOs (Community Policing Officers) who are specially trained to handle long-term community needs. This has developed as a reaction to the claim that the traditional crime control model has failed to address individual community needs and problems, and that this has consequently led to low morale among officers. It is argued that CP can help improve morale and offer more choices to the front-line officer.

Various components, such as proactive versus reactive policing and empowerment of both the public and front-line officers in crime prevention decision-making, are detailed as key ingredients to successful CP practice (Bayley, 1988). For CP to work, there must be constant interaction and cooperation between the police and the public. A central CP goal focuses on increasing front-line officers' autonomy and reclaiming neighbourhoods through organized community-police interactions (Trojanowicz, 1983; Trojanowicz and Bucqueroux, 1990; Bayley, 1988). CP can improve public attitudes towards the police. Moreover, decentralized decision-making empowers patrol officers to work with community leaders to identify problems, concerns, and solutions in specific communities (Chalom, 1993).

Similarly, Goldstein (1990, 1977) and Spelman and Eck (1987) assert that the traditional organizational style of police work must not be maintained. The police should not only focus on crime control but should also identify and examine the social disorders that may be directly related to crime. CP is seen as a unique perspective that encourages or rather operates successfully through problem-oriented approaches. Officers are expected to have good interpersonal skills and be trained in

121

problem identification, analysis, and solutions (Jurik and Martin, 2001). This method operates by assigning CP officers to a particular area in order to identify the problem; then together with the community they are expected to converse and attempt to create solutions that address the specific needs of that area.

Proponents of CP maintain that, organizationally, through the introduction of more visible foot patrol officers, there will be more verbal interaction between the police and community members. By empowering front-line officers, they will be able to offer suggestions and/or solutions to problems to their superiors and effect change in the communities in which they police. They further maintain that police-community relations are promoted through a shared responsibility in crime reduction, fear of crime, and/or recognition of social disorders that may lead to crime and/or deviance (Goldstein, 1977; Spelman and Eck, 1987; Bayley, 1988; Trojanowicz, 1990; Wilson and Kelling, 1982). In other words, the community becomes the informant. CP can assist the police in identifying "problem areas," and hence justify police decision-making powers (Marenin, 1989).

The claims made above parallel details described by Wilson and Kelling (1982) in their well-publicized "broken window" thesis. Their argument is that visible signs of "disorder," such as broken windows, panhandlers, beggars, and homeless people asleep on the street, are signs of crime or potential crime. These visible signs of disorder stimulate fear, which leads to further disorder as fearful people are not willing, or are less willing, to invest in their communities, and are less likely to interact positively or assist others in their communities. This leads to neighbourhood instability — people start to move out of these areas and serious crime increases. Claims made by some CP supporters (Bayley, 1988; Trojanowicz, 1990; Goldstein, 1990; 1977; Cordner, 1994) reflect the ideas of Wilson and Kelling in that CP initiatives, accomplished through proactive policing, will be able to "clean the streets," and therefore diminish visible signs of "disorder," ultimately reducing crimes and the fear of crime.

On the surface, these approaches appear to reflect the old policing styles of the so-called political era in the US, but, for many of CP's proponents, police today have evolved and learned lessons from the past that would prevent them from reverting back to the types of corruption associated with earlier times. They assert that police officers have become accountable to members of the public and no longer answer directly to the individual politicians who hired them.

Supporters and Their Different Community Policing Approaches

Some academics prefer the term "problem-oriented policing" (POP) over CP or COP. According to Goldstein (1990), POP is one of this century's most important innovations in policing. These methods of policing focus police attention on the problems faced by the community, rather than on the administrative problems faced by the department. They deal with a wide range of solutions and implement responses in collaboration with members of the public. POP differs from CP in that it focuses on specific crime problems and crime reduction, rather than on the means/methods of policing (Eck and Spelman, 1987; Goldstein, 1990). It incorporates the "broken window" theory in that it frequently targets environments and social disorders because they are believed to give rise to crime (Goldstein, 1990). Additionally, it advocates more indirect approaches to social control and limits the number of arrests made. The focus is on ecological solutions, such as cleaning abandoned lots, restoring condemned properties, and eliminating drug houses, all of which tend to attract certain types of crime.

Other criminologists focus on trying to make policing more efficient by promoting "crime-oriented policing" through the development of better enforcement tactics so that crime will not pay. This approach includes installing cameras on public streets and more aggressively deterring drug markets to increase the cost of doing business for criminals. A combination of community-oriented and crime-oriented policing is often referred to as order-maintenance policing. This would include stopping both lawful and unlawful disorderly behaviour in public places, which is believed to reduce the rate of more serious crimes (Wilson and Kelling, 1982; Skogan, 1990).

Reintegrative approaches to CP call on the police to play a greater role in crime prevention. The police can facilitate access to emergency social services for runaways, homeless persons, and the intoxicated. There have been several outreach teams made up of police officers and social and health care workers. For instance, some law enforcement officers identify youths at risk for delinquency and refer them to therapeutic agencies and programs (Wyrick, 2000). Other officers have diverted the mentally ill and domestic violence offenders to community-based rehabilitative programs (Morash and Robinson, 2002; Zdanowicz, 2001; Jolin and Moose, 1997; Eck, 1990; Eck and Spelman, 1987). These outreach approaches enable individuals who would otherwise end up incarcerated to be diverted to programs that are equipped to deal with their specific needs. The goal is to place them in the appropriate programs with professionals who can offer specialized assistance and hopefully decrease the likelihood of future police intervention.

This method has been referred to as "reintegrative community policing." This concept builds on Braithewaite's work (1989) on shaming. In reintegrative policing, a distinction is made between social control systems built on shaming through stigmatization and the means required to reintegrate offenders back into the community. Reintegrative approaches rely on the efforts of law enforcement agencies to address social disorders and prevent crimes. They also emphasize linkages with remedial services as a means of alleviating social strains, and move away from the notion of isolating an offender as a goal to crime control (Guarino-Ghezzi, 1994; Braithewaite, 1989).

Thacher (2001) discusses the conflicting values that arise in CP approaches, but calls for more strategic efforts to address and clarify them in order for departments to succeed in this type of policing. For example, he asserts that the police must address the definition of "public safety." Police tend to have a professionalized definition of public safety that is tied to serious crimes defined by criminal laws. Communities, on the other hand, are usually more concerned with less serious crimes and safety problems that are more visible and arise more often. In order to succeed in CP, Thacher contends that the police must pay more attention to less serious crimes and become more sensitive in their use of police authority. They must develop new strategies that are compatible with multiple values in order to resolve the conflicts that erupt in their community partnerships.

In examining officers' attitudes towards CP, proponents discuss the importance of training in this area, as well as officer designation to CP roles. Some research indicates that CP officers dedicate more time to COP activities, are more supportive of organizational change to accomplish CP goals, and tend to be more satisfied with their work in comparison to traditional police officers (Adams, Rohe, and Arcury, 2002). In Jackson's study (1997), both female officers working at the federal level (Royal Canadian Mounted Police [RCMP]), as well as at the municipal levels in the Atlantic Canada region believed that CP approaches such as proactive policing, public education, crime prevention, and referral measured good police work rather than the number of arrests made or the amount of tickets issued. All of the RCMP officers and 83 per cent of the municipal officers involved in the study favoured different methods other than arrest when dealing with community problems. Also, all of the RCMP officers in the sample and 84 per cent of the municipal officers believed that they could police more effectively by working closely with community agencies and services. In addition, 85 per cent stated that verbal and physical aggression in the performance of their policing duties was counterproductive. Overall, proponents support CP for a variety of different reasons and consider it central to the future of policing.

What Arguments Are Made by Opponents of Community Policing and/or What Criticisms Are Made against Particular Community Policing Approaches?

Opponents of CP present this policing perspective and/or method as one filled with problems and contradictions that maintain the power relations that produce and reproduce inequalities. They note that internal oppositions to CP initiatives exist creating different forms/levels of resistance within policing. Critics reject the claim that CP is the police brass's new creation in this wave of new-liberal reform of downsizing and restructuring (Stenson, 1993). Rather, they assert that this phenomenon creates the illusion that policing is somehow removed from politics. In Hodgson's (1993) study of Canadian police officers, he found that constables were hostile towards CP initiatives that claimed to reduce crime. They did not view CP as the instant simple solution to crime, and it was not seen as "real" policing. Officers perceived the new initiatives as a threat to the nature of their police work.

In *Policing the Risk Society*, Ericson and Haggerty (1997) present a theoretical analysis of CP that corresponds to today's "risk society." They claim that CP satisfies the police need for information and intelligence-gathering, and Ericson (1982) argues that the role of the front-line officer has not changed; their primary role is still to "patrol the petty." For Ericson and Haggerty, "risk" has become the obsession of today's society. Institutions such as policing are part of an emerging "risk society" in which knowledge of risk is used to control danger and reinforce social inequality. Police have become information brokers to institutions such as health and welfare organizations and insurance companies; they investigate, collect, produce, and disperse information to these institutions and are forced to constantly adapt and change their formats, rules, and technologies of communication to meet external demands for knowledge of risk in order to control danger. Therefore, they must remain committed to identifying "risky behaviour" and to "reducing" risk.

There are scholars who have dismissed CP as empty rhetoric (Klockars, 1988; Greene and Mastrofski, 1988) and claim that the term "community" is not defined by police departments, nor can it be used to refer to the existing parameters of patrol districts. For them, the goal of CP is to "conceal, mystify, and legitimate police distribution of non-negotiable coercive force" (Klockars, 1991: 531) and the rhetoric of CP is intended to "wrap police in ... powerful and unquestionable good images" (Klockars, 1988: 257). Some believe CP is intended to serve and protect the middle and upper classes while alienating the poor (Gordon, 1987; Neugebauer, 1999; 1996). It has been referred to as a "rhetorical giant" (Manning, 1997) that creates the illusion that the police are concerned with operating fairly and working to promote police-community relations. The police claim they engage in crime control and/or law enforcement rather than in politically and morally based ordering. Rather, it is argued that such rhetoric is a "resource" used by the police to justify their actions (Manning, 1997).

> External legitimation is maintained by withholding potentially damaging information from the public, maintaining complicity with the media to reveal and dramatize selectively certain stories presented in a positive "voice" or perspective, appealing to national symbols and ideologies, such as the rhetoric of crime control, and cultivating links with the legal profession and agencies and agents within the criminal justice system (Manning, 1992: 34).

Law enforcement is a form of social control that operates in a manner that discriminates against the less powerful and protects the power of the most powerful in society (Black, 1990). Police actions of social control reflect the hierarchical power structure in society. According to Ericson (1982; 1981), the organizational police system allows for the exercise of police authority and enhances officers' informal powers. It also shapes and defines the police occupational culture. For instance, the organization protects police actions from close scrutiny by the public and rarely calls for police accountability. CP can lead to police abuses by promoting the regulation of "disreputable" persons such as prostitutes, panhandlers, addicts, drunks, the mentally disturbed, loiterers, and rowdy teenagers because they are perceived as a threat to community stability.

A. Emphasis on Reactive Policing

Police departments today still advocate crime control, still engage primarily in reactive policing, and programs such as CP create impressions that the police are concerned with order maintenance only through law rather than also through organizational and occupational practices (Corsianos, 2007a; 2003; 2001). The front-line officer, to borrow Manning's term, is a "street bureaucrat" (1997) who constantly comes into contact with, and is visible to, the public. In order to continue to engage in policing reform, the role of the officer must continuously be redefined in order to maintain the illusion of law enforcement for all. The public is encouraged to believe that the concept of CP is futuristic and progressive and is primarily intended to improve police-community relations. In actuality, the CP rhetoric serves as an ideological tool used methodically by members of the brass to legitimate the police service to the community, the officers, and to themselves. Members of the brass must constantly reinvent themselves in an attempt to keep the public and their officers content. Another example of this would be the replacing of the word "force" with "service" in the renaming of Canadian police departments. For example, the Metropolitan Toronto Police Force was renamed the Metropolitan Toronto Police Service in 1992, and later became the Toronto Police Service. In the case of Toronto, members of the Metropolitan Toronto Police Services Board believed that the word "service" would appear less threatening and would be indicative of the police's new role in caring for and serving the community (Corsianos, 1997).

Moreover, several studies on CP in specific police departments (Manning and Singh, 1997; Hodgson, 1993; Corsianos, 1997) reveal that patrol officers have no special training in what CP is, nor what their apparent new roles are, nor do they receive supervision in problem-solving. However, the concept of CP, as will be discussed at the end of this chapter, has the potential to create specific goals that would require a redefinition of the police organizational structure and changes to the ideologies that have been maintained and promoted for years.

As demonstrated, organizationally, some changes have been made to large police departments across North America, which include the creation of community response units and more foot patrol and bicycle patrol units, to strive towards this apparent theoretical goal of building bridges between the police and communities and collectively working to decrease crime rates. Substantively, however, the role of the police has not changed, nor has there been any recorded improvement in the relations between the police and specific communities (Manning, 1997). Also, the concept of CP has obscured police discretionary powers, the potential for police abuse of these powers, and has created the illusion that police roles are being redefined and changed — that they are somehow progressive (Corsianos, 2003; 2001).

B. Community Policing Initiatives and Crime Control

MacDonald's research (2002) on the effectiveness of CP in reducing urban violence found that it had little effect on the control or decline of violent crime. This is despite attempts by the US federal government to increase the implementation and practice of CP under the 1994 Violent Crime Act. According to MacDonald (2002), police agencies with a more aggressive enforcement of disorderly conduct and driving under the influence had lower rates of robbery and homicide, but CP had no real influence on specific violent crimes (i.e., robbery and homicide). MacDonald and others conclude that CP, as it is defined and/or practiced in most police departments, has no effect on these specific types of crime. Yet, most agencies claim to promote this approach in order to receive federal funding, even though they do not necessarily "do" CP.

Aggressive policing styles (commonly referred to as "zero-tolerance" policing) do not involve community cooperation and lead to abuse, discrimination, and violation of people's liberties (MacDonald, 2002). Goetz and Mitchell (2003) found that police officers tended to reject reintegrative approaches to problems of substance abuse and illicit drug use because these were perceived as "social work" functions. Police perceived the role of the officer as one of a crime fighter and were anxious to make arrests to prove themselves among their peers. Officers resisted CP initiatives when they were seen as an attempt to redefine the police as "social workers." In both studies conducted in Norfolk, Virginia, and Baltimore, Maryland, officers opposed CP training unless it emphasized crime-fighting and order-maintenance goals (Goetz and Mitchell, 2003).

As stated, some agencies claim to endorse CP efforts in order to qualify for federal funding. In fact, however, many police agencies would have to first change many of their existing structures and operations in order to begin to legitimately adopt CP ideologies. To date, there is little evidence to suggest that CP, as it is currently being practiced, has reduced violent crimes. Until recently, the focus within police departments was to increase visibility and produce low response time. The research suggests that it is not the number of police officers that makes a difference in controlling crime, but rather the tasks the police are expected to perform (Sherman, 1995). Moreover, whereas advocates of CP believe the decreasing crime rate over the past decade is the result of CP strategies, opponents contend there has been little or no evidence to support this.

For instance, advocates of CP have praised the Boston Police Department for its CP program and have promoted it as a national model. However, contrary to reports of the success of its CP program, including decreasing crime rates, Saunders (1999) found that most of the department's operations remained untouched by CP initiatives and that the majority of Boston's residents were not part of the police-community partnership. In fact, the "policing body" reflected what Butler calls "bodies that matter" (1993: 16). In other words, all "bodies" are not prioritized by the police. "For many Bostonians, especially members of groups with long lists of grievances (Gays and African Americans, for example), the struggle to make 'bodies that matter' continues in the courts and media, in electoral and community politics, and in relations with police" (Saunders, 1999: 144).

CP approaches attempt to respond to the limitations of the public police to prevent and effectively investigate crimes by encouraging public participation. However, opponents point out that, at times, police believe that the information they receive from citizens is pointless because citizens lack the professional experience of police officers, rendering them incapable of making accurate observations (Saunders, 1999). The police remain doubtful as to the public's abilities to contribute effectively. Others are opposed to the idea of police roles going beyond crime control and law enforcement because of potential dangers such as officer burnout, personalization, and overcommitment. These would be the result of officers becoming too involved with the communities and citizens they serve (Buerger, Petrosino, and Petrosino, 1999).

Alternatively, some have focused on how CP enables processes of exclusion as they become hidden within desirable rhetoric such as "safe neighbourhoods" and "citizen empowerment." Fischer and Poland (1998) contend that processes of exclusion are emerging as crucial aspects of social control and governance in late modern societies. Public spaces become subject to surveillance and control by the authority of the public police and its resources. In addition, private policing emphasizes mechanisms of compliance or prevention rather than punitiveness and intrusive negative sanctioning (Cohen, 1985; Shearing and Stenning, 1987). CP can be used as a "tool" for the removal and banning of "problem people" from particular spaces. The concern is not with fairness and social justice but with the purification of public space (Sibley, 1988). As Ericson (1994) notes, surveillance and the management of risk factors are critical to the development of specialized knowledge, which is required to engineer community "safety." Emphasis is placed on the control and management of behaviour, and the mobility and whereabouts of "risky" individuals or populations. Thus, the exclusion of "risky" traits, behaviours, or individuals from identified environments of local control has become central to the operation of governance (Fischer and Poland, 1998). Policing in public versus private spaces addresses the centrality of social class, as those who own private property are given a voice, protection, and priority in the systems of social control and state power.

North American societies are currently experiencing the pluralizing of policing and the search by the public police to redefine themselves and discover new roles as they face the realization that they are neither effective at, nor efficient in, controlling crime. Policing today is performed by institutions other than the government. Policing is being offered by both private companies on a commercial basis and by communities on a volunteer basis. In the US there are three times more private security agents than public police officers (Maahs and Hemmens, 1998; Colby, 1995; Bayley, 1994) and in Canada there are 1.3 times as many (Statistics Canada, 2005b). In addition, individual communities have started to use volunteered resources and people.

The goal of the private police is to reduce the risk of crime by taking preventive actions, whereas the public police strive to deter crime by apprehending and punishing criminals. Private police are more responsive to the "bottom line" of safety and can be fired if they do not accomplish certain safety objectives, whereas the public police focus on arrest rates and are not fired for failing to achieve safety goals (Bayley and Shearing, 1996). The pluralizing of policing aims to improve public safety, but at a cost. It does not improve security equally for everyone but rather favours the wealthy. As it currently stands, the wealthy will be increasingly policed preventively by commercial security, while the poor will be policed reactively by the enforcement-oriented public police (Bayley and Shearing, 1996).

According to Greene (2004: 48):

> The best that can be said to date is that many police departments ... have adopted a framework for response that includes elements of problem solving .... But ... it is clear that the police imagination remains captured by nineteenth-century ideas about crime and police response, most particularly as zero-tolerance policing has gained popularity among the police and politicians in recent years.

As a result, CP initiatives cannot work within police systems that continue to overwhelmingly reflect the traditional paramilitaristic crime control model that produces and reproduces inequalities along several lines including gender, race, and class.

The Experiences of Women Police Officers and the Traditional Paramilitaristic Crime Control Model

As discussed above, despite CP rhetoric, initiatives, and some level of organizational changes, many police departments continue to reflect traditional paramilitaristic crime control structures and systems (Corsianos, 2007a; Zhao, He, and Lovrich, 2003; Ericson and Haggerty, 1997; Manning, 1997; Stenson, 1993), and there is not enough evidence to suggest that CP efforts, where implemented, have been successful (National Research Council, 2004). The current systems and structure continue to produce and promote different gendered realities for officers. Women officers continue to be subjected to stereotypes, prejudice, and ridicule. The gender roles displayed within the police culture are informed by what Fielding (1994) and others describe as "hegemonic masculinity." Masculine characteristics are assumed to be central to the roles of the police officer, and both police personnel and members of the public accept them as "common sense." All kinds of assumptions are made as to why they make sense and why they are justifiably legitimate to the job of policing.

Other studies have discussed the widely accepted mainstream image of police officers as "masculine" and "crime fighters," but also detail police operations as involving activities that are perceived as "feminine" (Martin, 1999; Martin and Jurik, 1996). Martin (1999) notes that policing has been defined in terms of enforcing laws or "catching criminals," although, in actuality, it involves a wide range of police activities. She also asserts that officers experience pressure to suppress their emotions, especially if they are perceived as appearing weak or vulnerable. However, a double standard exists. Women officers who violate their socialized gender roles and act "too masculine" are often not accepted by their fellow officers. Martin (1999) insists that women must ignore the double standards, but at the same time she says they must adopt new verbal, facial, and bodily displays to ensure their authority to the public and be taken seriously regardless of their physical stature. One particular facial expression she says women should avoid is smiling. Smiling at citizens could compromise their authority. Yet, this suggestion further supports the "double standard" she advises women officers to ignore. Rather, the response by the woman officer, whether smiling at citizens or not, should be, "Who cares what they think of me?" The officer is the one wearing the uniform and making the decision to give certain advice, offer a caution, or make an arrest. She should not be concerned with having to prove herself to anyone.

However, as the literature suggests, female officers continue to be criticized for not possessing the so-called necessary masculine traits of aggressiveness, rationality, bravery, objectivity, and brutality (Charles, 1981; Miller, 1999). These criticisms often lead to claims that women are inherently not competent to participate in the crime-fighting police model, and that they are better suited to police roles that deal with social-service-type functions (Heidensohn and Brown, 2000; Heidensohn, 1992; Bell, 1982; Drummond, 1976). Furthermore, despite the CP rhetoric that is used and promoted by the majority of North American police departments, police agencies continue to place a great deal of emphasis on arrest rates rather than crime prevention. We rarely hear about the crimes that were prevented in any given year due to the successful implementation of CP or victim-offender mediation.

Some research has indicated that female police officers have a less aggressive style than male officers and are better at de-escalating potentially violent situations (Belknap, 1991; Belknap and Shelley, 1993; Grennan, 1987; Bell, 1982), but this information is not utilized by police organizations to improve training or reward these officers. Also, female officers are more likely to have traits associated with "good policing," such as expressing empathy for victims of violence (Feinman, 1986; Homant and Kennedy, 1985; Kennedy and Homant, 1983; Price, 1974). Rather than supporting emotional communicative policing as a necessary tool in crime prevention and promoting related traits in police training classes, police departments continue to devalue and minimize "feminine" characteristics that are seen as an attempt to feminize policing. For these reasons, scholars such as Fielding (1994) and Miller (1999) support promoting areas such as CP in gender-neutral terms in order to gain support by male-dominated police agencies.

Under the current patriarchal paramilitaristic police structure and systems, one can find many commonalities in the experiences of women officers. This is well documented in literature on gender and policing. Shared experiences include being subjected to various sexist, heterosexist, and/or racist comments; derogatory comments made regarding physical strength, height, and/or the ability to protect themselves and other officers in physical confrontations with members of the public; chivalrous attitudes; the pressure to prove themselves and conform to the status quo; and discrimination in position assignments and promotions (Martin and Jurik, 2007; 1999; Corsianos, 2007a; 2005; 2004; Gerber, 2001; Heidensohn and Brown, 2000; Martin, 1999; Miller, 1999; Fielding, 1994; Belknap, 1991; Feinman, 1986; Morash and Greene, 1986; Homant and Kennedy, 1985; Kennedy and Homant, 1983; Price, 1974). Additionally, female officers who are seen as "deviant" or "rocking the boat" are closely policed by their supervisors. Alternatively, females in the department who frequently appropriate the patriarchal tools used to stroke the egos of those in the upper ranks are often rewarded with promotions, positive evaluation reports, specialized assignments, and specialized training courses (Corsianos, 2004).

Multicase Studies: Gender and Community Policing

Corsianos (2007a) conducted a case study of seasoned female officers representing two large urban police agencies; one in eastern Canada and one in the Western US. The purpose of the study was to gain a better understanding of female officers' reactions to CP within their departments, to the organizational structure in terms of whether it posed particular gender-specific challenges for women, and to the possibility of implementing the CP model in ways that would promote gender equalities. Both of the police agencies in the study have been proactive in promoting themselves as organizations dedicated to the CP model.

The study involved conducting a total of 120 formal interviews; 60 with American officers and 60 with Canadian. The officers also participated in focus groups at later dates. Respondents ranged in age from 28 to 51 and had at least seven years of experience as a police officer. All of the participants had either a college diploma or a university degree. Participants represented different racial and/or ethnic groups, including Aboriginal/Native persons, and people who were of African, Chinese, English, French, German, Greek, Indian, Irish, Italian, Jamaican, Mexican, Pakistani, Polish, Scottish, and Spanish descent, with the majority being of European descent. Moreover, the majority self-defined as being "heterosexual" or "straight," were married, and had children. A total of 15 participants planned to become parents at some point in the future, whereas 16 had no interest in becoming parents. A total of 13 participants self-defined as "gay" or "lesbian." In addition, all of the officers in the study represented different ranks within their organizations, which included police officer/police constable, sergeant, staff sergeant, and detective/detective constable.

Not surprisingly, all of the participants were supportive of the CP model, even though there were some variations in their definitions. However, several criticisms relating to CP in their departments were noted. These included a lack of CP training offered to police officers, a lack of clear direction and definition of the concept, a lack of organizational and ideological changes in how policing is performed, a lack of uniformity in who ultimately is given a voice in community-police partnerships, as well as a potential for abuse of power by not taking the necessary steps to monitor and evaluate police performance. Participants also noted a disparity between the promotion of CP objectives and the particular police roles that were valued and praised.

Many similarities emerged in terms of observed gender-specific challenges within the two police organizations in the study. Areas of concern for women specifically included the structure of shift work, the common practice of gender-specific assignments, discrimination in promotion, the emphasis on physical strength in hiring, and the role of management in rewarding only the "big arrests." For instance, not having family-friendly work schedules presented challenges to many women who were mothers. In the Canadian sample, 48 officers were mothers, nine of whom were single parents, and nine planned to become parents in the future. In the US sample, 41 officers were mothers, 10 of whom were single parents, and six planned to become parents in the future.

Officers who were mothers, whether single or living with a partner/husband, experienced difficulties in balancing shift work with child-rearing responsibilities (such as being able to pick up their kids from daycare or school, and spend time with their children after school in order to eat dinner together, work on homework, bond, attend their child's sporting event, school play, etc.). Many felt that if they had the choice to always work the day shift then they could be home with their children after school. These officers supported the idea of making this option available to officers with young children. On-site childcare facilities during the day shift were also supported in order to accommodate officers with preschool children throughout the year, as well as young school-age children during the summer months.

As a result of the conflict between work schedules and family responsibilities, these parents had to make childcare arrangements, which included having family members (e.g., husband/partner, grandparents, etc.) and/or friends care for their children, or arranging for a combination of family/friends and daycare centres to care for their children (daycare facilities typically operated only until 5 PM). Those who could not depend on family/friends had to hire live-in nannies. In these instances, a live-in nanny was seen as the only option, especially if the officer's husband/partner also did not have a permanent schedule (e.g., in the case when the husband/partner was also a police officer). Hiring outsiders as babysitters was very difficult given the constant change in police officers' work schedules and thus were rarely utilized. Eight of the Canadian officers had hired live-in nannies.

The lack of family-friendly schedules also presented challenges to women who wanted to become pregnant (regardless of whether they were going to become "first-time mothers," or parents once again). Many of the female officers supported the idea of women having the option to take time off on days of suspected ovulation in order to increase the likelihood of conceiving. There were concerns relating to increased stress resulting from the constant change in work schedules. Shift work was perceived as "taking a toll" on their bodies, making it difficult for them to relax and unwind. Their sleep patterns were also interrupted, since they did not have a daily sleep schedule. Moreover, their work schedule often did not coincide with that of their husband's/partner's, which also contributed to increased stress.

The promotional process presented various gender-specific challenges for women officers in the study. The process in both of the departments was not perceived as being objective. For the most part, participants believed that the decision to promote someone was made before the interview stage. "Who you knew" played a key role in the decision-making. Many women with childcare responsibilities believed that this put them at a disadvantage, since they could not regularly "hang out" with other officers at bars, and attend "tailgate" parties and other popular police events. It was at these "get-togethers" where people "got to really know each other" and ultimately this made the difference in who was promoted.

Other gender-specific challenges related to position assignments. When given the opportunity to work in specialized units, many women were frequently assigned to gender-specific positions. A disproportionate number of them had been assigned to areas/units that included CP, youth, domestic violence, and sexual assault units, as well as drug prevention/educational positions and court services. There was a lack of appreciation and recognition for their work in these units because it typically did not involve aggressive crime control. This prevented some officers from gaining the experiences frequently associated with "real police work," which in turn contributed to promotion, positive recognition from colleagues, and awards.

Another area of concern related to the continued emphasis on physical strength in hiring. Both of the departments in the study had a physical evaluation component in their hiring processes. The test used by the American agency consisted of an obstacle course that involved running, climbing, pushing weight, and dragging a mannequin over a specified distance, as well as a trigger-pull component. The first part of the test was based on a point system and was administered solely on a pass/fail basis. In the second component, candidates had to pull a gun trigger a specified number of times within a specific number of seconds in order to pass. The tests and set standards were the same for all applicants.

The Canadian physical test consisted of a somewhat similar obstacle course/circuit that involved running while carrying weight, climbing, scaling a fence, pushing weight, and dragging a 150-pound (68-kilogram) mannequin over a specific distance. The second component consisted of a shuttle run. The obstacle course component had to be completed by a specified time in order to pass. In the shuttle run, candidates had to reach and complete a particular stage in order to pass. The time set for the completion of the tests was the same for all applicants. The standards set for the police constable selection process for the Canadian agency had been created by the provincial government and endorsed by the Association of Chiefs of Police for the province.

When asked about their perceptions relating to the physical tests used for hiring, most participants in the study did not believe that physical strength (particularly upper body strength) determined one's ability to police effectively and felt that particular tests served to exclude some strong candidates. Some preferred to completely eliminate physical tests as a criteria for hiring, whereas others supported the implementation of more gender-neutral tests that would not attempt to measure "strength" or "muscle power," but rather aim to hire candidates who were "physically fit."

Interestingly, contrary to most of the literature, the pressure to "prove oneself" to male officers was not perceived as a gender-specific challenge. Most of the Canadian women (51) and American women (44) did not experience the pressure to prove themselves to their male counterparts. They felt that the increased visibility of women in the police services created a more supportive work environment as more women "teamed up" with other women to do patrol work. Many felt that they could relate to other women and/or receive support in ways that they could not with male officers.

However, when asked about their perceptions as to whether they thought the CP model could be used to promote gender equalities, there was a significant difference between the two groups. The American participants were generally pessimistic about CP being used by management to promote gender equalities. For the most part, middle management was perceived as being disinterested in CP initiatives. Ironically, members of upper management promoted CP and oversaw various organizational changes, but none of these were focused on achieving gender equality. Moreover, middle management (the participants' immediate supervisors) was more interested in aggressive crime control tactics and making arrests.

On the other hand, the responses from the Canadians in the study were more mixed. On some issues they were more optimistic about the CP model being used to recognize some of the needs of female employees and accommodate them. For instance, a few examples included discussions on the increased support offered to pregnant officers. Women were given the choice to perform "light duties" at the station during their pregnancy, and the department had to make accommodations for officers who were breastfeeding. Moreover, the department provided financial "top-ups" to the one-year unemployment insurance benefits paid by the federal government that covered approximately 55 per cent of an employee's salary, and ensured that officers on leave did not lose their seniority, sick leave, employer pension contributions, prorated annual vacation pay, court attendance benefits, and clothes and equipment allowances. Unit commanders were responsive to the needs of these women by ensuring that all of the available options were presented to them. Job-sharing was also seen in a positive light because it temporarily accommodated employees with particular difficulties related to childcare, maternity leave, health problems, and other family issues. However, many believed that the job-sharing policy should place the responsibility on upper management (i.e., the unit commander) to assist in making work arrangements. At that time, it was left up to the individual officers to first seek permission from the station's unit commander in order to participate in job-sharing, and, second, make the necessary work arrangements.

Furthermore, the majority of Canadian participants in the study believed that the continued increase in the number of women becoming police officers would lead to more discussions on various gender-specific challenges and ultimately bring more awareness to these issues. Over time, they felt this would lead to more substantive changes. However, some were more optimistic than others as to the degree of change.

Suggestions on How to Use the Community Policing Model as a Feminist "Tool"

Officers in Corsianos's study (2007a) were asked to make suggestions on how the CP model could be used to promote gender equalities, regardless of whether they felt there was organizational support to accomplish them. The popular responses were as follows:

1) Provide frequent in-house training in areas such as gender, race and ethnic relations, sexuality, and conflict resolution. These classes should be made mandatory for all officers in order to raise awareness of diverse groups and the relevant issues affecting different groups. Courses should be offered at the police college/academy to new recruits and to all other officers throughout their policing careers. Some even suggested that these courses should be taught by academics who specialize in these areas rather than police personnel.

2) Hire more officers with college diplomas and/or degrees and have police departments cover the tuition for officers who want to further their education. Hiring more people with college degrees who have taken courses or have majored in areas including gender, race/ethnicity, social stratification, sexuality, diversity issues, conflict resolution, and communities would encourage a new type of officer who is more tolerant and accepting of new progressive directions in policing. Exposure to these issues prior to becoming police officers would increase the likelihood of achieving long-term COP goals, rather than working with recruits who have had no prior exposure and/or are hostile towards them. Many believed that officers educated in these areas are more likely to express a level of sensitivity and understanding to the communities they serve and the people they work with, which over time would begin to change the police culture. This could also lead to an increase in officers' salaries, giving them more credibility and respect in the eyes of the public. (Interestingly, some research indicates that COP styles/approaches are treated with higher priority among front-line officers and managers who have a college degree [Hoover, 1995; Carter, Sapp, and Stephens, 1988]).

3) Clearly define CP initiatives within individual police departments and offer in-house training on what CP is and why it is important. This would send the message to all officers that CP is here to stay, and would begin to replace the traditional style of policing.

4) Recognize the good work of officers in meeting various CP goals. Successes should be noted in monthly police newsletters and the officers should be considered for internal awards, promotions, etc. Managers should promote CP at every level in the organization. This would send the message that arrest rates are not the only way to measure police performance and success (perhaps, an increase in arrest rates would need to be carefully assessed with respect to the individual officer and the needs of specific communities). This would initially have a direct positive impact on female officers as a disproportionate number of women are represented in CP units/roles. This would also begin to change the current image of the police as "crime fighters" and people's perceptions about the use of physical force in day-to-day police activities.

5) Create an objective promotion process. Some suggestions included creating a point system where equal points are awarded to all categories, including years of service, service in all specialized units, completion of internal specialized courses, completion of university/college courses, community service, awards received, letters of recommendation, etc. Some suggested that all applications for promotion be anonymous and that personal identity markers (e.g., gender, race/ethnicity, etc.) not be entered on the application form. Others suggested eliminating the interview process altogether, since it was this stage that was often the determining factor in one's promotion regardless of all other accomplishments. The interview stage was seen as the subjective element in the promotion process where certain individuals were favoured over others.

6) Allow officers with young children at home to work permanent shifts until their children are of an age where they no longer depend on adult supervision. In cases where both parents are police officers, only one parent should be given this option.

7) Provide on-site childcare centres during the day shift.

8) Allow officers part-time status for a set period of time for educational purposes and/or to meet family needs.

9) Introduce new criteria to determine competency in police performance. Police performance should no longer be measured in ways that promote crime-fighting and aggressiveness. Some suggested eliminating physical agility testing as a criteria for hiring, as historically this has not measured police effectiveness on the job, and this would help to change the current image of the police as "aggressive crime fighters." Others suggested creating gender-neutral tests that would determine one's "physical fitness" rather than attempt to measure "physical strength."

10) Officers should list their top choices of areas they want to serve in and should be awarded assignment to one or more of these areas within a particular time period. This would eliminate management's practice of making gender-specific assignments that "pigeonhole" people and limit them. This would improve morale by ensuring that officers are given the opportunity to work in traditionally female-specific assignments, or in male-specific ones. This would enable officers to work in desired units/areas, which would likely improve officers' work performance. As a result, communities would be better served. Also, by making the CP model central to police operations, more male officers would

begin to serve in specific CP units and/or take on specific CP roles. CP would be seen as a necessary part of the job, especially in terms of earning recognition, promotion, etc. Hostility expressed for CP objectives would be self-defeating and officers who refused to accept the changing structure and roles would ultimately quit.

11) A flatter power structure would ensure that front-line officers are given a voice (which affects a disproportionate number of women seeing that the majority currently occupy the lower ranks) and increase management's accountability to them. The success of CP depends largely on the efficacy of the front-line officer. Therefore, the CP platform should be used by female officers to voice concerns within the department and bring some of their issues and experiences to the forefront. Specific structural organizational changes should be introduced to address these concerns and provide officers with choices. These would give way to the creation of a more supportive work environment and improve morale. In turn, more women would be encouraged to become police officers and stay on until retirement. This would also help male officers who have similar experiences.

12) Police organizations should no longer promote authoritarianism, aggressiveness, secrecy, and respect for the chain of command. Also, the ideology of the "brotherhood of policing" must be replaced by a collective community-oriented one that promotes equality, partnerships, and transparency within policing. This would encourage more women to apply and ultimately lead to more female representation in all aspects of policing. There would be no place for chivalrous attitudes, stereotypes, and other discriminatory practices.

13) Job-sharing should be more structured and user-friendly in order to be accessible to more officers.

14) Departments must promote officers' accountability to the various diverse communities they serve. In order to create "community," the police should have monthly meetings with community organizations, community centres, schools, businesses, places of worship, etc. This approach to police operations would be essential for both police personnel and citizens in accomplishing specific goals. This, in turn, would promote community solidarity, mutual respect, and peace. All community members must be treated fairly by the police regardless of the groups they represent (i.e., gender, race/ethnicity, sexual orientation, class, etc.).

Can the Community Policing Model Be Used to Promote Gendered Justice?

The traditional paramilitaristic crime control model of policing continues to produce gendered experiences and does not encourage emancipatory systems, specifically freedom from sexist practices and ideologies. Patriarchal social forces continue to shape and influence society in general, and police organizations more specifically. In Canada and the US today, these forces may not be as obvious when compared to earlier decades, but nevertheless, they are reflected and embedded in various aspects of people's lives. The category "woman" or "women" is a product of patriarchal social forces. It has been socially constructed to imply various relatively fixed qualities by many people. There are different social processes where females become "women" with its multiple meanings, and the social construction of this category is connected to the social norms that are historically rooted, socially situated (Riley, 1988), and shaped and influenced by the current hegemonic social forces (Gramsci, 1957). Similarities are seen in officers' experiences regardless of whether or not they are conscious of them. They are reflected in the everyday work rhetoric (i.e., the patriarchal paramilitaristic rhetoric); in conversations with colleagues and/or supervisors; in police images, physical actions, and ideas; and in the expectations, assumptions, and decisions that are articulated (Corsianos, 2004). However, despite all the research on gender and policing to date, the question remains as to whether the CP model can be used to promote emancipatory politics within policing, specifically freedom from sexist ideologies. Can the philosophy of CP be used to promote gendered justice?

Admittedly, CP, as it is currently presented by police departments, serves as an ideological tool, as it is methodically used by members of the brass to legitimate their departments to the public, the officers, and to themselves (Corsianos, 2001). Yet, particular CP goals can be used to redefine the organizational structure and begin to change the ideologies that have been maintained and promoted over the decades. Substantive changes could lead to the re-examination of categories such as gender, race, ethnicity, class, sexual orientation, and age that create and sustain inequalities within traditional policing systems. Ideological and structural changes would have to be made at both the micro- and macro-structural levels to promote gendered justice goals. The continued promotion of democratic politics encourages democratic praxis, which in turn begins to lead to ideological shifts in gender constructions.

CP objectives have the potential of making the connection between gender, sexuality, culture, and economics, and promoting real change to the experienced realities of categories of different people. The misrepresentations and stereotypes of "women" and "men" must be acknowledged in order to move forward and begin to present new concepts and ideologies to police officers and to policing as a whole. Through CP, one could begin to ask different and critical questions relating to the purpose of policing, its organizational structure and culture, and the roles of police officers. This approach could enable individuals to think of the concept of policing in new and unprecedented ways and could lead them into new directions in the ways society ultimately polices its citizens.

These initiatives could be used to promote gender neutrality, and, over time, move towards creating the cultural space for a postgendered subjectivity. However, policing as it is currently understood must be redefined. Social categories such as "women police" or "policewomen," and "men police" or "policemen" must lose their essentializing qualities. Some would argue that the categories "woman/women" reduces women's sense of agency in their personal and professional lives (Riley, 1988). The same can be said for those representing the categories "man/men." These categories do not correspond to any unified and unifying essence, but in a patriarchal heterosexist society, they have been socially constructed to imply various relatively fixed qualities by many people. They have been constructed to represent various "truths" and regardless of how similar or different their personal experiences as "women" or "men" have been, there are overwhelming similarities in officers' perceptions of their work experiences, their police roles, and the overall police culture. Many officers accept the culturally historic, dominant, constructed "truths" about notions of "womanhood," "manhood," "femininity," and "masculinity," and how they impact the policing system and police roles. As products of their shared occupational culture, the wider socio-economic order, and personal identities such as gender, they have experienced consequences whether they are aware of them or not, and therefore share similarities in experience (Corsianos, 2004).

People are social beings and products of a patriarchal heterosexist social order that shapes and influences their thoughts and decisions, and that is why it is no surprise to find parallels in the consciousness of so many police officers, as has been demonstrated in the academic literature to date. These socially constructed and politically defined categories must lose their essentializing qualities; however, at present, experiential essentialist claims are deemed necessary because they address social "truths." For example, performance evaluations that are included in officers' evaluations for promotion lack procedures that recognize and reward officers' work outside of law enforcement roles. This produces gendered results, since accomplishments that are highly valued by many women officers are virtually unrecognized by the current police system and culture. This is very significant since law enforcement comprises only a small part of everyday police work (Walker and Katz, 2005). Moreover, looking at CP roles specifically, Miller (1999) found that, in comparison to male officers, women received less credit for their accomplishments in CP. The expectation is often that women should be better in CP roles given their gender roles and thus are not rewarded equally (Miller, 1999). Male officers continue to perceive CP as "women's work" that contradicts the image of the police as law enforcers and crime fighters, and they continue to turn down opportunities to work in these units (Miller and Hodge, 2004).

By completely abandoning universalism, one can see that there are a multiplicity of experiences among "women" and "men" that vary between and within races, classes, ethnic backgrounds, sexual orientation, education levels, religions, etc. However, this does not negate the fact that obvious parallels in the beliefs, attitudes, experiences, and understandings of gender and occupational performance can be found in groups and that these necessarily create consequences in people's lives generally and in their professional lives specifically (Corsianos, 2004). This is not to suggest there is a universal human nature that produces shared consciousness and experienced realities, but rather that individuals' consciousness is the result of social and cultural forces that lead to commonalities in the beliefs, attitudes, experiences, and understandings of gender (as well as other social categories such as race/ethnicity, class, and sexual orientation) among groups of female officers and male officers.

In order to successfully utilize the CP model to promote gender neutrality and, slowly, over time, move towards a postgendered subjectivity, a careful analysis of social and cultural institutions such as policing is required. There must be a careful examination of how policing currently functions and how it reproduces current ideologies. Essentialism searches for the intrinsic nature of things as they are in and of themselves. Essentialism makes "either/or" distinctions and posits polar opposites. It does not allow for variation. On the other hand, experiential essentialism recognizes the similarities in thought and praxis that exist among many police officers sharing a particular occupational culture and views them as products of the social world. Thus, it enables us to "see" that female officers share experiences of "oppression." They may not necessarily share the exact same experiences, or be "oppressed" in the same ways, but they certainly share experiences of "oppression" as a result of gender differences (see Chapter 7).

Police officers are individuals who make observations day in and day out. They are continuously observing and interpreting social systems, structures, images, and words. At the same time, it is important to note that the sociology of police culture cannot be separated from an analysis of the dominant ideologies in society that continue to promote many inequalities preventing individuals from experiencing independent subjectivity.

The possibility for a postgendered subjectivity within policing requires equality in society. Specifically, equality of opportunity can promote gender neutrality and a sense of agency; that is, the opportunity to think freely outside the box and to have the freedom to challenge normative expectations in order to make informed decisions about self-definitions relating to a wide range of identities including professional and personal ones (Corsianos, 2007b). The CP model can be used to help identify causes of experienced gender inequalities, including identifying the various instances of discriminatory police rhetoric commonly used in policing, police images, and police practices. These areas must first be identified and then removed. The current organizational police structure that produces and promotes difference in outcome of welfare among its officers undermines the potential for a postgendered subjectivity.

Furthermore, CP systems and structures must promote feminist ideologies, such as collectivity and accountability to the various diverse communities that the police serve. In the spirit of "community" and "building bridges," a collective feminist approach to police operations is essential for both police personnel and members of the public. Under the current traditional paramilitaristic structure, policing ultimately results in controlling lower socio-economic groups (Gordon, 1987); "policing the petty" (Ericson, 1982); protecting those who are privileged (Gordon, 1987; Manning, 1997; 1992; Visano, 1998); and operating in a manner that continuously attempts to legitimize itself to members of the public and to police officers themselves (Corsianos, 2003; 2001), regardless of social consequences and related ethical dilemmas. The concept of "equality" and "police service" must be re-evaluated and pursued simultaneously in association with an interrogation of the police organizational structure, the occupational culture, and the social economic order that sustain the current dominant policing ideologies and inequities. Collectively, the police and the public can begin to address the individual needs of different communities in order to determine possible solutions to specific problems. Feminist approaches to CP must be utilized to address the diverse and/or unique needs of neighbourhoods in cities and towns across the US and Canada.

For all of the reasons discussed above, CP could be feminist on a multitude of levels. Despite the different feminist approaches that can be taken to address, for instance, the experienced gendered realities within policing, the individual community needs, the ways to deal with the current police culture, and the different strategies for accomplishing gendered justice goals, they can also enable us to ask challenging, thought-provoking, and even what may be perceived as "threatening" questions, and to identify areas that the current policing organizational structure and operating systems have ignored.

The promotion of a feminist approach to CP requires time and well-planned strategic moves from progressive feminist and social justice advocates from both inside and outside policing, as well as from the various diverse communities the police serve. The current post-9/11 climate and the focus on terrorism in both the US and Canada may present even more challenges to the ones already in place. According to the National Research Council (2004) in the US, there has been an increase in the militarization of local police agencies and an increase in the sales of new military technologies. Large police departments today are allocating funds to assess security risks and gather intelligence in the post-9/11 climate. This means that the need for stronger feminist voices and well-planned decision-making is even more pressing as the police attempt to address and respond to recent "threats." Organizational changes must be made to all police agencies and must reflect feminist ideologies in order to promote gendered justice and move towards eradicating all other forms of inequalities between categories of people.

Questions
1. Do you favour or oppose the CP model? Why or why not?
2. What disadvantages do officers encounter within the current police structure?
3. Can the CP model be used to decrease gender inequalities?
4. Can the CP model accomplish its goals within the current socio-economic order? Why or why not?

CHAPTER 6

Gender, Detectives, and Discretionary Powers

Women continue to be under-represented in detective units such as homicide and robbery; they are more likely to work on patrol and in juvenile, community policing (CP), and sex crimes units (Boni, 1998; Ness and Gordon, 1995; Corsianos, 2007a; 2005; 2004). The purpose of this chapter is to address gendered differences as they relate to discretionary powers and detective work. Detectives, regardless of their individual differences, experience and learn to relate and identify on various similar levels within the police occupational culture. Yet, there are experienced differences resulting from particular social categories such as gender. The focus of this chapter is on detectives, as they are the ones expected to make all of the final investigative decisions on cases/investigations brought to the station by frontline officers, as well as on cases resulting from their own proactive police work.

Detectives are an integral part of the policing process. However, the majority of academic research is concentrated on patrol work. The first part of this chapter is intended to provide readers with a more descriptive account of the organizational structure, operational systems, and culture of detective units in Canada. These insights will enable readers to gain a better understanding of detective work, and to better evaluate the information presented in the second part of the chapter, which addresses the gendered differences relating to detectives' discretionary powers and decision-making. Much of the descriptive accounts of detective work in this chapter stem from Corsianos's studies (2005; 1999b). In Corsianos's earlier study (1999b), the relationship between detectives' decision-making and the police organizational structure and occupational culture was examined. Corsianos's more recent study (2005) evaluated the gendered experiences in detectives' investigative work as they related to case decision-making.

Detective Units: Roles and Processes

Detectives are responsible for thoroughly investigating all matters of a criminal nature assigned to them and preparing them for court or otherwise bringing them to a conclusion in a manner consistent with legal principles and established practices. Detectives who work in plain clothes are responsible primarily for processing prisoners who are arrested and brought to the station by the uniform police constables, and for investigating occurrences. "Occurrences" refer to reports submitted by the uniform constable to the duty sergeant in cases that require further investigation. For example, in a domestic assault case, when the suspect is not on scene upon the uniform officers' arrival, an occurrence is submitted by the uniform officers because the police are obligated to investigate and obtain all pertinent information such as statements from witnesses and/or victims, detailed descriptions of suspect(s), etc. (Corsianos, 2005; 1999b).

Processing Prisoners

From the moment a suspect is brought to the station after being arrested, he/she is taken through the sally port to the booking room and informed that all actions are monitored and recorded by audio and visual equipment. The officer in charge of the station (usually the staff sergeant working on that particular shift; or, if he/she is not available due to illness, vacation, etc., then a sergeant may be designated to be the officer in charge of the station) attends to the booking room to "parade the prisoner" and questions the arresting officer(s) and the suspect(s). The arresting officer at this time informs the staff sergeant as to the reasons for the arrest and whether the individual was notified of his/her rights and "cautioned" (i.e., understands that any information noted to an officer can be used as evidence in court).

Further, the arresting officer notifies the staff sergeant that the "prisoner" did not meet the requirements for release under the Bail Reform Act, thereby making the arrest and transport to the station mandatory. In turn, the staff sergeant is required to ask the suspect if he/she understood his/her rights. If the prisoner does not understand them, then the staff sergeant is directed to once again outline the reasons for the arrest, and reread the "right to counsel" and "caution." Furthermore, the officer in charge of the station is responsible for checking the suspect for any personal injuries and determining whether he/she is in need of any prescribed medications (if so, then arrangements must be made to provide treatment and/or make the medication available). The suspect is strip-searched, usually by the arresting officer and his/her partner to ensure that there are no concealed weapons, drugs, etc., for the safety of both the officers and the suspect. All of the information relating to a prisoner is entered into the police database system by the officer in charge of the station, and the individual is then taken to the division's general investigative unit and placed in an interview room (Corsianos, 1999b).

If, on the other hand, a person voluntarily comes into the station and admits to committing a crime, then a detective will be assigned to the case and will investigate the matter further. If it is determined that charges must be laid, then the detective will advise the suspect as to the reasons for the arrest and will read the "right to counsel" and "caution." According to the Canadian Charter of Rights and Freedoms (s. 10), every person "has the right on arrest or detention to be informed promptly of the reasons therefor; to retain and instruct counsel without delay and to be informed of that right; and to have the validity of the detention determined by way of habeas corpus and to be released if the detention is not lawful" (*Pocket Criminal Code*, 2002).

The suspect is then brought through the sally port and "paraded" in front of the officer in charge of the station in the manner outlined above. A property bag is issued to the suspect into which he/she is asked to place all of he/she personal belongings, such as jewelry, keys, cash, and any potential "weapons" that may be used to injure oneself or the police (e.g., shoestrings, belt). Following that, the prisoner is strip-searched and then taken to the divisions' general investigative unit and placed in one of the interview rooms.

The next available detective(s) is assigned to the investigation. Depending on the division, availability of officers, volume of cases, and sometimes the preference of the individual officers, detectives will either team up with different officers, work with the same partner, or less frequently, work on their own. When deciding what charges to lay, if any, the detective must first speak to the arresting officers, interview any eyewitnesses to the crime, interview victims or read victim statements recorded by the arresting officer, and assess any evidence collected by the arresting uniform officer (e.g., drugs, weapons), if relevant. The detective and/or detective constable will then make a decision as to what charge(s) to lay, or whether to release unconditionally (i.e., no charges laid) or release with certain conditions. When a decision to lay charges is made, the detective will inform the suspect as to the charges being laid against him/her (Corsianos, 1999b).

Once detectives determine whether charges should be laid, then the caution follows: "You (are charged, will be charged) with (briefly describe the charge). Do you wish to say anything in answer to the charge? You are not obliged to say anything unless you wish to do so, but whatever you say may be given in evidence." If the detective(s) wishes to speak to the now "accused" in relation to the charges, then a secondary caution is read: "If you have spoken to any police officer or to anyone with authority or if any such person has spoken to you in connection with this case, I want it clearly understood that I do not want it to influence you in making a statement" (Corsianos, 1999b: 73).

The detectives subsequently offer the accused the opportunity to contact an attorney. If he/she does not have a lawyer, then the detective will call a central number and leave a message for duty counsel to call the particular station. The individual is further given the opportunity to make other telephone calls; that is, if they are considered to be reasonable. If the detectives suspect that the accused may call someone to dispose of evidence, tip-off other suspects involved, or perhaps threaten an individual from cooperating with the police, the officers will take precautions to ensure these particular calls are prohibited. In these instances, full telephone privacy is guaranteed only after the detective determines the call is being made to the appropriate person. As for the call made to the duty counsel, sometimes it may take several hours for duty counsel to call back. In the meantime, the accused remains in the interview room unless the rooms are needed for new incoming prisoners, at which point, he/she is then transferred to the station's holding cells. Throughout this process, detectives are not prevented from asking the accused case-related questions. If he/she voluntarily decides to reply to any of them, then the detectives must interject and reread the secondary caution before listening to the responses that are given.

In instances where individuals wish to give statements, they are first taken to the Commissioner of Oaths in the station and asked to "swear to the truthfulness of the testimony." Subsequently, they are taken to a room that is equipped with audio and visual recording devices in order to record any statements. All of the information pertinent to the case is handled by the detective(s) in charge of the investigation and is entered into the station's database. Departments' software programs differ. They are designed to facilitate case preparations and typically provide several forms that must be completed by the detectives for the creation of "the dope sheet" (i.e., the file utilized by both the police and the Crown attorney in the prosecution of the accused). Recorded information includes personal information such as the accused person's name and any aliases, date of birth, height, sex, weight, place of birth, next of kin, place of employment, his/her automobiles, scars, tattoos, the names of the arresting officers, location and time of arrest, the court date if the accused is released, and the charges laid. A synopsis of the charge(s) is created that includes information pertaining to the details of the charge (e.g., what happened on the day of the incident, whether injuries were sustained, drinking was involved, children were present, etc.).

Information pertaining to the "show cause" is also recorded, entailing all of the information provided to the Crown attorney (equivalent to the district attorney in the US) for the accused person's bail hearing. There are primary and secondary grounds for a "show cause." The primary grounds are to ensure the accused individual's appearance in court on the set trial date; the secondary grounds are to prevent the accused from continuing or recommitting the offense. The accused must meet the criteria for P.R.I.C.E. (discussed below) in order to be released until his/her trial date. In other words, the officers must believe that by releasing the accused until his trial,

- the Public interest will be protected;
- there will not be any Repetition of the offense;
- the Identity of the accused is not in question;
- The officers are confident that the accused will be present in Court on the trial date;
- all Evidence has been collected for the trial.

Any previous criminal records, releases, as well as the present charge(s) are recorded under the "show cause." Following this information, the detectives outline their own recommendations (e.g., whether there should be a judicial release or whether there should be a detention order until the court date). Both the Crown attorney and the accused person's defense lawyer have access to the show cause. Therefore, detectives need to ensure that whatever information they include can be defended. If the detectives, for instance, recommend that the accused be detained until the trial because they are concerned about the possibility of a future assault on the victim, then they must be prepared to justify that assumption "on the stand." Similarly, if the detectives want the accused released with certain conditions, then they, too, must be noted in the show cause form. For example, if the accused is a known drug dealer, the detectives may ask the court to not allow him to carry a cell-phone; or if the offense occurred in a shopping mall, then the detectives may request that the accused be ordered to stay away from that location, or that a curfew be instated (Corsianos, 1999b). When charges are laid and the accused has satisfied P.R.I.C.E., then the detectives direct the accused to the officer in charge of the station, who must release the prisoner if he/she has been charged with a less serious offense (e.g., summary conviction offense).

One of several forms must be completed by the detectives when releasing an accused pending his/her first appearance in court. "Form 10," also referred to as a "promise to appear" (i.e., the accused promises to appear in court on a set date for trial) is completed. Detectives who release individuals under this process are expected to inform the accused that failure to appear in court on the set date will result in further criminal charges relating to "failing to appear." If the accused agrees, the promise to appear form is signed and he/she is subsequently released. In the alternative, a "Form 11" (a recognizance) can be entered into before an officer in charge or other peace officer. Under Form 11, the accused acknowledges that he/she will be responsible for payment of X amount of dollars (not exceeding $500) in the event that he/she fails to attend court on the set date (referred to as Form 11 without deposit), or he/she must deposit money or other valuable security not exceeding the amount or value of $500 (referred to as Form 11 with deposit), which will be for-feited if he/she fails to attend court on the set date (a Form 11 is always required for persons who are not ordinarily resident in the province in which they are in custody or who do not reside within 200 kilometres of the place in which they are in cus-tody) (*Pocket Criminal Code*, 2002).

When detectives set specific conditions for the release of the accused, then a sep-arate form (i.e., Form 11.1) accompanies Form 10. This additional form is also referred to as an "undertaking," because in order for an accused person to be released from custody, he/she must "undertake" to satisfy certain conditions (e.g., must notify the detective of any change in address; must not communicate directly or indirectly with the victim until the trial date; must surrender to the police any firearms; or must not apply for any firearm acquisition certificates, etc.). Alternatively, if no charges are laid, the person is released unconditionally (Corsianos, 1999b).

When detectives are not processing prisoners they are expected to investigate occurrences, which are submitted by the uniform constables to the duty sergeant. The occurrence is sent to the records bureau where it is given an occurrence number. It is then sent back to the division's general detective unit where it is assigned to a detective. In principle, detectives are expected to investigate all occurrences by making phone calls, driving to specific locations to speak to people, and searching for further evidence. In practice, however, detective offices tend to be swamped with cases, often resulting in little time to conduct follow-up work. Detectives often sit on piles of paper for a week or two, diminishing any chance of making prospective arrests as suspects become increasingly more difficult to locate. Often, some attempt is made (e.g., telephone calls) and if it is determined that the suspect cannot be located, then the case is deemed inactive. Alternatively, in occurrences where arrests are probable (e.g., the suspect and his/her address are known) or are considered "significant," summonses or warrants of arrest are issued. Also, when accused persons do not appear for trial on the assigned court date, a summons is served for the individual's arrest. If the case is considered serious by police, then an officer can have a warrant put out for the suspect's arrest, resulting in any officer coming in contact with this person being obligated to arrest him/her immediately rather than serving him/her with a summons to appear in court.

The arresting uniform officer is expected to create a synopsis of the events, while all of the other forms are completed by the detectives. Detectives create the "Information," which is the charge sheet (i.e., the charges laid against the accused), or, in addition to the Information, they will complete a show cause form when the accused is not released but is instead placed in a holding cell to be taken to the court for a bail hearing the next morning. The bail judge will then decide whether to release the accused until the trial date (provided the criteria for P.R.I.C.E. are met), or hold the accused in custody until trial. In addition, there are several other forms that must be completed by the detectives. For instance, if a person is charged with "failing to appear in court," then there are documents under the Canada Evidence Act that must be served on that person. Furthermore, there are documents relating to the "intent to present notices in court," which must be completed in order to introduce evidence.

Clearly, detectives need to have specific knowledge of legal procedures in order to adequately prepare a case for court. Once all of the paperwork is completed, then the detectives' work is considered finished. The officer in charge of the station will read over the report and ensure it was completed correctly. Very often, this is a speedy procedure as the officer in charge of the station has little time to look into all the details of the case and, hence, places his/her trust in the competence and expertise of the detectives handling the case. If the accused is charged and does not meet the criteria for P.R.I.C.E., then he/she is placed in a cell, and, in the morning, the police wagon will transport the prisoner to court for a bail hearing (Corsianos, 2005; 1999b).

The detectives produce the dope sheet, which includes the charge sheet (Information), the synopsis of the events, and all other pertinent information, and this is delivered to the Crown attorney. The dope sheet is placed in a pile, along with others, and every morning a detective from the warrant office in the division takes them to the courts and in the presence of a Justice of the Peace "swears to the Information." In turn, the Information is filed with the courts and then returned to the division, where it is subsequently filed under the particular court date set by the courts. Approximately one week before the court date, the division clerks working in the division's general investigative detective unit will send the Information back to the courts in preparation for court and possibly trial.

If, however, an accused person is kept overnight in custody for a bail hearing in the morning, then the entire file is sent to the courts with the prisoner by means of the wagon. In this instance, a detective working in the court office will have to "swear to the Information" in front of a Justice of the Peace, since a case cannot proceed without this being done. Even though this detective has not taken any part in the investigation, she/he is expected to read the synopsis of the charge before "swearing to it" and entering the courtroom to face the Justice of the Peace. This is to ensure that she/he can answer any questions posed by the justice; however, very often this detective does not have the time to read the file in any detail, especially when attending a courtroom with multiple cases. It is the responsibility of the court detective to ensure the file is taken to the initial bail hearing court.

With regard to the detective sergeant, one of his/her responsibilities is to monitor officers' court appearances and ensure the detective units are operating within their budget limitations. For instance, if court costs are high, it is the detective sergeant's job to find out which officers are going to court and why. In many police services, detectives who attend court during their off days are paid time and a half. If, however, they are required to attend court during their annual leave, then they are paid the equivalent of two days pay for one day of court. Because of this, the detective sergeant attempts to avoid police court appearances during officers' annual leaves. However, if a judge views a detective's testimony as significant in a case, she/he will order that detective to come to trial regardless of whether she/he is on leave. Subsequently, the budget is affected when a detective, who is on annual leave for an entire week or two, is expected to be in court for a lengthy trial. As a result, cutbacks are then made in other areas to compensate for these expenditures (Corsianos, 2005; 1999b).

Organizational Structure and Culture of Detective Units

In large police departments, every division has an investigative detective office/unit that is responsible for general investigative functions, such as support and direction to front-line officers on preliminary and follow-up investigations, management and administration of all criminal investigations, and the coordination of plainclothes functions. Typically, all police divisions maintain some criminal investigation function (i.e., general investigative function) and a youth bureau, while detective work in other specialized areas such as major crime, drugs, domestic violence, and missing persons is limited to those divisions that have the resources to operate such offices. However, the general investigative detective units may, at different times, include plainclothes, drugs, major crime, fraud, warrants, or other functions that upper management deems necessary. Depending on the size of these units, one or more detective sergeants may be assigned to manage them. Detectives may work either alone or in a team depending on the number of available detectives and the number of cases. Every divisional investigative unit operates differently due to the difference in the size of the division (i.e., the number of employees) and thus the different staffing levels. Some offices may operate 24 hours each day, while others may be only scheduled for a limited number of hours during the day. Specialized units, such as homicide, sexual assault, fraud, investigative special services (major crimes, auto theft rings, etc.), fugitive, and forensic identification, may be centralized and operate from one location, usually police headquarters, and service the entire city or region (Corsianos, 2005; 1999b).

Large police departments have multiple divisions spread throughout the city, and within each division there are a number of platoons. For example, one particular large urban police service operates with five platoons: A, B, C, D, and E. Each platoon works a particular shift within a 35-day cycle. The shift generally consists of a day shift, which consists of seven work days in a row (7:15 AM to 5:15 PM), followed by six days off. The evening shift is seven work days in a row (5:00 PM to 3:00 AM), followed by five days off, while the night shift is seven work days in a row (11:00 PM to 7:00 AM), followed by three days off (Corsianos, 1999b).

The structure of the detective offices will vary somewhat from division to division, depending on their resources, size, the number of police employed at the division, and the unique problems of the geographic area that the division polices. For instance, divisions that are considered "slower paced" have smaller detective offices, whereas areas with more visible crimes, such as street prostitution and street-level drug trafficking that require more proactive detective work, usually have larger detective offices (i.e., more personnel). The general investigative detective unit at a division may consist, for example, of one detective sergeant, two detectives (equivalent to a sergeant who oversees the uniform officers), and perhaps three detective constables (equivalent to a uniform police constable).

Some of the large police services structure the uniform patrol work to a 10-hour shift, which amounts to 21 days of work in a 35-day cycle, whereas the detectives work a 9-hour shift within a 22-day cycle. One day in the cycle is considered the "doubling up" or "coupling up" day when the platoon finishing on the last day of their shift is expected to catch up on any uncompleted investigations (e.g., paperwork, telephone calls, interviews). The platoon beginning their first day of the shift is expected to handle any cases that are brought to the attention of the detective unit (Corsianos, 2005; 1999b).

Detective units/offices are hierarchical and structured in terms of rank. The police department is paramilitaristic and demands respect for persons of higher rank. The detective constable who holds the temporary detective position must answer to the detective constables who hold the permanent positions (this is discussed in more detail below), and they must both answer to the detective. The detective, in turn, is accountable to the detective sergeant, who is accountable to those in high-level management positions, such as the inspector, superintendent, deputy chief, and chief. High-level management positions are ultimately accountable to the Police Services Board. The detective constables are expected to respect the decisions of the detective. In principle, all officers, regardless of their rank, are independent agents of the Crown and can therefore individually decide how to handle a case (e.g., what charges to lay, to release or not) (Corsianos, 2005; 1999b).

Corsianos (2003) found that in the majority of "typical" "ordinary" cases, detectives working together often agreed on how to handle specific investigations. It was in rare instances that detectives had serious concerns with the decisions made by the detective constables. Due to convincing arguments made on the part of the detective constables, detectives, at times, allowed them to proceed in the manner they believed was most appropriate (however, this did not apply in "high-profile" cases [Corsianos, 2003]). Despite this "support" from their "superiors," detective constables felt it was important to always protect their actions. They overwhelmingly believed that if they failed to protect themselves and became vulnerable to external scrutiny, then they would be left "on their own" to defend themselves.

For instance, in one example, a detective constable assisted a woman who had been defrauded of thousands of dollars. The detective constable was aware of the fact that the fraud office was overwhelmed with cases, some involving multimillion dollar frauds. He also asserted that the courts were not effective in providing restitution to victims. As a result, he "tracked down" the suspect and negotiated a deal. The agreement reached between the suspect and the officer was as follows: The suspect (who admitted to the crime) agreed to return all of the money to the victim, and the officer, in turn, agreed not to arrest him. Locating the suspect and negotiating the deal involved a great deal of time on the part of the officer, much of which was conducted while off duty. Some of the senior officers did not necessarily support his approach, but they did not object to it. However, if anything went wrong (e.g., a complaint was filed against the officer, if there was negative publicity by the media, etc.), then "there would be hell to pay" in the words of the detective constable, and he would be left on his own to defend himself (Corsianos, 1999b). The recurring theme voiced by all of the interviewed detectives was captured fully in the following statement: "Do what you wish providing your ass is always covered" (Corsianos, 2005; 1999b).

If, on the other hand, a detective objects to a detective constable's decision relating to an investigation, then the detective constable may unwisely take the issue to the officer in charge of the station (i.e., usually the staff sergeant). However, staff sergeants typically are not willing to "break rank" and take the side of a lower ranking officer, even though there may be times when they agree with the detective constable's position. Moreover, the detective constable only succeeds in "burning bridges" with the detective and possibly others in the office. The detective constable may also choose to speak to the unit commander, but, once again, the unit commander will most likely not "break rank" to support the officer. In addition, if she/he feels strongly about the investigation, the detective constable can go to the Justice of the Peace, like any other citizen, and lay the charge she/he deems appropriate. This course of action, however, would be highly unlikely and would be viewed negatively by the department. The officer would most likely be viewed as a troublemaker, disloyal to the department, and/or untrustworthy. In principle, no officer of any rank can tell another officer not to lay a charge with the Justice of the Peace because she/he could be charged with "obstructing justice" (i.e., a criminal offense). In practice, however, detective constables are expected to accept the decisions made by the detectives (and other senior officers) and not challenge them (Corsianos, 2005; 1999b).

If a detective constable attempts to "break rank," then typically she/he faces negative consequences ranging from being transferred back to uniform capacity, to being ostracized by fellow officers. Therefore, regardless of the fact that all detectives are independent agents of the Crown and, in principle, can individually decide the manner in which a case is processed, actual practice suggests the opposite is true. In numerous examples, detectives noted that "their detective constables" had never tried to override their authority. One detective described how, for as long as she had been on the job in the capacity of detective, this had never happened to her. In another example, a detective stated, "If he did, he would not last long in this unit, he would be chastised by his peers to the point where he'd be forced to leave" (Corsianos, 2005: 22; 2003; 1999b).

A great deal of discretion rests in the hands of detectives relating to how an investigation should be conducted. All cases are not treated in the same manner; the amount of time, energy, resources, money, and personnel utilized in a case will depend on whether the case is defined as "high-profile" or not. In other words, priority is always given to high-profile cases, which can include investigations involving serious criminal offenses (Corsianos, 2003). However, as noted above, in most cases, disagreement between detectives working in a reactive capacity is rare. Most cases are considered "ordinary," "typical," "everyday cases," where there is generally agreement relating to how they should be handled. Significant variance in decision-making usually occurs in relation to the fewer "high-profile" investigations (Corsianos, 2003).

A. Detective Units as Promotions

Detective positions are lateral entries but are considered prestigious in comparison to patrol work, and many officers perceive them as promotions to some degree. Firstly, detectives do not work in uniform capacity, but rather dress in business attire while in the office; if they work undercover, then they typically wear casual clothes. They receive a pay increase, a clothing allowance, and are able to earn a significant amount of money in court time when expected to attend court on their days off, or when they work overtime. Detective positions are desirable for these reasons, but also because of the level of autonomy given to individual detectives and the complexity and challenge attendant with particular investigations. However, most of the time as a detective is spent processing prisoners, preparing cases for court, and dealing with all of the relevant administrative tasks. Detective work often translates to significantly more responsibilities than uniform patrol work. Detectives are not under immediate supervision as are uniform officers, and they do not drive marked police cars responding to calls from the public.

The detective position, which is equivalent to the position of sergeant for patrol officers, is usually permanent. Meanwhile, detective constable positions can be permanent or temporary. Depending on the division, a permanent detective constable position typically translates to either a two- or three-year term, with the opportunity of extending the term for an additional year. The temporary position is typically considered a training position, and, again, depending on the department and the division, it can translate to a few months or even a one-year term.

In order to be able to attain one of the detective constable positions, an officer must apply whenever an opening comes up. Uniform police constables are typically given the opportunity to work in one of the temporary training positions. However, a permanent detective constable (usually a two-to-four year position) position is more difficult to obtain. Many times the permanent position is spoken for before "the call" is put out to the entire division. However, in order to create the illusion that an equitable system is in place, all applications are collected. The main players in the decision process are usually the detectives, the detective sergeant, and the unit commander. It is quite common for these actors to support their friends and/or the friends of friends and the friends of higher ranking officers.

The detectives and detective sergeant, in particular, have a strong voice in this process because they are the ones expected to work with the new person for the next several years. In one particular police department, the rule in some of its divisions was that a detective constable completing his/her second- or third-year term was expected to spend six months back "on the street" before applying to another detective office (Corsianos, 1999b). However, some of these individuals would often be removed from patrol status and sent back to the detective office within a month or two with the following common excuse provided by the detectives or detective sergeant, "We could not find anyone who was qualified" (Corsianos, 1999b: 65).

Detective sergeants and detectives frequently assigned permanent detective constables who were considered "friends" and were perceived as team players, competent, and trustworthy to another detective office for an additional two-to-four year term.

In the few rare instances where there is no one particular person in mind for the permanent position, the detectives and detective sergeant will carefully screen applicants for the job. This usually entails phone calls and meetings with sergeants, staff sergeants, and even uniform constables regarding the strengths and weaknesses of the applicants. More importantly, issues relating to loyalty to the job, trust, and the ability to work in a team environment without creating disruption are closely scrutinized. Additionally, due to the complexity of responsibilities in detective work and the pressure to work quickly in an environment that is at times "flooded" with a high volume of cases, the detectives will assess an applicant in terms of his/her experience in giving evidence in court, thoroughness in case preparation and case management, productivity "on the street" (e.g., arrests made), and note-taking abilities (Corsianos, 1999b).

Candidates who are able to conduct these duties effectively are considered, as one detective described them, the "cream of the crop," but more important is ensuring that they are "team players" and can be trusted. To reiterate, this screening process is only considered in the few rare instances when the position has not already been earmarked for a known applicant. Even when a position has been earmarked, formal procedures are followed in advertising the position and collecting applications to create the illusion that the application process is unbiased and fair. Whereas the training/temporary detective constable positions are more accessible to all officers, this is certainly not the case for the permanent positions. In fact, in some instances, the permanent position is temporarily converted into a training position until the detectives and detective sergeant can find the "right person" to fill the permanent spot (Corsianos, 2005; 1999b).

Detective offices are very cliquish and, in principle, as mentioned previously, are considered to be promotions rather than merely lateral moves. Therefore, a great deal of effort is invested in deciding who is afforded the opportunity to work in the detective office. Ultimately, the detectives and the detective sergeant seek to gain a "team player." Interview questions can range from work ethic and willingness to work in a team environment, to whether applicants are capable of "taking a joke" without "being offended racially, ethnically, sexually, religiously, politically, and so forth" (Corsianos, 1999b: 129). For instance, in Corsianos's studies (2005; 1999b), detectives spoke of their willingness to accept people of all races, ethnic backgrounds, and sexes; however, these individuals were expected to be able to conform to the dominant patriarchal Anglo-Saxon ideologies and identify as a homogeneous group regardless of individual differences. Overall, they experienced pressure "to fit in" and be a "team player."

Additionally, some officers in Corsianos's study (1999b) noted that detective positions should not be limited to a specified period, but rather should be open. Some of the arguments made in support of this included the following: It takes several years before an officer can "learn all the ropes" and become a "good detective." Therefore, officers felt it was unfair to be shifted around or moved back to uniform duty given the learning curve.

Other officers felt that it takes a unique individual to handle the wide range and complex responsibilities of the detective units. Some maintained that few officers had the "natural ability" to be effective detectives. A detective is seen as a person who can "schmooze"; she/he should be able to work with the courts, the judges, the justices of the peace, and the court clerks to build his/her reputation and gain the support of the various "players" (e.g., the court personnel who are needed to process the paperwork quickly and efficiently). This person is expected to be an effective communicator, as she/he deals with witnesses, accused persons, and victims of crimes, and is expected to build a rapport with the courts.

Furthermore, within the culture of policing, detectives are considered experts with respect to their knowledge of federal, provincial, and municipal laws. Detectives generally have more knowledge of the laws in comparison to front-line officers; they are aware of new case law and are often better able to determine appropriate charges. As a result of this, it is not uncommon practice for uniform police officers to call detectives for advice on current case law and/or suggestions on how to handle a case they are in the midst of investigating "on the street" (Corsianos, 2005; 1999b).

B. Detectives as "Experts"

Detectives are likely to express resentment and/or frustration with certain media and/or members of the public who are perceived as constantly trying to tell the police how to do their job and who paint a negative picture of the police. Detectives generally believe the wider public is ignorant of policing issues. They often claim the public does not realize the dangerous nature of their work, fails to understand that the police "chase criminals" in order to protect citizens and maintain peace, and that most people are unaware of how "some laws interfere with good police work," which puts the public at a disadvantage (Corsianos, 1999b). Interferences by external non-police agencies/institutions are often viewed as threatening and demeaning to their profession. One detective noted that "people are always trying to tell us how to do our work; I invite them to spend a single day with us out on the road and see what our job truly entails; that's when I guarantee you they'll begin to rethink some of the generalizations and assumptions they make" (Corsianos, 1999b: 131). Another detective was quoted as saying:

> Doctors, lawyers and other professionals are not exposed to the kind of scrutiny we are exposed to; I can't see why policing should be any different. I mean when was the last time you saw a passenger of a plane tell a pilot how to fly it? I think people believe they understand the complexity of our work yet they are completely clueless; for most of the public, detective work is what they see in Hollywood movies (Corsianos, 1999b: 131).

In Corsianos (2005; 1999b), several substantive examples of detectives' perceptions of themselves as "experts" were noted. One, in particular, related to a decision made by the municipal government in the 1990s to restrict officers from making court appearances on their days off. This created a great deal of outrage from the police department. All court dates were to be set on days when the officers worked day shift in order to avoid paying them time and a half on their off days (with the minimum guarantee of three hours). Detectives described this as an example of "nonpolice people" making a decision that significantly affected the lives of officers and the system in its entirety, without understanding the repercussions of that decision (i.e., with all of the detectives and uniform officers in court, there were few officers policing the streets and working the detective offices). Detectives explained how this approach completely failed and was ultimately eliminated.

C. Reactive versus Proactive Detective Work

Police strategies to control crime consist of reactive and proactive strategies. In reactive work, the police respond to crimes after they have taken place. The crimes and/or complaints are identified by others in the community, and they are the ones who notify the police. Often, citizens will call 911 to report a crime and the dispatcher will send the police to the scene. However, in proactive work, the police take it upon themselves to identify crimes. This involves the police stopping citizens and asking them questions to determine whether a crime has taken place (e.g., when an officer stops a motor vehicle to determine whether the driver is drinking and driving), or working undercover (e.g., when an officer poses as a drug buyer).

Most of the time, detectives are engaged in reactive policing in the processing of prisoners, preparing cases for court, and dealing with the relevant administrative responsibilities. As mentioned earlier, there is very little time for proactive work where the detectives can leave the station and investigate a case. Most of the detective units also primarily engage in reactive work. Typically, large police departments have only a couple of detective units that are primarily proactive. For instance, in one particular agency studied, a handful of undercover detectives were responsible for investigating liquor outlets, drug-selling, prostitution, car thefts, and other serious criminal activities. There were approximately four to eight detectives per shift, depending on the division, "out on the streets" engaging in undercover work, as well as plainclothes investigations. In these units, the detectives can allot time to thoroughly investigate cases and they are not confined to the office; they do not rely on uniform officers to make arrests but rather generate their own arrests based on their own proactive work. Detectives who work in these units clearly represent the minority and typically perceive all other detectives (i.e., the majority who work primarily in a reactive capacity) as "glorified secretaries" or "paper pushers" (Corsianos, 2005; 1999b).

Gender and Police Discretion

A. What is Police Discretion?

Police discretion refers to "the power conferred on criminal justice professionals to use their judgment to decide what action to take in a given situation. This includes the decision to take no action" (McLaughlin and Muncie, 2001: 95-96). Police discretion is an integral part of police work. Policing would not be possible without police discretionary powers. There are a multiplicity of rules and laws in existence, resulting in only a few being enforced due to the available time, resources, and lack of police knowledge of all of the rules/laws. Moreover, at times, many laws and procedures are themselves inconsistent, if not contradictory. Hence, policing involves a high level of discretion in the application of rules (Davis, 1969; Goldstein, 1964; LaFave, 1965), and as McNamara notes, "Police work does not consist of a standardized product or service" (1967: 185). It has been argued that "the source of police discretion lies with the legal powers they are given, the nature of the criminal law they have to enforce, the context within which police work takes place and limitations on resources" (McLaughlin and Muncie, 2001: 96).

Officers' decision-making relating to investigations depends on discretion and is made situationally. Initially, it is the front-line officers (the patrol officers) who apply their discretion in the handling of an investigation. Their choice of action or inaction in various circumstances partly depends on their discretion and interpretation of the laws (Corsianos, 1999b). Once a person is arrested and brought into the station/division, the case is "handed over" to the detectives working in the appropriate detective office and they will ultimately make decisions affecting the accused (Ericson, 1981; 1992). Several criminologists have discussed the high value that is placed on police discretion by police departments (Manning, 1997; McNulty, 1994; Dixon, 1992; Fyfe, 1991; Goldsmith, 1990; Hale, 1989; Shearing, 1981; Doig, 1978; Skolnick, 1966; Westley, 1953).

Officers' work is in most instances individualistic (Black, 1973). There tends to be a lack of uniformity in law enforcement; that is, which laws get enforced and to whom the laws are most applied, and which cases become prioritized and hence become subject to much investigative scrutiny internally by the police. Officers spend most of their time policing "minor crimes" where there is much more flexibility than in the more serious ones (e.g. indictable offenses in Canada; felonies in the US), and therefore, there is a heightened need for uniformity. Criminal statutes are not fully enforced. The statutes as drafted provide little or no enforcement guidance and even if certain sections of the law called for specific enforcement guidelines, police still have the power to enforce certain laws over others, and to apply selective law enforcement on particular groups of people.

Law enforcement does not provide equal protection, nor does it provide equal access to police services and to the quality of those services. In fact, police discretion can result in unequal treatment of people in similar situations (Neugebauer, 1999; 1996; Russell, 1998; Burtch, 1992; Harding, 1991; McLaughlin, 1991). Goldstein (1977), on the other hand, notes that the socializing process within police agencies accounts for some forms of discretion being uniformly applied; however, the majority of police discretionary powers are the result of the individual officer's decision. He further asserts that "persons who have accompanied several different police officers on routine assignments in the same area are often startled by the different ways in which similar incidents are handled," and "depending on work load and time constraints, officers' decisions in similar situations may not always be consistent" (1977: 101-02).

However, by attributing the majority of police discretionary powers to individual officers, Goldstein does not assess the impact of various social and political forces on the police occupational culture, as well as on "identity" categories such as gender in relation to officers' actions. Also, there is no acknowledgment of people's class, gender, and race/ethnicity regarding the differences in police actions in similar situations (Corsianos, 2001). Therefore, even though police work is in most instances individualistic (Black, 1973), that does not mean that officers necessarily act differently, as they are products of the occupational culture of policing (Corsianos, 2001). Yet, at the same time, some police actions may reflect patterns of differences relating to the "identity" categories of officers. For instance, gender, as a social category, produces differences in detectives' discretionary powers and decision-making relating to particular investigations (Corsianos, 2005; 1999b). The application of detectives' discretionary powers is ultimately an inquiry into expressions of power and cultural controls (Corsianos, 2001).

B. Gendered Discretion

In Corsianos's research (2005; 1999b), several gender differences were noted in relation to officers' discretionary powers and detective work. Most detectives seemed to be committed to quickly and adequately investigating a case, bringing it to a close, and moving on to the next one. However, women as a group were also more likely to be perceived as "going the extra mile" to ensure a case was handled properly, which included collecting and filing all of the relevant information and evidence in processing prisoners and in preparing cases for court. They were generally perceived as being more organized and more methodical in ensuring that "all the i's were dotted and the t's were crossed." When working in a reactive capacity, there tended to be agreement as to how a case should be handled, but women were seen as typically dedicating more time and effort to individual cases and seemed to have more in-depth knowledge of the details relating to the investigations. They appeared to be more organized, and paid more attention to detail when questioning witnesses, victims, and accused persons, and when completing reports. They were also reliable in filing reports on time and meeting other case-related deadlines. Women were further perceived as being more responsible and less likely to "take shortcuts." For instance, overall, they were less likely to avoid the laying of charges in less serious cases in an effort to avoid all the necessary paperwork.

When uniform officers arrested individuals for violating the conditions of their probation, male detectives were more often perceived as being reluctant to lay charges in comparison to females. For example, some cases involved individuals who were in violation of their probation for associating with a person(s) who had a criminal record and for not notifying their probation officer that their home address had changed. Male detectives tended to not want to spend the time processing the paperwork because it was viewed as a "waste of time," and because the accused person could notify the probation officer of the change of address at their next meeting together. For female detectives, however, these violations were important. In the above example, most of the women agreed that a charge for "associating with a criminal" should not be laid simply because it would be difficult to prove in court that the accused was aware of the individual's criminal record. However, they agreed that a charge should be laid for violating the second condition of his probation. The accused was expected to notify his probation officer of the change of address at his next meeting with his probation officer, but there was no guarantee of his attendance. If this individual chose not to attend his required scheduled meeting, then the probation officer would have no way of locating him. This would, in turn, lead to a warrant being issued for his immediate arrest. Thus, female detectives were committed to handling cases completely by laying charges when there were obvious violations of people's probation and the evidence against the accused was clear.

As discussed earlier, detectives working primarily in a reactive capacity for the most part agreed that in the vast majority of criminal cases, there was consensus in how a case should proceed (e.g., in the laying of specific charges, in releasing an accused person on several conditions, etc.). Frequently, the one or two detectives handling a case (i.e., in charge of the investigation) were "on their own" in their decisions, since other detectives were busy handling other investigations. In fact, detectives working primarily in a reactive capacity claimed that there was not much variance in their decisions relating to how a case should be handled. One exception, however, was in the number of charges laid. Some detectives felt it was their responsibility to lay every charge possible and let the courts decide which ones to convict on, seeing that their role was not one of judge and jury. Others claimed it was their job to lay only the most applicable charges. In either case, detectives laid more than one charge against an accused; this allowed the police, the courts, and the accused to engage in "plea bargaining," where the accused often pleaded guilty to the lesser charge and thus avoided trial. Cases were generally perceived as "clear-cut" in how they were investigated and in the subsequent laying of charges (if any). The detective office was described as an "assembly line" to some extent; that is, detectives were expected to quickly investigate a case, bring it to a conclusion via a decision on how to proceed, and move on to the next one (Corsianos, 2005; 2003; 1999b).

Both male and female detectives did not see a great deal of discretion in their decision-making as it related to reactive police work (with the exception of high-profile cases [Corsianos, 2003]). Detectives felt that cases would be handled similarly when they were considered "typical" or "ordinary," regardless of the investigating detective. Only in rare instances did differences in decision-making relating to reactive detective work become more exemplified and discretion moved up the hierarchy. These investigations were defined as "high-profile," in that they transcended "the ordinary" and involved a number of variables (i.e., relating to the accused or victim, the role of the media, political implications, questionable and/or illegal police conduct, or the public's reaction) (Corsianos, 2003).

C. Gendered Discretion in Proactive Detective Work

Disagreement between female and male detectives working primarily in a proactive capacity was identified in several areas (Corsianos, 2005; 1999b). This meant that there were times when detectives differed along gender lines in how the investigation should be conducted. In the district drug units, for instance, some male detectives expressed frustration with "let go's," whereas more female officers perceived them to be necessary to "getting the job done." Detectives working in the drug units were given a sum of money (i.e., "buy money") each week for their investigations. They worked undercover, which meant they would place themselves in situations where they would buy illegal drugs from different drug dealers and literally walk away from the situation without making any arrests. This was referred to as a "let go." The drug dealer would be arrested and charged a few months later.

The rationale for the "let go" strategy was that the dealer would not remember all of the people that she/he had sold to over the previous months, and, therefore, the undercover detective(s) could be utilized for longer periods of time in the same area. However, if the detectives made arrests immediately following particular sales, then the word would spread quickly to other drug dealers and the officers' work would come to an end. Interestingly, some of the male officers had concerns with these "let go's." They were eager to make the arrests and tended to feel awkward about "letting drug dealers walk free" after a sale had been made. Some also had concerns relating to being able to get a conviction in court because of the time that had elapsed between the offense and the arrest. They claimed that several questions could be raised by the defense lawyers to jeopardize the Crown's evidence (Corsianos, 2005; 1999b).

D. Proactive Detective Work and Its Relationship to Community Policing Initiatives

Proactive detective work relies heavily on the use of individual detectives' discretionary powers in deciding how best to proceed with an investigation. However, Corsianos (2005) found that discretionary powers are applied differently along gender lines when it concerns specific CP initiatives. Women detectives tend to be sympathetic to the needs of different communities and are supportive of various CP goals. Thus, they invest time and energy in investigating cases resulting from particular CP initiatives.

In one Canadian urban police department studied (Corsianos, 1999b), Community Response officers were expected to liaise with the detectives and provide information on what were deemed serious issues affecting the area, and identify problem areas that could lead to the undertaking of an investigation by the general investigative office, or even perhaps a joint project between the detective unit and the Community Response unit. Moreover, every division had developed a Crime Management team that consisted of the unit commander, inspector, detective sergeant, uniform staff sergeant, Community Response unit staff sergeant, crime analyst, front-line constable, detective or detective constable from the detective office, and the detective constable from the office of Domestic Liaison, Firearms, and Missing Persons. Once a month the team met to discuss current projects and to identify the need for new ones. In addition, there were lengthy discussions as to possible solutions to ongoing problems in the patrol parameters of specific divisions. This allowed each division to determine the concerns/problems that most affected the area they policed and to discuss and develop possible solutions, however, this was done without the public's input. The detective sergeant was expected to update the detective offices with respect to the decisions made in the meetings that took place once a month and from the information relayed by the crime analyst, who was responsible for compiling crime statistics and describing the crime trends within the patrol parameters of the division.

Furthermore, once a month, the mayor, along with his counsellors, organized a meeting where members of government (e.g., the police, the fire department, building inspectors, etc.), professional groups, and citizens who resided and/or worked in the area came together to listen to the public's concerns and/or complaints. The police were expected to respond to the policing concerns. In fact, the police were accountable to the mayor, and the mayor expected the police to investigate every situation noted in the meeting. However, detectives claimed that this restricted the police from investigating other matters that were considered much more significant, since there were only so many detectives working on any given shift with limited time, resources, and budgets. Some detectives referred to these mandatory investigations as "the politics of policing," because the mayor and the counsellors sought to maintain their popularity with their constituents.

The problems/concerns expressed at the public meetings were numerous and twofold: commercial concerns and residential concerns. They included complaints against certain businesses for selling drugs or running "booze camps," residents who played loud music, prostitution in certain areas that affected businesses and increased pollution and traffic, etc. All of these complaints were recorded. Detectives were then forced to respond to all of the cases on the list and update everyone during the following month's meeting. If certain incidents had not been investigated, then the mayor, who had the deputy's home phone number, would call her/him and complain. The deputy, in turn, would want an explanation from the detective units as to why these incidents had been ignored.

Both female and male detectives felt this requirement to investigate all complaints interfered at times with the investigation of other more important problems. However, at the same time, women were more committed to actually doing the work and ensuring that adequate attempts were made to respond to each complaint by the public in order to achieve some end result that was pleasing to the complainants. Yet, detectives noted that most cases remained on the list for months because frequently the police could only intervene to a certain point within the boundaries of the law and/or due to the available resources and budget. In fact, when a complaint was no longer considered an issue and was removed from the list, it was a call for celebration. Furthermore, drug concerns that were frequently voiced at these public meetings were considered difficult to bring to a close, since the district drug squads spent more time investigating "the big buys" and not the "street-level drug dealers," who were the drug players who concerned the local residents, schools, and businesses the most (Corsianos, 2005; 1999b).

Female detectives were also more supportive of CP initiatives relating to victims of violent crimes. Most complaints filed by victims were made against male officers for showing disrespect and/or a lack of compassion and understanding towards them. Some CP initiatives were established to address these concerns. Female detectives were more likely to take the lead on these and organize meetings at community centres or at the divisions to discuss various community concerns and provide support for victims of crimes by inviting them to voice their complaints relating to the police response (Corsianos, 2007a; 2005; 1999b).

E. Proactive Detective Work Relating to Domestic Violence Cases
Gender differences relating to discretionary powers and proactive detective work were also apparent in domestic violence cases. Reports from domestic violence victims included complaints against male officers for failing to see them as human beings and treating them as investigative "tools" that were temporarily needed to file reports. Also, many victims reported that they were made to feel as if they were wasting the police officers' time. Female detectives were more likely to treat domestic violence cases with priority and not perceive them as a "waste of time." They typically communicated with the victims prior to trial to explain the court process and to discuss the importance of the victim's court appearance and testimony. They provided support to the victims and took the necessary steps to attain a conviction in court (Corsianos, 2007a; 2005; 1999b).

Alternatively, some male detectives engaged in unethical tactics by using these cases to fulfill personal agendas. Some felt they were forced to lay charges in cases where they did not think a conviction was possible (e.g., because it was believed that the victim would not appear in court on the trial date and therefore the judge would dismiss the case, or because the victim would present conflicting evidence of the incident leading to a dismissal of the charges). Most of the male detectives seemed to be indifferent to these investigations, but some strategically utilized unethical means for their own personal benefit. Some wanted to ensure a conviction for their own self-promotion, or because they had a personal vendetta against the accused (e.g., had "run-ins" with the accused in the past). Aggressive "bully tactics" were used to ensure victim cooperation in court if they thought the victim might not attend. Sometimes they verbally threatened the witness, and some even lied about the possible legal consequences to not testifying (Corsianos, 1999b) (see Chapter 4).

Male detectives were also more likely to perceive themselves as "experts" in domestic violence situations; that is, in how to best handle these types of cases. Detectives were mandated to lay charges in all domestic violence cases provided there were "reasonable and probable grounds" that a criminal offense had occurred. Often at the trial level the case was resolved by the judge by issuing a peace bond (i.e., where both the accused and the victim agree not to communicate with each other; the accused is not criminally convicted). Many male detectives maintained that all of this could have been accomplished "at the scene," which would have saved a significant amount of time, energy, and resources on the part of the police and the courts. It was suggested that several processes had to be "revamped" and they necessarily required police input. One detective constable stated, "It's a waste of time; change is needed, but, they've got to hear our point of view. We know what the problems are. We know what works and what doesn't" (Corsianos, 2005: 24). Another detective stated, "We could have issued the peace bond ourselves and avoided waiting six to nine months for trial." Similarly, another officer noted, "Why go through all the paperwork for just a peace bond at the end of the day?" (Corsianos, 1999b: 130-31).

F. Proactive Detective Work and Unethical and/or Illegal Police Behaviour

Gender differences were observed in detectives' decisions to act in unethical ways, as was noted in some domestic violence cases, but unethical and/or illegal police acts also applied to other areas (Corsianos, 2005; 1999b). The reported illegal acts related only to male officers. Most male detectives believed that loyalty to other officers was very important, even if at times it meant acting in ways that were deemed unethical and/or illegal. Male officers who claimed they made a conscious effort to ensure that their sense of loyalty to other officers did not interfere with being ethical in their work constituted the minority. These detectives claimed that if officers followed the rules and proceeded in a lawful manner in the execution of police duties, then they never had to worry about being "discovered." Also, as discussed in Chapter 4, time and energy would not be wasted in sheltering any lies or fabrications on their part (e.g., collectively working with one's partner on the information they would record in their memorandum books to ensure their "stories" did not contradict in any way). Ironically, however, these same detectives had admitted to doing things "against their better judgment" for the sake of "loyalty." Female detectives maintained that being ethical in the execution of their police duties (i.e., following the administrative rules and obeying the laws) was crucial even if it meant being "disloyal" to another officer for refusing to lie or "cover" for him/her.

As noted in Chapter 4, male detectives admitted to acting unethically and/or illegally by taking on the role of "disciplinarians," or acting in ways they believed were necessary in order to "teach the suspect a lesson." These cases typically involved suspects who either showed no remorse for their actions and/or disrespected the police by being uncooperative, arrogant, or by using obscene language. Sometimes detectives falsified charges when dealing with individuals who were deemed "career criminals." "Trumped-up" charges did not seem to be the norm, however, detectives had the power to falsify evidence for the sake of charging if the need arose. This was perceived as being justified in order to punish the individual and "teach him/her a lesson."

Other detectives used physical force to silence these individuals and utilized witnesses to protect their illegal actions. For instance, some detectives used physical force to control individuals who were perceived as troublemakers, but the use of force was not warranted and was illegal. When witnesses were in the near vicinity, these detectives often yelled out orders/commands and repeated them continuously in order to suggest to citizens that they were trying to apprehend a suspect. Subsequently, they would proceed to strike the individuals with their batons. If a complaint was ever filed, witnesses who worked and/or lived in the area could be called to verify the police "attempts" to control the suspect before being "forced" to apply "legitimate" physical force (Corsianos, 1999b).

In addition, other male officers conducted illegal searches of cars. If they suspected criminal activity, they would use a number of different "justifications" to search a motor vehicle. These included making false claims about smelling alcohol on the driver's breath, or tossing a beer cap in the car and claiming they had found it (this suggested possible open liquor). These "justifications" allowed the officers to search the vehicle because they constituted offenses under a provincial statute (see Chapter 4) (Corsianos, 1999b).

The statement "cover your ass" was often repeated by several detectives, both male and female. "Covering your ass is the cornerstone of policing; it's about self-preservation regardless of how you conduct yourself as an officer," noted one detective constable. This referred to being able to protect themselves when acting legally, but also when acting inappropriately and/or illegally. Most officers sought to protect themselves by ensuring their legal actions did not put them in positions where they could later be criticized for their choices or falsely accused of illegal behaviour (Corsianos, 2005; 1999b).

Both female and male detectives discussed the importance of recording detailed notes in order to protect themselves from being falsely accused of acting negligently or failing to act altogether. Several detectives made it a habit to always record various events and discussions in their memo books in order to create a paper trail. Many protected themselves by not placing themselves in situations where they could be falsely accused of illegal behaviour. For instance, male detectives never entered an interview room to speak to a female suspect without either being accompanied by another detective, taping the discussion, or leaving the door to the room wide open so others could hear the conversation. These strategies were utilized to protect themselves from being falsely accused of any sexual misconduct and they were carefully detailed in their memo books. For those acting illegally, however, detailed notes were considered equally important in order to protect themselves. These officers ensured their notes were strategically crafted, with the cooperation of their police partners to "cover" their actions (see Chapter 4) (Corsianos, 1999b).

G. Proactive Detective Work and Competition for "the Big Arrest"

Certain criminal investigations involved heightened pressure to make arrests and these appeared to be more important to male officers in comparison to females. For instance, the district drug squads were eager to investigate cases that involved prominent drug dealers, drug trafficking, drug distribution, and drug importation. These investigations could lead to the discovery of large amounts of illicit drugs and could, in turn, benefit officers professionally.

However, the competition and/or pressure for "the big arrest" often meant the less sensational cases were ignored by the detectives who worked in this proactive capacity. The few female detectives working at the district level were committed to these "big cases," but also considered the street-level drug offenses to be important. They noted that there were numerous public complaints made about the street-level drugs in particular areas and felt that the department should make more strategic attempts to respond to them, or return the drug squads to the division level (Corsianos, 2005; 1999b).

H. Proactive Detective Work in Maintaining the Peace

At times, detectives were faced with making decisions relating to arrests in order to avoid confrontations with the public. These actions were commonly referred to as "judgment calls." Decisions had to be readily made to determine whether making an arrest would lead to upheavals or further social unrest and perhaps result in more serious consequences. Typically, the possibility of jeopardizing the social peace was confronted in situations where a large number of people were involved and thus detectives scrutinized the possible ripple effects attendant with making arrests. For example, undercover detectives who monitored the overall peaceful activities of people at various festivals, picnics, parades, and rallies at times observed minor criminal violations. In these instances, some felt compelled to charge, but women detectives seemed to favour avoiding arrests when they felt it could lead to negative reactions from the public. Both the police and innocent bystanders could be hurt by individuals who intervened to prevent the arrest and this possibility was viewed as not worth risking for minor offenses (Corsianos, 2005; 1999b).

However, arrests were deemed necessary by both male and female officers when they involved serious crimes (e.g., aggravated assault, serious damage to property, etc.). Interestingly, most females and males believed it was important to ensure that arrests were not made against one particular group over another (e.g., in peaceful demonstrations and rallies, or in "ethnic" marches/gatherings that included two or more opposing groups). Officers agreed this tactic was necessary in order to avoid being perceived as supporting one group over another, which could turn an incident into a potentially violent situation (Corsianos, 2005; 1999b).

Alternatively, in violent situations that involved large crowds of people, where serious criminal violations were observed by the police, both male and female detectives tended to avoid arrests for the safety of the officers themselves and innocent bystanders. Some examples included bar fights that had "spilled out into the streets," and violent demonstrations. Detectives generally agreed that making arrests would not be wise, unless, of course, there was "adequate backup" (i.e., a high number of officers responding to the scene). Yet, even then, the number of officers in many of these types of situations was not enough to safely and effectively deal with the mobs of people (Corsianos, 2005; 1999b).

Indeed, there are gender differences in how officers respond to situations relating to maintaining the peace. Male detectives tended to use tactics that escalated situations and promoted negative confrontations between the police and the public. Whereas, female detectives were more likely to de-escalate potentially violent situations and maintain the peace. Some of the male detectives used tactics such as speaking in a condescending manner or using "humour" to deal with "uncooperative individuals." Others opted to make "jokes" to his partner relating to the suspect, while some appeared to be condescending in their use of language.

In one example, detective constables were investigating possible criminal violations at a frat party. While the detectives were speaking to the owner of the house, several intoxicated males started to berate the detectives, saying they were law students, knew their rights, and thus could not "be touched." A detective constable asked the most vocal of the group to identify himself. The individual responded by approaching the detective. As he moved towards the officer, he stepped over the border of the frat house's private property onto public property. This enabled the detective to immediately arrest him for intoxication in a public place. While arresting him, the officer, in a condescending manner, suggested to the law student that he should perhaps go back and reread the laws, seeing as how his law education had failed him here. These remarks outraged the intoxicated student, and he responded violently by kicking and pushing the officer. Subsequently, other officers intervened to assist in restraining him.

Another tactic used by male detectives to obtain information from belligerent, uncooperative, but otherwise lawful individuals was to provoke confrontations in order to make arrests. Some detectives antagonized individuals and encouraged them to be more vocal and vulgar to the point where pedestrians noticed and became onlookers. This subsequently empowered the detectives to legally arrest the individuals and perhaps lay the charge of "cause disturbance." Women officers were less likely to use these types of tactics and typically tried to reason and connect with citizens on a human level via the use of supportive, empathetic, and/or calming rhetoric (Corsianos, 2005; 2004; 1999b).

Gender differences in relation to officers' discretionary powers and detective work cannot be ignored. Gender differences become apparent when evaluating the power dynamics within the detective units and the police department overall, as well as the officers' interpretations of their roles as detectives and their relations and sense of commitment to members of the public. Female detectives share particular experiences as a result of their gender identity, and as the following chapter will demonstrate, their gender status ensures shared experiences of "oppression," regardless of how they are perceived by individual officers.

Questions
1. What role does gender play in officers' discretionary powers and detective work?
2. How can detective units become more accountable and transparent when choosing officers for detective assignments?
3. What is involved in becoming a "team player" within the detective culture?

CHAPTER 7

Gender Identity and Shared Policing Experiences

As products of the occupational culture of policing (McNulty, 1994; Dixon, 1992; Fyfe, 1991; Manning, 1997; Goldsmith, 1990; Hale, 1989; Shearing 1981; Doig, 1978; Davis, 1969; Skolnick, 1966), women officers share certain work-related experiences. However, as individuals representing the category "women" or "woman," they also share experiences of "oppression" relating to their gender. What becomes clear in all of the literature presented in the previous chapters is that what "oppresses" "women" officers is not the same as what "oppresses" "men" officers. "Women" and "men" may share experiences of "oppression" as members of the police culture, but female officers share different experiences of oppression as a result of their particular gender identity. This is different from the shared experiences of men as a result of their gender status.

The purpose of this chapter is to engage in a theoretical exercise to demonstrate how the category "women" or "woman" ensures shared experiences of "oppression" for all female officers, regardless of whether individual female officers identify them as such, and regardless of the different social categories they may represent (e.g., race, ethnicity, sexual orientation, age, etc.). The focus is on officers' perceptions of oppression which includes an analysis of female officers who fail or are reluctant to acknowledge they have experienced instances of oppression relating to their gender and to their roles as police officers. Perceptions of oppression are evaluated, since, in the field of criminology, many researchers will often accept the conclusions of their studies at face value, rather than exploring the relevance of various social and power dynamics at work within particular social relationships and social organizations. Perceptions of oppressive work experiences, or the lack thereof, relating to gender identity are explored in order to better understand how women share experiences of oppression, why some women define particular instances as oppressive whereas others do not, and what the implications of these dynamics may be.

Multiple Experiences versus Shared Experiences

Female officers represent diverse social categories including race, ethnicity, age, and sexual orientation, and criminological research must reject the essentialism inherent in treating women as part of a unitary category (Simpson, 1989). Studies examining criminal justice agents are starting to focus on the individual and organizational constructions of gender relating to both women and men (Britton, 1997; Miller, 1999; Pierce, 1995). As discussed in Chapter 3, postmodern feminists have been instrumental in identifying the multiple experiences of women. Postmodern feminism is often discussed as a theoretical perspective, but it also reflects an epistemological position because it raises questions about the nature of knowledge itself. This perspective can be understood as a philosophy or a critical method that challenges the values, ideals, and beliefs that dominated modernity and represent a specific period in the history of the Western world (Flax, 1990).

Postmodern feminists view individuals as contradictory and socially constructed. Thus "knowledge" is the result of multiple social forces and has varied meanings and interpretations. There is no one "truth," no universal essence. History is not necessarily progressive, it is nonlinear, and individuals are not rational beings who can provide an objective universal basis for knowledge (Flax, 1990). Moreover, history is read or understood through the limited perspective of the present (Lather, 1991). For these reasons, postmodern feminists challenge modernism's ethnocentric domination of "others" and are committed to utilizing nonuniversalizing nonessentialist theories of women. They assert there are multiple experiences among women and that not all women share the same experiences just because they belong to, or, represent, the category "women."

Experiences among women often vary depending on their social class, sexual orientation, race, ethnicity, age, disability, religious beliefs, level of formal education, etc., and differences among women who share certain social categories also exist. All social categories, including that of "women," must be questioned and deconstructed (Butler, 1992). According to postmodern feminists, modernist conceptions of gender, patriarchy, truth, and the social categories "women/woman" have been oppressive to women. They frequently serve to pigeonhole many women in terms of societal expectations and thus deny individual agency. These feminists assert that gender identity categories do not correspond to any unified and unifying essence. They are committed to grounding theory in lived experience and, therefore, understanding the world through subjective experiences while at the same time raising questions about the nature of knowledge.

However, while they address multiple identities and concerns with identity politics, in the process, postmodern feminists fail to recognize the current gendered social realities throughout the world generally, and in specific social arenas such as policing. This has disempowered people from coming together to advocate for social change and engage in political praxis (Ackoff, 1988; Flax, 1987; Harding, 1986a).

Gendered social realities in policing have been identified by a number of criminologists (Martin and Jurik, 2007; Corsianos, 2007a; 2005; Schulz, 2004a; 2004b; 1995; Heidensohn and Brown, 2000; Martin, 1990; 1980; Miller, 1999). Indeed, one should criticize the idea of a universal human nature, a universal canon of rationality that leads us to the "truth." However, this does not negate the fact that there are obvious similarities in the perceptions and/or experiences of women officers and that these necessarily create consequences in people's lives generally and in their policing lives specifically.

The concept of "women/woman" connotes particular images and characteristics that serve to define, influence, and control individuals assumed to be "women," and these categories serve to position females according to mainstream society's standards. For example, in Corsianos (2004), the majority of female officers identified "oppressive" experiences as defined by the researcher. Oppressive situations included instances where female officers were denied a voice or opportunity to act in their work as police officers and where this was perceived to be because of their sex. They also identified as oppressive certain situations where they were subjected to negative attitudes, ideas, or acts by their colleagues because of their status as women. Even the minority of female police officers who claimed they had not experienced oppression had indeed experienced it as defined by the researcher.

Experiential Essentialism

An individual's consciousness is shaped by social and cultural institutions. Through socialization, people develop their perceptions of the social world around them and learn the patterns of their culture. An individual's sense of self develops only with social experiences. In other words, the "self" is not innate and it does not exist at birth (Mead, 1962). Social experiences and interactions shape a person's fairly consistent patterns of acting and thinking. Thus, essentialist claims cannot be applied to explaining and understanding gender, since they do not allow for variation. Opponents of essentialism assert that gender is socially constructed. According to Spelman (1997), gender identity must be understood in terms of the imposition of classification systems, not in terms of individuals' psychological or biological states. For Spelman (1997: 176–77),

> positing an essential "womanness" has the effect of making women inessential in a variety of ways. First of all, if there is an essential womanness that all women have and have always had, then we needn't know anything about any woman in particular. For the details of her situation and her experience are irrelevant to her being a woman. Thus if we want to understand what "being a woman" means, we needn't investigate her individual life or any other woman's individual life. All those particulars become inessential to her being and our understanding of her being a woman. And so she also becomes inessential in the sense that she is not needed in order to produce the "story of woman." If all women have the same story "as women," we don't need a chorus of voices to tell the story.

"Experiential essentialism," on the other hand, allows for the recognition of shared experiences of oppression as products of the social world. It enables us to consider the similarities in thought and praxis that exist among categories of people sharing a particular culture. Individuals are observers who are continuously interpreting social systems, structures, images, and words. Yet, the sociology of culture cannot be separated from an analysis of the dominant ideologies in society that continue to promote inequalities along gender lines (as well as class, race, ethnicity, sexual orientation, etc.), preventing the majority from experiencing independent subjectivity. For instance, given historical patriarchal social forces, it is not surprising to see that so-called masculine traits, which are often defined in positive terms in North American society, are typically associated with males, while so-called feminine characteristics, which are often defined in negative terms, are often associated with females.

Experiential Essentialism and Policing

Women police officers continue to be criticized for not possessing the perceived necessary masculine traits required of "effective" crime-fighting police officers, and these attitudes impact them in their professional experiences (Charles, 1981; Miller, 1999). Others have discussed how policing is often viewed as masculine work that focuses on fighting crime (Martin, 1999; Martin and Jurik, 2007). They show how these perceptions often lead to claims that women are inherently not competent to participate in the crime-fighting/aggressive crime control model of policing (Heidensohn and Brown, 2000; Heidensohn, 1992; Bell, 1982; Drummond, 1976).

As mentioned earlier, even though studies on female police officers' performance have been conducted since 1972, and most report that female officers are as capable as male officers (Bartol et al., 1992; Grennan, 1987; Sichel et al., 1978; Bartlett and Rosenblum, 1977; Sherman, 1975; Bloch and Anderson, 1974), few studies have attempted to evaluate female police officers' performance in ways that do not emphasize situations and characteristics associated with definitions of "masculinity" (Corsianos, 2007a; 2005; Gerber, 2001; Morash and Greene, 1986). In other words, most studies assume that male police officers are the standard to which female officers must be compared. Alternatively, some research has indicated that female police officers (and female prison workers) have a less aggressive style than male officers and are better at de-escalating potentially violent situations (Corsianos, 2005; Belknap, 1991; Belknap and Shelley, 1993; Grennan, 1987; Bell, 1982), and that female officers may be more likely to have traits associated with "good policing," such as expressing empathy for female victims of rape and domestic abuse (Feinman, 1986; Homant and Kennedy, 1985; Kennedy and Homant, 1983; Price, 1974).

Additionally, female officers who are mothers are also often seen as not being "team players" within the organization and that they often "put the job second." This perception is linked, in part, to their roles as "mothers." For instance, there are times when they have to call in sick to care for their sick children on days when they cannot attend school/daycare, or when they have to deal with other family emergencies. This image of female officers as "working moms" can work against them when seeking promotions within the organization, while men's status as "fathers" is not so considered (Corsianos, 2007a).

Not surprisingly, further research suggests that women experience increased stress related to their token status (Bartol et al., 1992; Wertsch, 1998), sexist practices associated with gender-specific assignments (Britton, 1997), and harassment from male coworkers (Morash and Haar, 1995; Pogrebin and Poole, 1997). Moreover, a study of female police officers conducted in Canada examined the effects of personal discrimination on two forms of psychological disengagement from police work: discounting and devaluing. The study found that women officers were more likely to discount personnel evaluations when they experienced more personal discrimination, which, in turn, led them to devalue the importance of their job (Tougas et al., 2005). Also, Corsianos (2004) found that all female officers shared experiences of oppression, whether or not they defined them as such. Other feminist criminologists are committed to raising questions relating to whether women officers can experience agency when they appropriate patriarchal definitions of occupational performances of female bodies as promoted in traditional male arenas such as the paramilitaristic policing system.

Gender has been socially constructed to imply various relatively fixed qualities by many people. It has been constructed to represent various "truths" and regardless of how different female officers' personal experiences as individuals have been, there are overwhelming similarities in certain experiences that impact their lives (Corsianos, 2004). Gender differences can only be understood relationally and situationally, and regardless of individual differences in social experiences, all female officers, despite differences in race, ethnicity, age, sexual orientation, etc., have at various levels shared experiences of oppression as a result of being defined or "seen" as women. As representations of these social categories (i.e., "women" or "woman"), they have experienced forms of oppression directly and/or indirectly, whether consciously recognized or not; that is, in the police organizational structure and its social systems, in everyday police rhetoric, in particular conversations with colleagues and/or supervisors, in police images, and in officers' assumptions about them.

All of these forms of oppression are related to particular social constructions of gender, which in turn have been shaped and influenced by patriarchal social forces historically and continue to be shaped and influenced by these hegemonic social forces presently (Gramsci, 1957). Unlike postmodern feminists, experiential essentialist claims allow for a critique of unjust macro-structures like the institution of policing, and do not repudiate broad categories like gender. Specifically, experiential essentialism allows us to consider various social "truths" as not natural.

For instance, in Corsianos's study (2004), various forms of oppression were experienced by all 60 female detectives in the study's sample. Sixty-three per cent of the participants believed they had experienced "oppressive" experiences as defined by the researcher. The concept of "oppression" was used to refer to unjust treatment within policing, which included exclusion from participating in particular areas within the field and being subjected to other forms of sexist and misogynistic acts and ideas. More specifically, oppressive experiences relating to gender and policing were defined by Corsianos as instances where female officers were denied a voice or opportunity to act in their work as police officers and where this was perceived to be because of their status as "women," or where they were subjected to negative attitudes, ideas, or acts by their colleagues because of their status as "women." However, 37 per cent of the respondents in Corsianos's study said they had not experienced oppression as defined by the researcher.

Similarities in oppressive experiences were identified by approximately two-thirds of the female officers in Corsianos's study (2004). Oppressive experiences shared by the majority of the participants were numerous. Many were frustrated with the lack of women in policing generally (approximately 15 per cent of the department studied consisted of female officers) and in specialized and/or high-level decision-making positions. In particular, they were troubled by the lack of female detectives, and, more specifically, the lack of females in permanent detective positions versus the temporary ones, as well as the lack of females in upper management positions.

Other female officers in Corsianos's study (2004) discussed incidents relating to male officers' sexist attitudes or intolerance of female officers, particularly if they were physically smaller. All 38 female officers (i.e., the 63 per cent who identified being oppressed) shared stories of having to put up with various sexist comments voiced by some male officers (e.g., unwanted comments about their physical appearance, comments relating to higher ranking female officers who had "probably slept their way to the top," etc.). One detective constable noted, "On any given shift, I could expect one of them to make some ridiculous comment on how I looked" (Corsianos, 2004: 72-73).

Others voiced concerns relating to male officers "second-guessing" their abilities to defend themselves and other officers in potentially dangerous situations, therefore preferring to have male officers offer them assistance. They shared stories about overhearing male officers talking about not wanting to work with some of the smaller females on the job because they felt they would "not receive adequate backup," or making "jokes" about women's "lack of physical strength" and height (Corsianos, 2004). One officer stated, "I hated the comments about my shoe size; hey (officer's name), they'd say, I wouldn't want to run into you in a dark alley … (laugh)" (Corsianos, 2004: 73). Alternatively to the male officers who resented being paired with the females, some of the male officers did not support the pairing of two women together because this was perceived as a "weakness"; rather, they preferred that women be paired with men.

Interviewees also shared stories of male officers who tried to make it their business to learn about the female officers' private sexual relationships. According to one officer, she was constantly dealing with personal questions from male colleagues about her "love life" and whether she was "getting any." Another officer stated, "Because I made every effort to keep my private life private, then it was assumed that I must be lesbian." Another officer noted that it was not uncommon to hear male officers talking about who they thought was "hot" and "whose pants they thought they had a chance of getting into" (Corsianos, 2004: 73).

Oppressive experiences also involved more senior male colleagues who took on the role of "mentor," frequently giving unsolicited "advice" to some of the newer female officers. The females in the department who frequently appropriated the patriarchal tools used to stroke the egos of those above them were often rewarded via job support, such as obtaining positive evaluation reports, invitations to important informal gatherings with other police personnel, promotions, enrollment in training courses, etc. However, female officers who were seen as "deviant" or "rocking the boat" were closely policed by their supervisors. One female officer noted, "I know they can't stand me. I consider myself a strong woman and would like to see many changes in this department as far as women are concerned. I make my opinions known and they can't stand it. In the meantime, I have to put up with a lot of nonsense" (Corsianos, 2004: 74).

This majority of female officers (63 per cent) who, at various levels, recognized oppressive instances relating to their gender believed that systemic gender discrimination and sexist attitudes were part of the policing system (Corsianos, 2004). They were also often reminded of the negative consequences of being "different" and/or challenging the "status quo." Others were merely dismissed as being "deviant," troublesome, angry, or confused by both male and female colleagues, the latter of whom failed or were reluctant to recognize the impact of particular patriarchal social forces on the politics of gender constructions, or who had at various degrees accepted it consciously.

Interestingly, those who professed that their status as women did not lead to any oppressive work experiences had convinced themselves there is gender equality in policing (Corsianos, 2004). Examples here included female officers who stated they had never seen or experienced sexism within the police department. For instance, one officer stated that throughout her policing career, she had always been treated as "one of the guys." Some felt that women could move up the ranks if they worked hard enough, and others believed that it was just a matter of time before the department witnessed its first female chief of police.

Many of these same officers were unaware of the number of women employed as officers within their own department, or how many had served in detective units and in management positions. Some of these same officers had at times apologized and/or tried to explain to male officers the reasons for their various actions, ideas, speech, or for being "too aggressive" or confident. They had even apologized for, or tried to explain, their style of dress while off duty and socializing with their peers.

Yet, they claimed they did not feel silenced in their work because of their status as women. They believed they had a voice and were not subjected to negative attitudes, ideas, or acts because of their gender status. They, therefore, rejected the idea of women's "oppressions" within policing specifically, as well as the general concept of patriarchy.

The assertions of these officers signify the power of patriarchal conditioning and the socially created need for some female officers to belong to the "boy's club." However, even though they did not consciously recognize "oppressive" experiences, they all shared stories that qualified as "oppressive" as defined by the researcher (Corsianos, 2004). The majority of the participants occupied low-level ranks within the organization, even though the vast majority had served as police officers for more than eight years. They were subjected to various forms of oppression, which included paternalistic acts and attitudes; derogatory or "humorous" comments made against female officers; inquiries made by male officers regarding their sexual relationships; and exclusion from various specialized units, promotions, and even from various formal and informal social gatherings.

The majority of female officers (85 per cent) in the study, which included the 37 per cent who said they had never experienced oppression, believed that there were certain innate differences between women and men that often made women more effective in their roles as officers (Corsianos, 2004). These included the belief that women are naturally more nurturing and emotional than men, and that women have a "maternal instinct" and therefore are better able to deal with particular "sensitive" issues relating to both older and younger children. Interestingly, none of these officers consciously recognized that these particular beliefs served to create oppressive instances. Perhaps these attitudes explain why more women served in particular detective units that relied on women to perform various gender-specific tasks.

Shared Experiences of "Oppression" and Real Consequences

What is clear here is that one cannot abandon the idea of shared experiences of oppression as a result of the category "women/woman" as some postmodern feminists have done. To fail to acknowledge the similarities means that we must then dismiss all of the feminist and critical criminological literature that identifies several shared experiences among female officers. Officers share experiences of oppression relating to their gender whether they consciously recognize them or not. They do not necessarily have the exact same experiences, nor are they oppressed in the same ways, but they certainly share experiences of oppression. An experience can still be considered "oppressive," even if not recognized by the individual as such, because there are accompanying effects to that oppression (e.g., not being invited to participate in police-strategic planning; not being invited to important social gatherings; not being promoted and/or not getting into certain specialized units that have a significant impact on salary due to the change in rank, possibilities for overtime, etc.; not being allowed to "pair up" with other females, etc.). These impact female officers' lives on a variety of levels, regardless of whether or not they define them as "oppressive" and recognize the influencing factors relating to the cause of their experiences.

The dominant perceptions of gender that define "women," for example, as weaker, emotional, irrational, and passive, and "men" as stronger, aggressive, courageous, and rational privilege males in the vast majority of social arenas and produce significant consequences for the lives of all women officers regardless of their differences in race, age, sexual orientation, etc. Unfortunately, some female officers are unaware of these hegemonic (Gramsci, 1957) social forces and thus fail to see how the above mentioned "truths" affect their lives directly and/or indirectly.

Shared Experiences and Patriarchal Social Conditioning

As discussed in Chapter 4, female officers either accept the patriarchal social order or various aspects of it consciously or not, or they challenge the various aspects of patriarchal positions of power. Some are able to recognize the power of patriarchal conditioning. They realize that at times they are being silenced in their professional lives, however, they learn to tolerate or accept a degree of disempowerment in order to survive and be accepted. Therefore, they perform (i.e., physically, verbally, emotionally, and/or ideologically) in specific ways in order to be rewarded and accepted in various dominant social circles They conform to the various aspects of patriarchal dominant ideologies, which are embedded within the paramilitaristic organizational police structure, because there is an investment in conforming and the investment can be financial, emotional, and/or socio-psychological. However, others have accepted certain levels of disempowerment for survival and/or social acceptance while at the same time challenging various aspects of patriarchal conditioning where resistance does not necessarily have negative consequences to their overall lives within policing.

Then there are the female officers who do not identify as having experienced oppression in their positions as police officers. Some, for instance, believe that certain gender differences are innate, or that there are no gender differences today because women have gained equality with men and have moved into a post-feminist era where the politics of feminism are no longer necessary. These women are not aware of any particular power dynamics and accept the patriarchal social order as genuine. This may also be because changes have been made to various department rules, social structures, and systems to create the image of a progressive egalitarian police department and the illusion of equality between the sexes. However, sexist ideology is so pervasive in our society that it makes it difficult and challenging for many to recognize that dominant ideologies have been born and bred within patriarchal social structures and systems.

There is also a small percentage of female officers who will not accept the current positions of patriarchal power and will make strong attempts to challenge them. They are the ones who, for instance, will not tolerate sexist comments or accept being denied entrance into certain units or training courses. These are the women who will voice their opinions, verbally complain to immediate supervisors, write letters to members of management, act alone in their investigative decisions if need be, file complaints with their police associations, and even file lawsuits against their departments.

Penny Harrington and Lenna Bradburn are excellent examples of these types of women. Harrington sued the Portland Police Department 22 times for a number of gender discriminatory practices, including the denial of promotions for women, as well as the denial of access to certain areas in the policing field and unequal pay. As was noted in Chapter 1, Harrington would ultimately become the first woman chief of a large police agency in the US in the modern policing era (Harrington, 1999). Similarly, Bradburn was very vocal in her complaints against systemic gender discrimination that prevented women from gaining access into certain units, wearing the forage hat, and participating in the annual police march, to name but a few. Bradburn would ultimately become the first woman chief of police in Canada (again, see Chapter 1). Both Harrington and Bradburn achieved positions of power by obtaining the highest rank within the police organization. Similarly, there have been other women who have moved into high-level decision-making positions through promotions, political networking, training courses, awards, community appreciation letters, etc. However, they remain a minority.

One must not forget that even the changes that have been created to apparently work towards a gender-neutral society have been produced within a patriarchal society and complement patriarchal systems like policing. Also, identification within these patriarchal ideologies is so pervasive, so internalized, that as individuals speak, act, think, and feel, many are not only unaware of the origins of the politics of the gendered body but often believe these to be their own "truths." Many female officers believe they have choices that are somehow removed from social conditions and are the result of individual agency. Also, many women, regardless of race, ethnicity, age, sexual orientation, etc., internalize many of the mainstream ideologies that promote the gender hierarchy.

Futhermore, it is a common practice to categorize people based on gender-specific, as well as heterosexist stereotypes. For example, some single female officers who have very short hair, do not wear makeup, perform in more aggressive ways, and resist being in intimate relationships with any male officers at work are often perceived to be "dykes" by many of their male colleagues. For instance, in Corsianos (2004), four officers in particular had short "butchy hair," did not wear makeup, and did not share their private lives with anyone at work, nor did they date any of their colleagues. All of this led some of their fellow officers to conclude they were lesbians, but they were wrong in all four of these cases.

Questioning Constructions of Gender

It is important to continuously question modernist constructions such as gender and deconstruct them in order to learn more about the processes by which they are formed. This constant critical exercise can begin to challenge many of the assumptions, beliefs, attitudes, and values that many officers and citizens have of female and male police officers. It also allows us to question whether increases in female representation can change policing systems. Can the presence of more women serve to redefine policing, or will the image of inclusion serve to promote a feminized social control discourse while hiding the fact that policing remains committed to preserving the so-called masculine characteristics of aggressive crime control, discipline, and punishment? Gendered findings, assumptions, and expectations must cease to exist in order to gain certain freedoms.

Postmodern feminists assert that their insistence on continuous questioning will free us from oppressive socially constructed categories. However, at this time, it is dangerous to accept claims that dismiss the use of any categories of subjects that can convey some type of homogeneous meaning with regard to the perceptions and experiences of "women" and "men." These claims suggest a political naïveté, and they disempower groups of individuals from engaging in political practice, especially given the evidence of shared experiences of oppression relating to gender constructions.

Admittedly, many feminists have relied on praxis to advocate consciousness raising and change and, in the process, have adopted modes of theorizing that embrace the foundationalist "objective" metanarratives criticized by postmodernists. However, it is important to not rely on normative theories that utilize metanarratives, but rather to depend on social theories grounded in the particular histories of women's experiences, thought processes, and ideas as products of the patriarchal social order. This can allow us to depend on social theories of power in society in order to better understand people's perceptions and social experiences within policing (and in other institutions), in order to show the very real effects of patriarchy (i.e., the social consequences).

For Butler, the body becomes its gender through a series of acts that are renewed and revised through time. "Just as a script may be enacted in various ways, and just as the play requires both text and interpretation, so the gendered body acts its part in a culturally restricted corporeal space and enacts interpretations within the confines of already existing directives" (i.e., the social norms) (Butler, 1997: 410). She states (1997: 403) that

> for both Beauvoir and Merleau-Ponty, the body is understood to be an active process of embodying certain cultural and historical possibilities, a complicated process of appropriation which any phenomenological theory of constitution needs to describe. In order to describe the gendered body, a phenomenological theory of constitution requires an expansion of the conventional view of acts to mean both that which constitutes meaning and that through which meaning is performed or enacted.

According to de Beauvoir (1974: 38), "One is not born, but rather, becomes a woman." Similarly, Merleau-Ponty (1962) asserts the body is a "historical idea" and not a "natural species." However, Merleau-Ponty's phenomenological analysis has been criticized by feminists for its failure to recognize gender differences. For Butler (1997: 404-405),

> to be a woman is to have become a woman, to compel the body to conform to an historical ideal of "woman," to induce the body to become a cultural sign, to materialize oneself in obedience to an historically delimited possibility, and to do this as a sustained and repeated corporeal project ... indeed, those who fail to do their gender right are regularly punished. Because there is neither an "essence" that gender expresses or externalizes nor an objective ideal to which gender aspires; because gender is not a fact, the various acts of gender creates the idea of gender, and without those acts, there would be no gender at all. Gender is, thus, a construction that regularly conceals its genesis.

Riley (1988) examines, in the manner of Foucault (1979), shifting historical constructions of the category "women" in relation to other categories such as "the mind," "the body," "nature," and "the social." In addition, she asserts that "'women' is a simultaneous foundation of and an irritant to feminism, and that is constitutionally so" (Riley, 1988: 17).

To reiterate, all "women" share experiences of "oppression" even if they feel differently. Clearly, there are various consequences to being perceived and defined as representing particular so-called feminine characteristics in organizations such as policing that overwhelmingly support and promote so-called masculine traits. It is important to recognize that when studying "women" and "men" in the policing field, one must always be aware of the politics of the gendered body. It is important to consciously recognize the experienced differences along gender lines, analyze them and their consequences, and work towards making the necessary changes ideologically, socially, and structurally. This constant push to raising consciousness can help us move from a society of socially constrained "women" and "men," to a society that ceases to produce shared experiences of oppression among groups/categories of people.

Questions

1. How does the category "women/woman" currently ensure shared experiences of oppression among female officers?
2. Does the category "men" produce shared experiences of oppression for male officers? Explain.
3. What are the implications to suggesting there are no shared experiences among "women" in fields such as policing?

CHAPTER 8

Effecting Change through the Use of Feminist Methods and Action-Research

This chapter addresses the importance of feminist methods in identifying exclusionary practices in the production of "knowledge" as they relate to policing, as well as the need for action-research. The use of feminist methods can enable individuals to begin to reconceptualize "knowledge" as it relates to gender and policing. Equally important is action-research, as it aims to convert research into action to make a positive difference in the lives of many people. In other words, in addition to the need for new interpretations of "knowledge" is the commitment to creating equitable practices in policing and making deliberate attempts to introduce feminist findings into the policing arena where access to this information has been nonexistent. In the process of effecting change, one must focus on the materialist analyses while at the same time operating at the level of ideas and ideology that are embedded in material institutional systems and practices.

Effecting Change through the Use of Feminist Methods

Feminists are aware of the impact that exclusionary practices have on the conduct of research, the areas being studied, and the societal effects. Through the use of feminist methods, one can effect change by utilizing different approaches to discuss social experiences relating to gender and policing and to the production of academic knowledge. One can also encourage change through the use of feminist methods, as they relate not only to matters of inclusion but also to an analytical and methodological reconceptualization of research topics, methods, and knowledge.

As discussed in Chapter 2 (feminist methods), there is no one set of methodological approaches that are distinctly feminist, but rather feminists use a variety of means in collecting data. Interviews, surveys, participant observation, secondary analysis, and experiments can all be feminist methods depending on how they are approached and utilized. Feminist researchers use any and every means available for investigating the social conditions of women in a sexist society. Even though there are no specific methods/techniques or theoretical frameworks (views of society that guide thinking and research) that are seen as distinctly feminist, feminist researchers are unified in the topics they research, the questions they raise, and the ways they position themselves.

Feminist research also encourages individuals to recognize that in social research studies notions of objectivity and subjectivity are false dichotomies. These concepts are the products of social and institutional practices. Feminist research on the police, and in other areas, presents them as such and aims at deconstructing them. Feminists, such as Smith (1990), encourage individuals to engage in an alternative way of thinking about research and knowledge building by refuting the positivist notion that there is a fixed social reality that cannot be changed. Interpretation and subjectivity become part of the process of producing new forms of knowledge. Many feminist researchers (Smith, 1990; Haraway, 1991; Jaggar, 1997; Longino, 1999) are committed to presenting new forms of inquiry outside of the positivist empirical framework that embrace the idea of objective value-free research methods and the possibility for neutral generalizable research findings.

Feminist research is not limited to topics on or about women, but rather questions are framed, results are interpreted, and suggestions for social change are made in ways that recognize the need for social justice and equitable practices, and the relevance of gender categories in our social world. For example, in Corsianos's research on the police (2003; 2001; 1999b; 1997), the majority of participants were men, but feminist approaches to the research were key. They enabled the researcher to give recognition to the centralized patriarchal ideologies reflected in current policing systems and structures.

In the pursuit for social change, identity categories remain necessary components of feminist research on the police. They are socially and politically constructed categories that speak to gendered experiences and forms of "oppression." As discussed in Chapter 7, it is important to recognize the different kinds of experiences and forms of oppression among "women'; that is, for those representing different social categories (e.g., race, class, sexual orientation, etc.), as well as for those who share particular social categories. This statement does not suggest, as do positivist researchers, that there is objective value-free knowledge that can be attained through the application of neutral value-free instruments of measurement. As stated earlier, it is not suggested here that all women have the exact same experiences or that they are oppressed in the same ways, but rather that they share experiences of oppression. This is very different from empiricists who are committed to the basic epistemological and methodological characteristics of positivist research; that is, the application of value-free research methods and the attainment of objective research findings. Empiricists strive to achieve knowledge that is "objective" and "truthful." They seek to understand the social world by grounding their methodologies in what can be experienced and measured by their senses and through the use of "value-free" methods.

With regard to policing, one can assert that all female officers, regardless of individual differences in experience, share particular experiences. They have shared similarities in work experiences and in the experiences of other women in the paid work force. By recognizing shared experiences, as well as understanding how women are historically situated and strongly influenced and shaped by current patriarchal social forces, individual officers have the potential to challenge many current inequities and encourage social change.

Women are not powerless in bringing forth change. By recognizing shared experiences of oppression, people have the ability to recognize various "truths" about their material realities, and are then able to analyze them and make necessary changes. Wise and Stanley (1984; 1987: 14) note that "'oppression' should be seen as an extraordinarily complex process in which women are only rarely and in extremis totally powerless and in which, ordinarily, women utilise a range of resources — verbal, interactional and other — in order to 'fight back.'" Similarly, Anleu (1992) notes that social systems and structures simultaneously limit and permit variation and resistance in the workplace. Making arguments that assume that all women are passive victims of masculine dominance, or presenting all women as being the "same" or "different" are very one-dimensional actions that ignore class, race, cultural, and situational differences among women, as well as personality differences (Martin and Jurik, 2007). As Smith (1990; 1987; 1981) states in her writings, feminist research practice should always recognize women as actively "constructing" and interpreting the social processes and relations that constitute their everyday realties.

Furthermore, feminist research insists on the need for useful knowledge, theory, and praxis, as well as "unalienated knowledge." According to Stanley (1990), this type of knowledge is that which locates the product of the academic feminist labour process within a concrete analysis of the process of production itself. In feminist terms, unalienated knowledge refers to the following:

- the researcher/theorist is grounded as an actual person in a concrete setting;
- understanding and theorizing are located and treated as material activities and not as unanalysable metaphysical 'transcendent' ones different in kind from those of 'mere people';
- the 'act of knowing' is examined as the crucial determiner of 'what is known' (Stanley, 1990: 12).

Moreover, feminist approaches shift the epistemological basis of the completed research by presenting alternative, or different kinds of knowledge. As Stanley (1990) recognizes, nonfeminist research can produce "unalienated knowledge" and also propose a different kind of knowledge than that provided by Cartesian scientism, however, what makes certain types of research "feminist" is the relation between epistemology and ontology.

That is, 'feminism' is not merely a 'perspective', a way of seeing; nor even this plus an epistemology, a way of knowing; it is also an ontology, or a way of being in the world. What is distinctly 'feminist' about a concern with research processes is that this constitutes an invitation to explore the conditions and circumstances of a feminist ontology, with all its slips and contradictions certainly, but a feminist ontology nonetheless (Stanley, 1990: 14).

There is not an ontology attached to the social category of "women," and there is no one universal nature that leads us to a particular "truth." Rather, there exist many diverse human experiences that vary between and within classes, races, ethnic backgrounds, sexual orientation, education levels, etc. Yet, at the same time, one can make "experiential essentialist claims" that deal with social "truths" and not natural ones. For instance, experiential essentialism enables us to recognize commonalities in the perceptions of experienced differences between police officers. It also allows for a critique of unjust macro-structures, such as the institution of policing, and does not repudiate broad categories like gender, sexual orientation, class, race, etc.

As discussed in Chapter 7, Corsianos (2004) noted there are similarities in officers' perceptions and/or experiences relating to their gender status. These shared experiences are seen in the beliefs, attitudes, and behaviour of the police who work within a particular police structure and culture, and they necessarily create consequences in female officers' personal and professional lives. However, Corsianos's study (2004), as a feminist ontology, focused on and analyzed the perceptions individuals have of their personal experiences and the world around them and utilized a feminist epistemology as this approach became embedded in the research process. Feminist epistemology raises a series of questions relating to what qualifies as "knowledge" and who has the power to possess and determine "knowledge." Moreover, many feminist researchers have examined the relationship between epistemology and ontology (Harding, 1986a; 1986b; Hartsock, 1983; Flax, 1983; Smith, 1981).

The use of feminist methods can help identify the exclusionary practices used in the production of academic knowledge, and analyze the impact they have on the conduct of research, the areas being studied, and the societal effects. Feminists methods can also offer a reconceptualization of knowledge. Unfortunately, some feminists' writings present unique challenges to social action. For instance, postmodern feminists have heavily relied on social constructionism, interpretation, difference, and plurality to the extent that they can no longer identify commonalities in social experiences. These have attracted much criticism for moving feminist issues out of the realm of methodology and into the realm of epistemology. This, in turn, makes it very difficult, if not impossible, to work to promote social change.

Postmodern feminists are viewed as being "the opposite" of empiricists. They recognize the limitations of grand theories as explanations about social reality. They make the argument that these "truths" are socially constructed and that they are self-legitimating explanations that serve particular interests. As a result, postmodern feminists aim to deconstruct totalizing categories and make room for multiple inter-pretations and "truths."

However, the recent attention given to the multiple interpretations of social real-ity does not address some of the common experiences shared by women, nor does it promote social change that can make a real positive difference in the quality of people's lives today. As some feminists point out, there are risks and dangers with the increasing fragmentation among and between feminist researchers, theorists, and activists (Hesse-Biber, Gilmartin, and Lydenberg, 1999). It is important to not lose sight of the feminist struggle to introduce new forms of knowledge by documenting the realities of gender differences in different social arenas, and, in turn, to promote positive changes in the quality of people's lived realities. By recognizing the many differences in experiences between and among categories of women, one moves away from the idea that there is one "truth" for all women; that is from presenting or viewing women as a group of people with uniform experiences. Multiple voices are vital in feminist research and praxis, but this does not change the fact that different realties emerge in particular social arenas like policing that lead individuals repre-senting various social categories to having shared experiences, whether consciously recognized or not.

The need to encourage changes in policing along gender lines is ongoing and is itself subject to change. Women's experiences in particular settings such as policing may change over time, which does not make them any less real. For instance, in the 1960s and 1970s, women fought to gain entry as sworn officers in policing. Today, female officers are engaged in struggles related to a number of issues that include eliminating some of the physical requirement policies that emphasize upper body strength, creating supportive childcare policies, promoting gender-neutral assign-ments, etc. As Brooks (2007: 57) asserts, "We can treat women's standpoints on a particular issue or set of issues as legitimate, as serious, as grounded in social reality while also acknowledging these standpoints' location within a moving historical context; that is, that they can change over time."

Action-Research: Exploring Possibilities

Action-research is an important step in the pursuit for social change. It is important to conduct feminist research, but it is equally important to convert the research into action. Smart (1995), one of the founders of feminist criminology, encourages indi-viduals to rethink conceptions of justice as a strategy for change. Thus, the goal should be to redefine and transform the nature and operation of our current polic-ing system and structure, as well as the socio-economic and political system, and feminist analysis is central in this quest.

Action-research that pursues feminist goals can "raise consciousness"; that is, introduce people to alternative possibilities that can bring about more equitable practices. It can also change consciousness when people consider situations and "realities" in a new light. According to Bologh (1984), the goal of feminist action is the process of continuous change that can be accomplished by using theoretical frameworks and methods that are antipositivist and antipatriarchal. For Smart (1995), a deconstructionist approach to the study of criminology and the criminal justice system is necessary. By thinking of alternate conceptions of "justice," one can recognize the limitations of, and problems with, focusing solely on the law as an instrument for change. Moreover, Bristow and Esper (1988) argue that feminist action-research must be tied to specific implementation goals.

Feminist action-research should first strive to evaluate individual and organizational behaviour to look for biases from within. Kamens (1981) asserts that evaluation in mainstream research often involves using the stated goals or purposes of the research as the criteria for evaluation and does not typically question them (i.e., the goals and purposes). She further adds that in order for the work to be feminist, the evaluator must articulate her justice values and apply them to the process, not only the content, of the evaluated program. According to Fetterley (1978:42), "At its best, feminist criticism is a political act, whose aim is not simply to interpret the world but to change it by changing the consciousness of those who read and their relation to what they read." Some feminists (Epstein, 1986; 1973) believe that feminist research is inherently linked to action, while others (Lather, 1988) claim that research is feminist only if it is linked to action.

Feminist action-research raises consciousness and is political because it demystifies. It raises alternative explanations for some of the current problems in policing. In the demystification framework, by obtaining knowledge of various patriarchal social forces as a first step, one can create the potential for change. As stated earlier, feminist research is not limited to topics on or about women, but rather questions are framed, results are interpreted, and suggestions for social change are made in ways that recognize the need for equitable systems and practices, as well as the relevance of gender categories in how their use and acceptance produce differences in experiences between the sexes.

A. Action-Research in Policing

Action-research on the police should be committed to documenting the activities and experiences of particular groups, conceptualizing people's behaviour and social systems and structures as an expression of power, and utilizing the research to help officers and others understand and change their situations. Introducing feminist findings into arenas such as policing, where these types of "knowledge" are not presented, is needed to encourage change among the officers themselves, as well as future officers. This demands the use of feminist approaches in presentation and strategic use of rhetoric, as well as reference to feminist academic studies to begin to repudiate the status quo. Indeed, it takes a lot of energy, patience, tactfulness, dedication, and time to present individuals with scenarios that they can ultimately understand and use, and to inform them of the patriarchal origins and operations of policing as linked to many of the current police societal problems. Clearly, these are not the scenarios presented in police departments, police colleges, and police academies. Equally important to the commitment to critical evaluation and new interpretations of "knowledge" is the commitment to creating equitable systems and practices and making deliberate attempts to introduce feminist findings into policing fields where access to this kind of research has been nonexistent.

This dedication to change includes introducing feminist findings in formal and informal presentations to officers and students in police departments, colleges/academies, law enforcement programs, and policing classes. Action-research is necessary to offer officers and/or students a different theoretical and ideological framework that can hopefully lead them to make changes in their individual roles as current or future police officers in terms of how they address gender issues, how they "see" and ultimately treat people, and how they view policing and their respective roles. These findings should be strategically structured, and the discussions and materials should be presented in ways that do not make them appear to be threatening and/or antipolice. Undoubtedly, the terms "feminism" and "feminists" continue to be perceived, to varying degrees by the mainstream culture as being synonymous with "antimen," or "man-hating." This is clearly apparent to the thousands of academics who discuss gender-related issues in their criminology classes. According to the National Opinion Research Center (2003), 20 per cent of American adults express attitudes in opposition to feminism. There has been little improvement in feminist attitudes in recent years, and more men than women are antifeminist in their behaviour and beliefs. Thus, significant time and careful attention must be dedicated to critically evaluating the relevance of gender in individuals' lives in order for officers and students to gain a new appreciation for feminism and feminist theories and learn to apply them to people's experiences in multiple areas, including the criminal justice system and policing more specifically.

Action-research should aim at encouraging officers to think "outside the box" and to think of possible tangible tools they can use in their day-to-day police work to apply more equitable practices. Action-research should strive to accomplish this while recognizing that officers currently continue to work in a very traditional policing structure and system that promotes particular perceptions on the part of the police, especially pertaining to the purpose and function of policing, as well as to who should be policed. In many ways, this calls on officers to begin to deconstruct "crime" and "criminals" and commit to the social transformation of society to make it more egalitarian. By being exposed to feminist research, officers can begin to think critically of their individual policing roles, the function of policing, and the relevance of the police image to various members of the public.

Research on policing may lead officers (and students) to question why they became police officers in the first place (or why they want to pursue a policing career). It may lead them to question why many officers continue to perceive community policing (CP) as not constituting "real police work." Why is CP viewed as being "feminine"? Where does this perception come from and why is it threatening to so many officers? These questions are meant to help them begin to think critically about the contradictions within police departments and address some of the contradictions in their personal perceptions of policing, including the focus on crime control versus their desired professional goals. They may come to realize that specific CP initiatives can actually accomplish specific desired results that cannot be achieved by traditional aggressive law enforcement. Effective CP approaches can make a real difference in areas such as crime control, the quality of police service, and in improving the public image of the police.

In responding to particular crimes, feminist writings can help officers "see" people as human beings (including the ones who come across as bitter, angry, and/or antipolice). On many levels, they may come to recognize "the sociology" of people's choices; that is, the social factors that influence/guide, allow, and/or prevent choices. For instance, officers and/or students may come to recognize the social realities of some of the survivors/victims of domestic violence. Some women are without the necessary options to help them leave violent relationships; that is, housing may be difficult, there may not be any shelters in the area to offer them short-term support, jobs may be scarce, they may not have emotional and/or financial support from relatives and/or friends, etc.

Officers and students should be exposed to research on the power of socialization and how it influences so-called life choices. For instance, a history of familial violence as a child, being subjected to verbal abuse, and growing up without love and stability or positive role models can contribute to levels of low self-esteem and instability. These experiences can leave some people feeling lost, without the emotional strength to leave their abusive partners. These experiences can also shed some light on why some women "choose" to appeal to the salvation ethic, where the abuser is seen as troubled and where the woman believes she can take care of him and "make him better," or why some women "choose" to see the violence as being beyond the abuser's control. These women often blame external forces for their own violent experiences. Alternatively, other women come to accept the abuse as part of their lives. This knowledge would serve to expose officers and/or students to some of the difficulties encountered by individuals living in abusive relationships, as well as help them realize that in a different set of social circumstances, "those women" could very well be people they know and love. This exposure to the research can help eliminate the common police practice of victim-blaming and of not viewing these domestic violence cases as crimes.

By introducing gender stereotypes relating to police officers in policing arenas, gender neutrality in policing can be promoted. The message that both men and women have the equal potential of being capable police officers must be clearly articulated. By learning about some of the concerns relating to the heavy reliance on upper body strength as a predictor of officer competence and effectiveness, and how intelligence and strategic decision-making promotes officer safety, one can begin to critically assess some of the physical tests used in the application process. Officers and students would become better informed as to the applicability, or lack thereof, of particular physical tests to the job of police officer. Discussions could be had on how officers on the job are no longer subject to physical tests; the role of adrenaline in dangerous situations; the role of officer safety training and defensive tactics; the research showing that female officers are less likely to be involved in violent confrontations due to their ability to communicate more effectively; and the standard operating procedures that dictate police conduct in particular situations.

In addition, through consciousness raising around gender stereotypes, officers may come to realize the double standard that exists when male and female officers make mistakes on the job. When serious mistakes are made by male officers, the mistakes are not used to "paint all male officers with the same brush," but rather criticism is offered to the individual officer regarding his actions. However, the opposite is often true with female officers, particularly in small police departments. An increased awareness of the hurtful and negative effects of gender stereotypes can encourage positive change.

Research showing the effects of gender stereotypes and gossip concerning officers' private lives, including their sexual lives and sexual orientation, must also be made available to current and future officers. Research that describes the problems with the paramilitaristic police style that encourages "war-like" ideologies and respect and loyalties to the hierarchical "chain of command" can raise consciousness and increase the likelihood that individuals will consider the importance of a system and structure that promotes team work, accountability, and equal quality of service to all communities. Once again, the goal is to share knowledge about the different possibilities available in the hope that these individuals will make positive changes to policing systems and organizational structures in how they address gender issues, in how they perceive and respond to different groups of people, and in how they view policing and their respective roles.

Action-research strives to expose the discourse that reinforces social and cultural stereotypes. By documenting the androcentric biases and stereotypes in police work and police research, the effects of these biases and stereotypes begin to lessen. Moreover, action-research can make a difference at some level, whether it impacts one person or thousands of people. There is no point in just talking about the issues without making deliberate attempts to bring about change; that is, change that can create a better society. As Denzin (2000: 898) states, "Writing is not an innocent practice"; it is a powerful tool that can help change the world. Research and academic writings can serve as significant tools that shape and influence our culture, and can be "central to the workings of a free democratic society" (Denzin, 2000:

899). However, it is important to introduce these writings into arenas such as policing that have been reluctant and/or hostile to considering and accepting alternative ways of thinking about policing and "doing" policing.

Over the years, the author has learned of and/or witnessed degrees of social action resulting from feminist writings, presentations, and/or discussions on policing issues. Sometimes, it involved individual officers who were able to make changes to their everyday police work; in how they viewed their roles as police officers, and in how they responded to calls and dealt with diverse groups of people and problems. In other instances, a group of officers collectively created positive change. For example, some officers shared stories of how particular "knowledge" inspired them to produce "how-to" manuals for fellow front-line officers that aimed to answer specific CP questions. These manuals provided the police with substantive examples on how to act in particular instances with members of the public and were intended to serve as a response to management's eagerness to promote CP initiatives within their departments. Other officers were successful in creating monthly newsletters acknowledging those who proactively engaged in CP initiatives. Their intention was to send the message that the CP ideology would be supported and that the officers embracing it would be recognized for their efforts. Other examples included individual officers who had convinced members of management to develop a structured system whereby patrol officers could voice their concerns about various policing matters and offer suggestions on how to deal with the problems. The intention here was to give voice to the front-line officer, who was often the most knowledgeable about matters "on the streets," versus members of upper management.

B. "Hidden Work" in Action-Research

It is important to note that background preparations involved in certain research processes to retrieve data are often not recognized by readers but are relevant to the quality of work and commitment to action-research. It is this "hidden work" that can enable and enrich formal research and commitment to action-research. Some researchers hope to demystify the research process and provide their readers the opportunity to "see" the decisions they make and the reasons behind some of them, as well as help their readers come to understand the reasons behind their commitment to social action and change (McLean and Leibing, 2007). For instance, before the formal research began on any of her projects, the author spent years networking with police officers from different police departments in both Canada and the US, attending police conferences, and attending social events with police officers. As a university student, the author started working for police departments in various volunteer capacities. She gained first-hand knowledge about police operations and responses and was able to witness police interactions with members of the public, as well as the police response to particular crimes. She was introduced to many police officers and socialized with some of them after work, which often translated into being exposed to countless hours of police-related stories. Through all of this, she was introduced to officers from other police departments across Canada and was invited to participate in a series of formal and informal meetings at the Canadian Police College in Ottawa, Canada. These experiences would eventually provide her with a long roster of police contacts and participants for some of her future research projects that included officers representing different ranks and police departments across Canada and the United States. Gaining access to study the police is often very difficult for many researchers, and when they do gain access via permission from members of upper management, they are often not able to obtain complete data on particular sensitive issues relating to officers' individual units and/or departments. This ambiguous border, where life and research overlap, can help erase the presumed separation between these spheres and can help explore the paths through which researchers learn about the social categories that define them and others around them, as well as help them to explore their personal commitments to action-research.

Being able to achieve authentic data (i.e., achieve honest accounts of individual experiences) from officers employed in a culture that is, for the most part, secretive and frowns upon any possible negative exposure requires significant time spent networking with the police in order to develop a level of trust. The researcher's reputation as a trustworthy scholar in search of writing a comprehensive account of police issues without compromising participants' anonymity is vital. This is significant in the quality of the information collected and in its purpose and effectiveness as action-research. In addition, purposive, targeted, referral, and snowball sampling are oftentimes the most appropriate, beneficial, and practical sampling techniques to use in obtaining data that brings to light particular oppressive practices and ideologies. According to Biernacki and Waldorf (1981), certain nonprobability sampling methods are notably applicable to researching deviant and/or illegal behaviour. Purposive sampling allows the researcher to utilize her/his expert judgment to select units that are representative or "typical" of the population. With referral and snowball sampling, the researcher utilizes a process of chain referral. Members of the target population are contacted and asked to provide the name and contact information of others representing the target population (Singleton, Jr. and Straits, 1999). Finally, targeted sampling (Watters and Biernacki, 1989) provides researchers with a different approach for sampling "hidden" populations (e.g., officers willing to discuss sensitive police-related issues concerning their departments).

In the pursuit of change, feminist methods must be utilized to identify exclusionary practices in the production of police "knowledge," but, in addition, research must be converted into action in order to promote positive change in the quality of people's lives. Feminist approaches and findings are committed to the promotion of new knowledge, but equally important is the commitment to making deliberate attempts to introduce this information to policing arenas where ideological and structural changes are needed. Action-research can promote change and indicate motivation, direction, and opportunity, and police officers and students who become receptive to feminist writings and ideas can serve as an access to others for consciousness raising.

Questions

1. Why is action-research important in relation to policing and gender inequalities?
2. Provide some examples of how studies of the police can be converted into action-research.

Bibliography

Abernathy, A., and C. Cox. 1994. "Anger Management Training for Law Enforcement Personnel." *Journal of Criminal Justice*. 22: 5: 459-466.

Ackoff, L. 1988. "Cultural Feminism versus Post-Structuralism." *Signs: Journal of Women in Culture and Society*. 13: 3: 406-436.

Adams, R.E., W.M. Rohe, and T.A. Arcury. 2002. "Implementing Community-Oriented Policing: Organizational Change and Street Officer Attitudes." *Crime and Delinquency*. 48: 3: 399-430.

Adamson, N., L. Briskin, and M. McPhail. 1988. *Feminists Organizing for Change*. Toronto: Oxford University Press.

Adler, F. 1975. *Sisters in Crime: The Rise of the New Female Criminal*. New York: McGraw-Hill.

American Civil Liberties Union. 22 March 2007. *ACLU Letter to Representatives Nadler and Franks Exploring the Current State of Civil Rights Enforcement within the Department of Justice*. <http://www.aclu.org/racialjustice/gen/29139leg20070322.html>.

Anderson, D.J. 1976. *Evaluation of the Methodological and Policy Implications of the District of Columbia Policewomen on Patrol Study*. Ann Arbor, MI: University of Michigan Microfilms.

Anleu, S.R. 1992. "Women in Law: Theory, Research and Practice." *Australian and New Zealand Journal of Sociology*. 28: 391-410.

Appier, J. 1998. *Policing Women: The Sexual Politics of Law Enforcement and the LAPD*. Philadelphia: Temple University.

Aristotle. 1962 [1934]. *The Nichomachean Ethics*, translated by H. Rackman. Cambridge, MA: Harvard University Press.

Arnold, R.A. 1995. "Processes of Victimization and Criminalization of Black Women." In *The Criminal Justice System and Women: Offenders, Prisoners, Victims and Workers*, edited by Barbara Raffel Price and Natalie J. Sokoloff. New York: McGraw Hill.

Austin, R. 1995. "'The Black Community,' Its Lawbreakers, and a Politics of Identification." In *After Identity*, edited by D. Danielsen and K. Engle, 143-164. New York: Routledge.

Balfour, G., and E. Comack, eds. 2006. *Criminalizing Women: Gender and (In)Justice in Neo-Liberal Times*. Halifax, NS: Fernwood.

Bannerji, H. 1993. *Returning the Gaze: Racism, Feminism and Politics*. Toronto: Sister Vision Press.

Bannerji, H., et al. 1991. *Unsettling Relations: The University as a Site of Feminist Struggle*. Toronto: Women's Press.

Barak, G. 2003. *Violence and Nonviolence: Pathways to Understanding*. Thousand Oaks, CA: Sage.

Barak, G., J.M. Flavin, and P.S. Leighton. 2001. *Class, Race, Gender and Crime: Social Realities of Justice in America*. Los Angeles: Roxbury.

Bartell and Associates. 1978. *The Study of Police Women Competency in the Performance of Sector Police Work in the City of Philadelphia*. State College, PA: Bartell.

Bartlett, H.W., and A. Rosenblum. 1977. *Policewomen Effectiveness in Denver*. Denver, CO: Civil Service Commission.

Bartol, C.R., et al. 1992. "Women in Small-Town Policing: Job Performance and Stress." *Criminal Justice and Behavior*. 19: 3: 240-259.

Bashevkin, S. 1985. *Toeing the Lines: Women and Party Politics in English Canada*. Toronto: University of Toronto Press.

Baskin, D.R., and I.B. Sommers. 1998. *Casualties of Community Disorder: Women's Careers in Violent Crime*. Boulder, CO: Westview Press.

Bass, M. 1982. "Stress: A Woman Officer's View." *Police Stress*. 5: 1: 30-33.

Baudrillard, J. 1993. *The Transparency of Evil*, translated by James Benedict. Paris: Verso.

Bayley, D.H. 1994. *Police for the Future*. New York: Oxford University Press.

———. 1988. "Community Policing: A Report from the Devil's Advocate." In *Community Policing: Rhetoric or Reality*, edited by J.R. Greene and S.D. Mastrofski, 225-238. New York: Praeger.

Bayley, D., and J. Garafalo. 1989. "The Management of Violence by Police Patrol Officers." *Criminology*. 27: 1: 1-25.

Bayley, D.H., and C.D. Shearing. 1996. "The Future of Policing." *Law and Society Review*. 30: 3: 585-606.

Becker, H.S., and B. Geer. 1957. "Participant Observation and Interviewing: A Comparison." *Human Organization*. 16: 28-32.

Beirne, P., and J. Messerschmidt. 1991. *Criminology*. San Diego: Harcourt Brace Jovanovich.

Belknap, J. 2007. *The Invisible Woman: Gender, Crime and Justice*, 3rd edition. Belmont, CA: Thomson Wadsworth.

———. 2001. *The Invisible Woman: Gender, Crime and Justice*, 2nd edition. Belmont, CA: Wadsworth/Thomson Learning.

———. 1991. "Women in Conflict: An Analysis of Women Correctional Officers." *Women and Criminal Justice*. 2: 89-115.

Belknap, J., and J.K. Shelley. 1993. "The New Lone Ranger: Policewomen on Patrol." *American Journal of Police*. 12: 47-75.

Bell, D.J. 1982. "Policewomen: Myths and Realities." *Journal of Police Science and Administration*. 10: 1: 112-120.

Bertrand, M.A. January 1969. "Self-Image and Delinquency: A Contribution to the Study of Female Criminality and Women's Image." *Acta Criminologia: Etudes sur la Conduite Antisociale*. 2: 71-144.

Biernacki, P., and D. Waldorf. 1981. "Snowball Sampling: Problems and Techniques of Chain Referral Sampling." *Sociological Methods and Research*. 10: 141-163.

Birzer, M., and R. Tannehill. 2001. "A More Effective Training Approach for Contemporary Policing." *Police Quarterly*. 4: 2: 233-252.

Black, D. 1990. "The Elementary Forms of Conflict Management." In *New Directions in the Study of Justice, Law, and Social Control*, 43-69. Prepared by the School of Justice Studies, Arizona State University. New York: Plenum Press.

Black, D.J. January 1973. "The Mobilization of the Law." *The Journal of Legal Studies*. 2: 125-149.

Bloch, P., and D. Anderson. 1974. *Policewomen on Patrol: Final Report*. Washington, DC: Urban Institute.

Bologh, R.W. 1984. "Feminist Social Theorizing and Moral Reasoning: On Difference and Dialectic." In *Sociological Theory*, edited by the American Sociological Association. San Francisco: Jossey-Bass.

Boni, N. 1998. *Deployment of Women in Policing*. Payneham, South Australia: National Police Research Unit.

Bottcher, J. 2001. "Social Practices of Gender: How Gender Relates to Delinquency in the Everyday Lives of High-Risk Youth." *Criminology*. 39: 893-931.

Bradburn, L. 20-23 May 1997. "Moving Beyond Obstacles and Constraints." A presentation made at the Women in Policing in Canada: The Year 2000 and Beyond—Its Challenges workshop, Canadian Police College, Ottawa, ON.

Braithewaite, J. 1989. *Crime, Shame, and Reintegration*. Cambridge: Cambridge University Press.

Brand, D. 1993. "A Working Paper on Black Women in Toronto: Gender, Race, and Class." In *Returning the Gaze: Essays on Racism, Feminism and Politics*, edited by Himani Bannerji, 220-241. Toronto: Sister Vision Press.

Brandl, S. 1996. "In the Line of Duty: A Descriptive Analysis of Police Assaults and Accidents." *Journal of Criminal Justice*. 24: 3: 255-264.

Breci, M. 1997. "Female Officer on Patrol: Public Perceptions in the 1990s." *Journal of Crime and Justice*. 20: 2: 153-165.

Breines, W., and L. Gordon. 1983. "The New Scholarship on Family Violence." *Signs: Journal of Women in Culture and Society*. 18: 490-531.

Brenzel, B. 1983. *Daughters of the State*. Cambridge, MA: MIT Press.

Brisken, L. 1994. "Feminist Pedagogy: Teaching and Learning Liberation." In *Sociology of Education in Canada*, edited by L. Erwin and D. MacLennan, 443-470. Toronto: Copp Clark Longman.

Bristow, A.R., and J.A. Esper. 1988. "A Feminist Research Ethos." In *A Feminist Ethic for Social Science Research*, edited by the Nebraska Sociological Feminist Collective. Lewiston, NY: The Edwin Mellen Press.

Britton, D.M. 1997. "Gendered Organizational Logic: Policy and Practice in Men's and Women's Prison." *Gender and Society*. 11: 6: 796-818.

Brooks, A. 2007. "Feminist Standpoint Epistemology: Building Knowledge and Empowerment through Women's Lived Experience." In *Feminist Research Practice*, edited by Sharlene Nagy Hesse-Biber and Patricia Lina Leavy, 53-82. Thousand Oaks, CA: Sage.

Brush, L.D. 1997. "Harm, Moralism, and the Struggle for the Soul of Feminism." *Violence Against Women*. 3: 237-256.

Buerger, M.E., A.J. Petrosino, and C. Petrosino. 1999. "Extending the Police Role: Implications of Police Mediation as a Problem-Solving Tool." *Police Quarterly*. 2: 2: 125-149.

Bureau of Justice Assistance. 2001. *Recruiting and Retaining Women: A Self-Assessment Guide for Law Enforcement*. Washington, DC: Bureau of Justice Assistance.

Burgess-Proctor, A. 2006. "Intersections of Race, Class, Gender, and Crime. Future Directions for Feminist Criminology." *Feminist Criminology*. 1: 27-47.

Burris, J.L., and C. Whitney. 1999. *Blue vs. Black: Let's End the Conflict Between Cops and Minorities*. New York: St. Martin's Griffin.

Burtch, B. 2000. "Racial Discrimination in Law: An International Perspective." In *Criminal Injustice: Racism in the Criminal Justice System*, edited by R. Neugebauer, 65-81. Toronto: Canadian Scholars' Press.

——. 1992. "Racial Discrimination in Law: An International Perspective." In *Sociology of Law: Critical Approaches to Social Control*, edited by Brian Burtch, 108-123. Toronto: Harcourt Brace.

Busson, B.A. 20-23 May 1997. "Women and Policing." A presentation made at the Women in Policing in Canada: The Year 2000 and Beyond—Its Challenges workshop, Canadian Police College, Ottawa, ON.

Butler, J. 1997. "Performative Acts and Gender Constitution: An Essay in Phenomenology and Feminist Theory." In *Writing on the Body: Female Embodiment and Feminist Theory*, edited by Katie Conboy, Nadia Medina, and Sarah Stanbury, 401-417. New York: Columbia University Press.

——. 1993. *Bodies That Matter*. New York: Routledge.

——. 1992. "Contingent Foundations: Feminism and the Question of Postmodernism." In *Feminists Theorize the Political*, edited by Judith Butler and Joan W. Scott. New York: Routledge.

Campbell, H. 1892. *Darkness and Daylight*. Hartford, CT: Roberts Brothers.

——. 1890. "Both Sides of the Sea." In *Prisoners of Poverty Abroad*. Boston: Roberts Brothers.

——. 1883. *Prisoners of Poverty: Women Wage-Workers, Their Trades and Their Lives*. New York: Garrett Press.

Canada. Intergovernmental Affairs. 2008. *The Canadian Constitution*. Government of Canada, Privy Council Office. <http://www.bcppco.gc.ca/aia/index.asp?lang=eng&page=canada&sub=constitution&doc=constitution_e.htm>.

The Canadian Encyclopedia: Historica. 2007. <http://www.thecanadian encyclopedia.com/index.cfm?PgNm=TCE&Params>.

Cao, L., X. Deng, and S. Barton. 2000. "A Test of Lundman's Organizational Product Thesis with Data on Citizen Complaints." *Policing: An International Journal of Police Strategies and Management*. 23: 3: 356-373.

Caputi, J. 1992. "To Acknowledge and Heal: 20 Years of Feminist Thought and Activism on Sexual Violence." In *The Knowledge Explosion: Generations of Feminist Scholarship*, edited by C. Kramarae and D. Spender, 340-352. New York: Teachers College Press.

Carter, D., A. Sapp, and D. Stephens. 1988. *The State of Police Education: Policy Direction for the 21st Century*. Washington, DC: Police Executive Research Forum.

Cassidy, B., R. Lord, and N. Mandell. 1998. "Silenced and Forgotten Women: Race, Poverty, and Disability." In *Feminist Issues — Race, Class, and Sexuality*, 2nd edition, edited by Nancy Mandell. Scarborough, ON: Prentice Hall Allyn and Bacon Canada.

CBC News. 28 July 2006. "Controversial OPP Commissioner Stepping Down." <http://www.cbc.ca/canada/toronto/story/2006/07/28/boniface.html>.

Chalom, M. Autumn 1993. "Community Policing: Toward a New Paradigm of Prevention?" *International Review of Community Development*. 30: 70: 155-161.

Charles, M.T. 1981. "The Performance and Socialization of Female Recruits in the Michigan State Police Training Academy." *Journal of Police Science and Administration*. 9: 209-223.

Charles, M.T., and A.G. Copay. 2001. "Marksmanship Skills of Female Police Recruits: Impact of Basic Firearms Training." *International Journal of Police Science and Management*. 3: 4: 303-308.

Chesney-Lind, M. 1995. "Girls, Delinquency, and Juvenile Justice: Toward a Feminist Theory of Young Women's Crime." In *The Criminal Justice System and Women: Offenders, Prisoners, Victims, and Workers*, edited by Barbara Raffel Price and Natalie J. Sokoloff. New York: McGraw Hill.

——. July 1974. "Juvenile Delinquency: The Sexualization of Female Crime." *Psychology Today*. 43-46.

——. 1973. "Judicial Enforcement of the Female Sex Role: The Family Court and the Female Delinquent." *Issues in Criminology*. 8: 2: 51-69.

Chesney-Lind, M., and N. Rodriguez. 1983. "Women under Lock and Key." *Prison Journal*. 53: 47-65.

Chesney-Lind, M., and R.G. Shelden. 2004. *Girls, Delinquency, and Juvenile Justice*, 3rd edition. Florence, KY: Thomson/Wadsworth.

Cochran, C.C., P.A. Frazier, and A.M. Olson. 1997. "Predictors of Responses to Unwanted Sexual Harassment." *Psychology of Women Quarterly*. 21: 2: 207-226.

Cohen, S. 1985. *Visions of Social Control: Crime, Punishment and Classification*. Cambridge: Polity Press.

Colby, P.W. 1995. "Contract Police." In *The Encyclopedia of Police Science*, 2nd edition, edited by W.G. Bailey, 120-122. New York: Garland.

Coles, F.S. 1986. "Forced to Quit: Sexual Harassment Complaints and Agency Response." *Sex Roles*. 14: 81-95.

Collins, P.H. 1990. *Black Feminist Thought: Knowledge, Consciousness and the Politics of Empowerment*. New York: Routledge.

Comack, E., ed. 2006. *Locating Law: Race/Class/Gender/Sexuality Connections*, 2nd edition. Halifax, NS: Fernwood.

——. 1996. *Women in Trouble: Connecting Women's Law Violations to Their Histories of Abuse*. Halifax, NS: Fernwood.

Comack, E., V. Chopyk, and L. Wood. 2002. "Aren't Women Violent Too? The Gendered Nature of Violence." In *Marginality and Condemnation: An Introduction to Critical Criminology*, edited by B. Schissel and C. Brooks. Halifax, NS: Fernwood.

——. December 2000. *Mean Streets? The Social Locations, Gender Dynamics, and Patterns of Violent Crime in Winnipeg*. Winnipeg, MB: Canadian Centre for Policy Alternatives.

Commission on Systemic Racism in the Ontario Criminal Justice System. 1995. *Racism in Justice: Perceptions*. Toronto: Queen's Printer for Ontario.

Comstock, G.D. 1991. *Violence Against Lesbians and Gay Men*. New York: Columbia University Press.

Connell, R.W. 1995. *Masculinities*. Cambridge: Polity Press.

Cordner, G. 1994. "Foot Patrol without Community Policing: Law and Order in Public Housing." In *The Challenge of Community Policing: Testing the Promises*, edited by D. Rosenbaum, 182-191. Thousand Oaks, CA: Sage.

Corsianos, M. 2007a. "Promoting Gendered Justice Using the Community-Oriented Policing Model." A paper presented at the Annual Meeting of the American Society of Criminologists, Atlanta, Georgia.

——. 2007b. "Mainstream Pornography and 'Women': Questioning Sexual Agency." *Critical Sociology*. 33: 863-885.

——. 2007c. "Police Corruption." In *Battleground: Criminal Justice*, volume 2, edited by G. Barak, 508-515. Westport, CT: Greenwood Press.

——. 18 November 2005. "Gender and Detectives: Working Towards Social Justice." A paper presented at the Annual Meeting of the American Society of Criminologists, Session: Feminist Empowerment in Criminal Justice, Toronto, ON.

———. 2004. "'Women' Detectives and Perceptions of 'Oppressive' Experiences: Exploring Experiential Essentialism and Phenomenology." *Critical Criminology*. 12: 1: 67-85.

———. 2003. "Discretion in Detectives' Decision Making and 'High Profile' Cases." *Police Practice and Research: An International Journal*. 4: 3: 301-314.

———. 2001. "Conceptualizing 'Justice' in Detectives' Decision Making." *International Journal of the Sociology of Law*. 29: 2: 113-126.

———. 1999a. "Freedom versus Equality: Where Does Justice Lie?" In *Interrogating Social Justice: Politics, Culture and Identity*, edited by Marilyn Corsianos and Kelly Amanda Train, 1-22. Toronto: Canadian Scholars' Press.

———. 1999b. "Detectives' Decision Making Within a Police Organizational Structure and Occupational Culture: Examining the Social Construction of 'High Profile' Cases." Ph.D. Dissertation, York University, Toronto, ON.

———. 1997. "Recognizing Power within Paramilitarism and Language: A Case Study of the Metropolitan Toronto Police Service." In *Policing the New Millennium: Critical Essays on Social Control*, edited by the Critical Criminology Association, Centre for Police and Security Studies. Toronto: York University.

Crank, J. 1998. *Understanding Police Culture*. Cincinnati, OH: Anderson Publishing.

Crenshaw, K. 1995. "Mapping the Margins: Intersectionality, Identity Politics, and Violence Against Women of Color." In *After Identity*, edited by D. Danielsen and K. Engle, 332-354. New York: Routledge.

Crites, L. 1973. *Women in Law Enforcement*. Management Information Service Report: 5, 9. US: International City/County Management Association.

Culbertson, A.L., et al. 1992. *Assessment of Sexual Harassment in the Navy: Results of the 1989 Navy-Wide Survey*. San Diego, CA: Navy Personnel Research and Development Center.

Cupit, G. 1996. *Justice as Fittingness*. New York: Oxford University Press.

Dahler, D. 2008. "Pregnant N.J. Cop Denied Bid For 'Light Duty.'" CBS Broadcasting Inc. <http://wcbstv.com/local/pregnant.cop.patrol.2.716881.html>.

Daly, K., and M. Chesney-Lind. 1988. "Feminism and Criminology." *Justice Quarterly*. 5: 497-538.

Danner, M.J.E. 1989. "Socialist Feminism: A Brief Introduction." In *New Directions in Critical Criminology*, edited by B.D. MacLean and D. Milovanovic, 51-54. Vancouver: The Collective Press.

Dansky, B.S., and D.G. Kilpatrick. 1997. "Effects of Sexual Harassment." In *Sexual Harassment: Theory, Research and Treatment*, edited by W. O'Donohue, 152-174. New York: Allyn and Bacon.

Das Gupta, T. 1995. "Families of Native People, Immigrants, and People of Colour." In *Canadian Families: Diversity, Conflict and Change*, edited by Nancy Mandell and Ann Duffy, 141-174. Toronto: Harcourt Brace.

———.1994. "Towards an Anti-Racist, Feminist Teaching Method." *Feminism and Education: A Canadian Perspective*. 2: 17-42.

Davies, M. 1994. *Violence and Women.* Atlantic Highlands, NJ: Zed.

Davis, K.C. 1969. *Discretionary Justice.* Baton Rouge: Louisiana State University Press.

de Beauvoir, S. 1974. *The Second Sex,* translated by H.M. Parshley. New York: Vintage.

Dei, G.J.S. 1994. "Reflections of an Anti-Racist Pedagogue." In *Sociology of Education in Canada,* edited by L. Erwin and D. MacLennan, 290-310. Toronto: Copp Clark Longman.

DeKeseredy, W.S., and R. Hinch. 1991. *Woman Abuse: Sociological Perspectives.* Toronto: Thompson Educational Publishing.

DeKeseredy, W.S., and M.D. Schwartz. February 1998. "Measuring the Extent of Woman Abuse in Intimate Heterosexual Relationships: A Critique of the Conflict Tactics Scales." <http://www.vaw.umn.edu/Vawnet/ctscrit.html>.

Dell, C.A. 1999. "Crimes of Violence: An Examination of the Identification of Women as 'Violent' Offenders in the Canadian Criminal Justice System." In *Interrogating Social Justice: Culture, Politics and Identity,* edited by Marilyn Corsianos and Kelly Amanda Train, 109-142. Toronto: Canadian Scholars' Press.

Denfield, R. 1996. *The New Victorian: A Young Woman's Challenge to the Old Feminist Order.* New York: Warner Books.

Denzin, N.K. 2000. "The Practices and Politics of Interpretation." In *Handbook of Qualitative Research,* edited by Norman Denzin and Yvonna Lincoln, 897-922. Thousand Oaks, CA: Sage.

Department of Defense. 1996. *Defense 96.* Washington, DC: US Government Printing Office.

Dick, P., and A.D. Jankowicz. 2001. "A Social Constructionist Account of Police Culture and Its Influence on the Representation and Progression of Female Officers: A Repertory Grid Analysis in the UK Police Force." *Policing: An International Journal of Police Strategies and Management.* 24: 2: 181-199.

Dixon, D. December 1992. "Legal Regulation and Policing Practice." *Social and Legal Studies.* 1: 4: 515-541.

Dobash, R.E., and R.P. Dobash. 1992. *Women, Violence and Social Change.* New York: Routledge.

Dobash, R.P., et al. 1992. "The Myth of Sexual Symmetry in Marital Violence." *Social Problems.* 39: 71-91.

Dodge, M., and M. Pogrebin. 2001. "African-American Policewomen: An Exploration of Professional Relationships." *Policing: An International Journal of Police Strategies and Management.* 24: 4: 550-562.

Doerner, W.G. 1995. "Officer Retention Patterns: An Affirmative Action Concern for Police Agencies." *American Journal of Police.* 14: 205.

Doig, J.W. 1978. "Police Policy and Police Behavior: Patterns of Divergence." *Policy Studies Journal.* 7: 436-442.

Downes, D. 1966. *The Delinquent Solution.* New York: Free Press.

Dreifus, C. 1982. "Why Two Women Cops Were Convicted of Cowardice." In *The Criminal Justice System and Women*, edited by Barbara Raffel Price and Natalie J. Sokoloff. New York: Clark Boardman Company.

Drummond, D.S. 1976. *Police Culture*. Thousand Oaks, CA: Sage.

Dworkin, A. 1987. *Intercourse*. New York: Free Press.

Eaton, M. 1986. *Justice for Women? Family, Court and Social Control*. Milton Keynes, UK: Open University Press.

Eck, J.E. July 1990. "A Realistic Approach to Controlling Drug Harms." *Public Management*. 7-12.

Eck, J.E., and W. Spelman. 1987. "Who Ya Gonna Call: The Police as Problem-Busters." *Crime and Delinquency*. 33: 1: 31-52.

Elliott, J.L., and A. Fleras. 1992. *Unequal Relations: An Introduction to Race and Ethnic Dynamics in Canada*. Toronto: Prentice Hall.

Elliot, P., and N. Mandell. 1998. "Feminist Theories." In *Feminist Issues: Race, Class and Sexuality*, 2nd edition, edited by N. Mandell, 2-25. Scarborough, ON: Prentice Hall Allyn and Bacon Canada.

Eng, S. 20-23 May 1997. "Policies for Women in the Justice Field—Need or Necessity." A presentation made at the Women in Policing in Canada: The Year 2000 and Beyond—Its Challenges workshop, Canadian Police College, Ottawa, ON.

Engle, K. 1995. "Female Subjects of Public International Law: Human Rights and the Exotic Other Female." In *After Identity*, edited by D. Danielsen and K. Engle, 210-228. New York: Routledge.

Epstein, C. Fuchs. 1986. "Symbolic Segregation: Similarities and Differences in the Language and Non-Verbal Communication of Women and Men." *Sociological Forum*. 1: 27-45.

——. 1981. *Women in Law*. New York: Basic Books.

——. 1973. "Positive Effects of the Multiple Negative: Explaining The Success of Black Professional Women." *American Journal of Sociology*. 78: 913-918.

——. 1970. *Woman's Place: Options and Limits in Professional Careers*. Berkeley: University of California Press.

Ericson, R. 1994. "The Division of Expert Knowledge in Policing and Security." *The British Journal of Sociology*. 45: 2: 149-175.

——. 1992. "The Police as Reproducers of Order." In *Understanding Policing*, edited by K. McCormick and L.A. Visano, 163-208. Toronto: Canadian Scholars' Press.

——. 1982. *Reproducing Order*. Toronto: University of Toronto Press.

——. 1981. *Making Crime: A Study of Detective Work*. Toronto: Butterworth.

Ericson, R., and K. Haggerty. 1997. *Policing the Risk Society*. Toronto: University of Toronto Press.

Faith, K. 1994. *Unruly Women: The Politics of Confinement and Resistance*. Vancouver: Press Gang Publishers.

Farkas, M., and P. Manning. 1997. "The Occupational Culture of Corrections and Police Officers." *Journal of Crime and Justice.* 20: 2: 51-68.

Feinman, C. 1986. *Women in the Criminal Justice System.* New York: Praeger.

Felkenes, G.T., and J.R. Schroeder. 1993. "A Case Study of Minority Women in Policing." *Women and Criminal Justice.* 4: 65-89.

Feminist Daily News Wire. 8 May 2008. "Pregnant Police Officer Request to Go on Light Duty Granted." Feminist Majority Foundation. <http://feminist.org/news newsbyte/uswirestory.asp?id=10992>.

———. 21 June 2006. "Pregnant Police Officers Win Discrimination Case." Feminist Majority Foundation. <http://www.feminist.org/news/newsbyte uswirestory. asp?id=9720>.

Ferguson, K.E. 1984. *The Feminist Case Against Bureaucracy.* Philadelphia: Temple University Press.

Ferraro, K.F. 1995. "Cops, Courts, and Woman Battering." In *The Criminal Justice System and Women: Offenders, Victims and Workers,* 2nd edition, edited by Barbara R. Price and Natalie J. Sokoloff, 262-271. New York: McGraw-Hill.

Ferraro, K.J., and T. Boychuk. 1992. "The Court's Response to Interpersonal Violence: A Comparison of Intimate and Non-Intimate Assault." In *Domestic Violence: The Changing Criminal Justice Response,* edited by E. Busawa, 209-225. Westport, CT: Greenwood.

Ferree, M., and B. Hess. 2000. *Controversy and Coalition: The New Feminist Movement Across 4 Decades of Change.* New York: Routledge.

Fetterley, J. 1978. *The Resisting Reader: A Feminist Approach to American Fiction.* Bloomington: Indiana University Press.

Fielding, N. 1994. "Cop Canteen Culture." In *Just Boys Doing Business? Men, Masculinities and Crime,* edited by T. Newburn and E.A. Stanko. London: Routledge.

Fine, M., et al., eds. 1997. *Off White: Readings on Race, Power and Society.* New York: Routledge.

Fischer, B., and B. Poland. 1998. "Exclusion, 'Risk', and Social Control—Reflections on Community Policing and Public Health." *Geoforum.* 29: 2: 187-197.

Fitzgerald, L.F. 1993. "Sexual Harassment: Violence Against Women in the Workplace." *American Psychology.* 48: 1070-1076.

Flax, J. 1990. "Postmodernism and Gender Relations in Feminist Theory." In *Feminism/Postmodernism,* edited by L.J. Nicholson. New York: Routledge.

———. 1987. "Postmodernism and Gender Relations in Feminist Theory." *Signs: Journal of Women in Culture and Society.* 12: 4: 621-643.

———. 1983. "Political Philosophy and the Patriarchal Unconscious: A Psychoanalytic Perspective on Epistemology and Metaphysics." In *Discovering Reality: Feminist Perspectives on Epistemology, Metaphysics, Methodology and Philosophy of Science,* edited by Sandra Harding and Merrill Hintikka, 245-281. Boston: Reidel Publishing.

Fletcher, C. 1995. *Breaking and Entering.* New York: HarperCollins.

Forcese, D. 1999. *Policing Canadian Society*, 2nd edition. Scarborough, ON: Prentice Hall Canada.

Foucault, M. 1979. *The History of Sexuality, Volume 1: An Introduction*, translated by R. Hurley. London: Allen Lane.

——. 1977. *Discipline & Punish: The Birth of the Prison*. New York: Vintage Books.

Frager, Ruth. 1993. "Class, Ethnicity, and Gender in the Eaton Strikes of 1912 and 1934." In *Gender Conflicts: New Essays in Women's History*, edited by F. Iacovetta and M. Valverde, 189-228. Toronto: University of Toronto Press.

Freedman, E. 1981. *Their Sisters' Keepers: Women's Prison Reform in America, 1830-1930*. Ann Arbor: University of Michigan Press.

Freeman, J. 1984. "The Women's Liberation Movement: Its Origin, Structure, Activities and Ideas." In *Women: A Feminist Perspective*, 3rd edition, edited by Jo Freeman, 543-556. Palo Alto, CA: Mayfield Publishing.

Frost, S.N. 20-23 May 1997. "Gender Equality Analysis." A presentation made at the Women in Policing in Canada: The Year 2000 and Beyond—Its Challenges workshop, Canadian Police College, Ottawa, ON.

Frug, M.J. 1995. "A Postmodern Feminist Legal Manifesto." In *After Identity*, edited by D. Danielsen and K. Engle, 7-23. New York: Routledge.

Fyfe, J.J., et al. 1997. *Police Administration*, 5th edition. New York: McGraw-Hill.

Fyfe, N.R. September 1991. "The Police, Space and Society: The Geography of Policing." *Progress in Human Geography*. 15: 3: 249-267.

Gadamer, H. 1976. *Philosophical Hermeneutics*. Berkley: University of California.

Garcia, V. 2003. "'Difference' in the Policing Department: Women, Policing, and 'Doing Gender.'" *Journal of Contemporary Criminal Justice*. 19: 330-344.

Garner, J., et al. 1996. *Understanding the Use of Force By and Against Police*. Washington, DC: National Institute of Justice.

Garrison, C.G., N. Grant, and K. McCormick. 1988. "Utilization of Police Women." *Police Chief*. 55: 9: 32-35.

Gerber, G.L. 2001. *Women and Men Police Officers: Status, Gender and Personality*. New York: Praeger.

Gerden, R. 1998. *Private Security: A Canadian Perspective*. Scarborough, ON: Prentice Hall Canada.

Gere, A.R., and S.R. Robbins. 1996. "Gendered: Turn of the Century African-American and European-American Club Literacy in Black and White Women's Printed Texts." *Signs: Journal of Women in Culture and Society*. 21: 3: 643-678.

Gilligan, J. 1996. *Violence: Reflections on a National Epidemic*. New York: Vintage.

Ginzberg, L.D. 1990. *Women and the World of Benevolence: Morality, Politics, and Class in the Nineteenth-Century United States*. New Haven: Yale University Press.

Glaser, B., and A. Straus. 1967. *The Discovery of Grounded Theory*. Chicago: Aldine.

Goetz, B., and R. Mitchell. 2003. "Community-Building and Reintegrative Approaches to Community Policing: The Case of Drug Control." *Social Justice*. 30: 1: 222-247.

Goldsmith, A. 1990. "Taking Police Culture Seriously: Police Discretion and the Limits of Law." *Policing and Society*. 1: 2: 91-114.

Goldstein, H. 1990. *Problem-Oriented Policing*. New York: McGraw-Hill.

——. 1977. *Policing a Free Society*. Cambridge, MA: Ballinger.

——. September 1964. "Police Discretion: The Ideal vs. the Real." *Public Administration Review*. 23: 140-148.

Gordon, P. 1987. "Community Policing: Towards the Local Police State?" In *Law, Order and the Authoritarian State*, edited by P. Scraton, 121-144. Philadelphia: Open University Press.

Goudar, R. 1989. "Adjusting the Dream." *Saskatchewan Multicultural Magazine*. 8: 3: 5-8.

Gramsci, A. 1957. *The Modern Prince and Other Writings*. New York: International Publishers.

Grana, S.J. 2002. *Women and (In)Justice: The Criminal and Civil Effects of the Common Law on Women's Lives*. Boston: Allyn and Bacon.

Grant, D.R. 2000. "Perceived Gender Differences in Policing: The Impact of Gendered Perceptions of Officer-Situation 'Fit.'" *Women and Criminal Justice*. 12: 1: 53-74.

Greene, J.R. 2004. "Community Policing and Police Organization." In *Community Policing: Can it Work?*, edited by Westley G. Skogan. Florence, KY: Wadsworth.

Greene, J., and S.D. Mastrofski. 1988. *Community Policing: Rhetoric or Reality*. New York: Praeger.

Grennan, S.A. 1987. "Findings on the Role of Officer Gender in Violent Encounters with Citizens." *Journal of Police Science and Administration*. 15: 78-85.

Greschner, D. 1985. "Affirmative Action and the Charter of Rights and Freedoms." *Canadian Woman Studies*. 6: 4: 34-36. <http://pi.library.yorku.ca/ojs/index.php/cws/article/viewFile/12800/11883>.

Grossman, J. 2002. "What Defines 'Business Necessity' in the Discrimination Context? A Federal Appellate Case Grapples with How Fast Transit Police Officers Must Run." FindLaw. <http://writ.lp.findlaw.com/grossman/20021119.html>.

Gruber, J.E. June 1998. "The Impact of Male Work Environments and Organizational Policies on Women's Experiences of Sexual Harassment." *Gender and Society*. 12: 3: 301-320.

——. 1992. "A Typology of Personal and Environmental Sexual Harassment: Research and Policy Implications from the 1990s." *Sex Roles*. 22: 447-464.

——. 1990. "Methodological Problems and Policy Implications in Sexual Harassment Research." *Population Research and Policy Review*. 9: 235-254.

——. 1989. "How Women Handle Sexual Harassment: A Literature Review." *Sociology and Social Research*. 74: 3-9.

Guarino-Ghezzi, S. 1994. "Reintegrative Police Surveillance of Juvenile Offenders: Forging an Urban Model." *Crime and Delinquency*. 40: 131-153.

Gutek, B.A. 1985. *Sex and the Workplace: The Impact of Sexual Behavior and Harassment on Women, Men, and Organizations*. San Francisco: Jossey-Bass.

Gutek, B.A., and M. Koss. 1993. "Changed Women and Changed Organizations: Consequences and Coping with Sexual Harassment." *Journal of Vocational Behavior*. 42: 28-48.

Haar, R.N. 1997. "Patterns of Interaction in a Police Patrol Bureau: Race and Gender Barriers to Integration." *Justice Quarterly*. 14: 1: 53-85.

Haar, R.N., and M. Morash. 2005. "Police Workplace Problems, Coping Strategies and Stress: Changes from 1990 to 2003 for Women and Racial Minorities." *Law Enforcement Executive FORUM*. 4: 3: 165-185.

Hale, D.C. 1989. "Ideology of Police Misbehavior: Analysis and Recommendations." *Quarterly Journal of Ideology*. 13: 2: 59-85.

Hale, D.C., and C.L. Bennett. 1995. "Realities of Women in Policing: An Organizational Cultural Perspective." In *Women, Law and Social Control*, edited by A.V. Merlo and J.M. Pollock, 41-54. Boston: Allyn and Bacon.

Halliday, C.A. N.d. "Many Minnies Later." Unpublished paper, available from the Vancouver Police Museum.

Hamilton, S. 1993. "The Women at the Well: African Baptist Women Organizations." In *And Still We Rise: Feminist Political Mobilizing in Contemporary Canada*, edited by Linda Carty, 189-206. Toronto: Women's Press.

Haraway, D.J. 1991. *Simians, Cyborgs, and Women: The Reinvention of Nature*. New York: Routledge.

Harding, J. 1991. "Policing and Aboriginal Justice." *Canadian Journal of Criminology*. 33: 3-4: 363-383.

Harding, S. 1986a. "The Instability of the Analytical Categories of Feminist Theory." *Signs*. 11: 645-664.

——. 1986b. "Introduction: Is There a Feminist Methodology?" In *Feminism and Methodology*, edited by Sandra Harding, 1-14. Milton Keynes, UK: Open University Press.

——. 1986c. *The Science Question in Feminism*. Ithaca: Cornell University Press.

Harrington, P., and K.A. Lonsway. 2004. "Current Barriers and Future Promise for Women in Policing." In *The Criminal Justice System and Women: Offenders, Prisoners, Victims, and Workers*, 3rd edition, edited by Barbara Raffel Price and Natalie J. Sokoloff. New York: McGraw Hill.

Harrington, P.E. 1999. *Triumph of Spirit*. Chicago: Brittany Publications.

Hartsock, N. 1983. *Money, Sex, and Power*. New York: Longman.

Heidensohn, F.M. 1992. *Women in Control? The Role of Women in Law Enforcement*. New York: Oxford University Press.

——. 1985. *Women and Crime: The Life of the Female Offender*. New York: New York University Press.

——. 1968. "The Deviance of Women: A Critique and an Enquiry." *British Journal of Sociology.* 19: 2: 160-176.

Heidensohn, F., and J. Brown. 2000. *Gender and Policing: Comparative Perspectives.* New York: St. Martin's Press.

Henry, S., and D. Milovanovic. 1999. *Constitutive Criminology at Work.* Albany: State University of New York Press.

Hess, B., and M. Ferree. 1987. *Analyzing Gender: A Handbook of Social Science Research.* Newbury Park, CA: Sage.

Hesse-Biber, S., C. Gilmartin, and R. Lydenberg, eds. 1999. *Feminist Approaches to Theory and Methodology: An Interdisciplinary Reader.* New York: Oxford University Press.

Heywood, L., and J. Drake. 1997. *Third Wave Agenda: Being Feminist, Doing Feminism.* Minneapolis: University of Minnesota Press.

Hickman, M.J., and B.A. Reaves. 2001. *Community Policing in Local Police Departments, 1997 and 1999.* BJS Special Report NCJ 184794.Washington, DC: US Department of Justice.

Hilton, J. 1976. "Women in the Police Service." *Police Journal.* 49: 2: 93-103.

Hodgson, J. 1993. "Police-Community Relations: An Analysis of the Organizational and Structural Barriers Inhibiting Effective Police-Community Relations." Ph.D. Dissertation, York University, Toronto, ON.

Homant, R., and D. Kennedy. 1985. "Police Perceptions of Spouse Abuse: A Comparison of Male and Female Officers." *Journal of Criminal Justice.* 13: 1: 29-47.

hooks, b. 1984. *Feminist Theory: From Margin to Center.* Boston: South End Press.

Hoover, L. 1995. "Education." In *The Encyclopedia of Police Science,* 2nd edition, edited by W.G. Bailey, 245-248. New York: Garland.

Horne, P. 1980. *Women in Law Enforcement,* 2nd edition. Springfield, IL: Charles C. Thomas.

Human Rights Program. 2007. *The Canadian Charter of Rights and Freedoms.* Canada: Canadian Heritage. <http://www.pch.gc.ca/progs/pdp-hrp/canada/freedom_e.cfm>.

Hunt, J. 1984. "The Development of Rapport through Negotiation of Gender in Field Work among Police." *Human Organization.* 43: 283-296.

Hurtado, A. 1989. "Relating to Privilege: Seduction and Rejection in the Subordination of White Women and Women of Color." *Signs.* 14: 833-855.

Husserl, E. 1960. *Cartesian Meditations: An Introduction to Phenomenology,* translated by Dorion Cairns. The Hague: Martinus Nijhoff.

Iacovetta, F. 1993. "Making 'New Canadians': Social Workers, Women, and the Reshaping of Immigrant Families." In *Gender Conflicts: New Essays in Women's History,* edited by Franca Iacovetta and Mariana Valverde, 261-303. Toronto: University of Toronto Press.

Inciardi, J. 1987. *Criminal Justice,* 2nd edition. New York: Harcourt, Brace, Jovanovich.

Independent Commission on the Los Angeles Police Department. 1991. "Summary of Report." Unpublished manuscript.

International Association of Chiefs of Police (IACP). November 1998. *The Future of Women in Policing: Mandates for Action.* <http://72.14.205.104/search?q=cache:X9j6wGIvY1sJ:www.theiacp.org/documents/pdfs/Publications/ACF830.pdf+International+Association+of+Chiefs+of+Police+1998+the+future+of+women+in+policing&hl=en&ct=clnk&cd=2&gl=ca>.

Itwaru, A. 1989. *Critiques of Power.* Toronto: Terebi Publications.

Jackson, L.D. 20-23 May 1997. "Crossing the Thin Blue Line: A Study of Female Police Officers in Atlantic Canada." A presentation made at the Women in Policing in Canada: The Year 2000 and Beyond—Its Challenges workshop, Canadian Police College, Ottawa, ON.

Jaggar, A., and P. Rothenberg. 1984. *Feminist Frameworks: Alternative Theoretical Accounts of the Relations Between Women and Men,* 2nd edition. New York: McGraw-Hill.

Jaggar, A.M. 1997. "Love and Knowledge: Emotion in Feminist Epistemology." In *Feminisms,* edited by Sandra Kemp and Judith Squires, 188-193. Oxford: Oxford University Press.

James, J., and J. Meyerding. 1977. "Early Sexual Experiences and Prostitution." *American Journal of Psychiatry.* 134: 12: 1381-1385.

Jolin, A., and C.A. Moose. 1997. "Evaluating a Domestic Violence Program in a Community Policing Environment: Research Implementation Issues." *Crime and Delinquency.* 43: 279-297.

Josiah, H. 20-23 May 1997. "Innovative Policy Development Approaches." A presentation made at the Women in Policing in Canada: The Year 2000 and Beyond—Its Challenges workshop, Canadian Police College, Ottawa, ON.

Jurik, N.C., and S.E. Martin. 2001. "Femininities, Masculinities and Organizational Conflict: Women in Criminal Justice Occupations." In *Women, Crime and Criminal Justice,* edited by C.M. Renzetti and L. Goodstein. Los Angeles: Roxbury.

Juristat—Canadian Centre for Justice Statistics. 2001. *Private Security and Public Policing in Canada in 2001.* Statistics Canada Catalogue No. 85-002, Vol. 24, No. 7. Ottawa, ON.

——. 1996. *Female Police Officers in Canada.* Statistics Canada Catalogue No. 85-002, Vol. 16, No.1. Ottawa, ON.

Kamens, L. 1981. "Evaluating Evaluation Research from a Feminist Perspective." A paper presented at the Annual Meeting of the Association for Women in Psychology, Boston, MA.

Kanter, R.M. 1976. "The Impact of Hierarchical Structures on the Work Behavior of Women and Men." *Social Problems.* 23: 415-430.

Kelling, G.L., and M.H. Moore. 1988. *The Evolving Strategy of Policing.* Washington, DC: US Department of Justice.

Kendall, K. Spring 1991. "The Politics of Premenstrual Syndrome: Implications for Feminist Justice." *The Journal of Human Justice.* 2: 2: 77-98.

Kennedy, D., and R. Homant. 1983. "Attitudes of Abused Women toward Male and Female Police Officers." *Criminal Justice and Behavior.* 10: 391-405.

Kinsman, G. 1987. *The Regulation of Desire*. Toronto: Black Rose Books.

Klein, D. Fall 1973. "The Etiology of Women's Crime: A Review of the Literature." *Issues in Criminology*. 8: 3-30.

Klockars, C. 1991. "Blue Lies and Police Placebos: The Moralities of Police Lying." In *Thinking about Police: Contemporary Readings*, 2nd edition, edited by C. Klockars and S. Mastrofski. New York: McGraw-Hill.

———. 1988. "The Rhetoric of Community Policing." In *Community Policing: Rhetoric or Reality*, edited by J.R. Greene and S.D. Mastrofski, 239-258. New York: Praeger.

Kolm, S.C. 1996. *Modern Theories of Justice*. Cambridge, MA: MIT Press.

Komarovsky, M. 1988. "The New Feminist Scholarship: Some Precursors and Polemics." *Journal of Marriage and the Family*. 50: 585-593.

———. 1985. *Women in College: Shaping New Feminine Identities*. New York: Basic Books.

Kome, P. 1983. *The Taking of the Twenty-Eight: Women Challenge the Constitution*. Toronto: The Women's Press.

Koons-Witt, B.A., and P.J. Schram. 2003. "The Prevalence and Nature of Violent Offending by Females." *Journal of Criminal Justice*. 563: 1-11.

Krieger, S. 1985. "Beyond 'Subjectivity': The Use of the Self in Social Science." In "Innovative Sources and Uses of Qualitative Data," edited by Meredith Gould. Special Issue of *Qualitative Sociology*. 8: 309-324.

Kruger, Karen J. 2006. "Pregnancy Policy: Law and Philosophy." *The Police Chief*. 73: 3.

LaFave, W. 1965. *Arrest*. Boston: Little Brown.

Langworthy, R.H., and L.F. Travis III. 2003. *Policing in America:. A Balance of Forces*, 3rd Edition. Upper Saddle River, NJ: Prentice Hall.

Larsen, E. 7 May 2008a. "Ocean Township, Police Union Reach Agreement on Patrolwoman: Deal on Light Duty Awaits Approval Today." Asbury Park Press. <http://www.app.com/apps/pbcs.dll/article?AID=/20080507/NEWS/805070471/0/>.

———. 6 May 2008b. "Pregnant Cop Denied Bid to Get Office Duty: Recommended by Her Doctor." Asbury Park Press. <http://www.app.com/apps/pbcs.dll/article?AID=/20080506/NEWS/805060450&>.

Lather, P. 1991. *Getting Smart. Feminist Research and Pedagogy With/in the Postmodern*. New York: Routledge.

———. 1988. "Feminist Perspectives on Empowering Research Methodologies." *Women's Studies International Forum*. 11: 569-581.

LeBeuf, M.E. 1996. *Three Decades of Women in Policing: A Literature Review*. Ottawa, ON: Canadian Police College.

Leonard, E.B. 1982. *Women, Crime, and Society: A Critique of Criminology Theory*. New York: Longman.

LeSueur, E. September 1928. "Can Women Do Active Police Work in Vancouver?" *Social Work*. 10: 12: 41-50.

Linden, R. 1984. *Women in Policing: A Study of the Vancouver Police Department*. Ottawa, ON: Ministry of the Solicitor General.

Linden, R., and C. Fillmore. 1993. "An Evaluation Study of Women in Policing." In *Evaluating Justice*, edited by J. Hudson and J. Roberts, 93-116. Toronto: Thompson Educational Publishing.

Lloyd, A. 1995. *Doubly Deviant, Doubly Damned: Society's Treatment of Violent Women.* London: Penguin Books.

Logan, E. 1999. "The Wrong Race, Committing Crime, Doing Drugs, and Maladjusted for Motherhood: The Nation's Fury over 'Crack Babies.'" *Social Justice.* 26: 1: 115-138.

Lombroso, C., and W. Ferrero. 1895. *The Female Offender.* London: Fisher Unwin.

Longino, H.E. 1999. "Feminist Epistemology." In *The Blackwell Guide to Epistemology*, edited by John Grecco and Ernest Sosa, 327-353. Malden, MA: Blackwell.

Lonsway, K.A. 2000. *Hiring and Retaining More Women: The Advantages to Law Enforcement Agencies.* Washington, DC: National Center for Women and Policing.

Lord, L.K. 1995. "Policewomen." In *The Encyclopedia of Police Science*, 2nd edition. New York: William Bailey.

Los Angeles Police Commission. 2000. *Police Academy and Probationary Officer Attrition.* <http://www.lacity.org/oig/documents/OIG2001annual.pdf>.

Los Angeles Police Department—Women in the LAPD. N.d. "LAPD Had the Nation's First Police Woman." <http://www.lapdonline.org/history_of_the_lapd/content_basic_view/833>.

Los Angeles Police Historical Society. N.d. *Los Angeles Police Department—Women in the LAPD.* Los Angeles, CA: Los Angeles Police Historical Society. Museum and Community Education Center.

Lundman, R. 1980. *Police and Policing: An Introduction.* New York: Holt, Rinehart and Winston.

Lynch, G. 1976. "Contributions of Higher Education to Ethical Behavior in Law Enforcement." *Journal of Criminal Justice.* 4: 4: 285-290.

Lyotard, J.F. 1984. *The Postmodern Condition: A Report on Knowledge*, translated by G. Bennington and B. Massumi. Minneapolis: University of Minnesota Press.

Maahs, J.R., and C. Hemmens. 1998. "Guarding the Public: A Statutory Analysis of State Regulation of Security Guards." *Journal of Crime and Justice.* 21: 1: 119-134.

Maas, P. 1973. *Serpico.* New York: Viking.

MacDonald, J.M. 2002. "The Effectiveness of Community Policing in Reducing Urban Violence." *Crime and Delinquency.* 48: 4: 592-618.

Macionis, J.J. 2005. *Sociology*, 11th Edition. Upper Saddle River, NJ: Prentice Hall.

MacKinnon, C. 1989. *Toward a Feminist Theory of State.* Cambridge, MA: Harvard University Press.

———. 1987. *Feminism Unmodified: Discourses on Life and Law.* Cambridge, MA: Harvard University Press.

Maden, A., M. Swinton, and J. Gunn. Spring 1994. "A Criminological and Psychiatric Survey of Women Serving a Prison Sentence." *British Journal of Criminology.* 34: 2: 172-191.

Maher, L., and K. Daly. 1996. "Women in the Street-Level Drug Economy — Continuity or Change?" *Criminology*. 34: 4: 465-491.

Mann, C.R. 1995. "Women of Color and the Criminal Justice System." In *The Criminal Justice System and Women: Offenders, Prisoners, Victims, and Workers*, 2nd edition, edited by Barbara Raffel Price and Natalie J. Sokoloff. New York: McGraw Hill.

Manning, P.K. 1997. *Police Work: The Social Organization of Policing*, 2nd edition. Prospect Heights, IL: Waveland Press.

——. April 1992. "The Police, Symbolic Capital, Class and Control (Bourdieu on the Beat)." Prepared for a Conference on Class and Social Control, University of Georgia, Athens, Georgia.

——. 1990. "Policing and Technology: Technologies and the Police." Draft intended for *Modern Policing*, volume 5 of *Crime and Justice Annuals*, edited by Michael Tonry and Norval Morris. Chicago: University of Chicago Press.

——. 1977. *Police Work*. Cambridge, MA: MIT Press.

Manning, P., and M.P. Singh. 1997. "Violence and Hyperviolence: The Rhetoric and Practice of Community Policing." *Sociological Spectrum*. 17: 339-361.

Marenin, O. Summer 1989. "The Utility of Community Needs Surveys in Community Policing." *Police Studies*. 12: 2: 73-81.

Martin, S.E. 1999. "Police Force or Police Service? Gender and Emotional Labor." *Annals of the American Academy of Political and Social Science*. 561: 111-126.

——. 1994. "Outsider within the Station House: The Impact of Race and Gender on Black Women Police." *Social Problems*. 41: 3: 383-400.

——. 1990. *On the Move: The Status of Women in Policing*. Washington, DC: Police Foundation.

——. 1980. *Breaking and Entering: Policewomen on Patrol*. Berkeley: University of California Press.

——. 1979. "Police Women and Police*women*: Occupational Role Dilemmas and Choices of Female Officers." *Journal of Police Science and Administration*. 7: 314-323.

Martin, S.E., and N.C. Jurik. 2007. *Doing Justice, Doing Gender—Women in Legal and Criminal Justice Occupations*, 2nd edition. Thousand Oaks, CA: Sage.

Marx, K. 1978 [1852]. "The Eighteenth Brumaire of Louis Bonaparte." In *The Marx-Engels Reader*, edited by Robert C. Tucker. New York: W.W. Norton.

Marx, K., and F. Engels. 1970 [1846]. *The German Ideology*, edited by C.J. Arthur. New York: International Publishers.

Mathieson, Chris. 2005. "Woman Officer Goes 4000 Miles Beyond the Call." In *Beyond the Call — Annual Report 2005*. Vancouver Police Department.

McDermott, J.M. 2002. "On Moral Enterprises, Pragmatism, and Feminist Criminology." *Crime and Delinquency*. 48: 283-299.

McKinley-Floyd, L.A. 1998. "The Impact of Values on the Selection of Philanthropic Clubs by Elite African American Women: An Historical Perspective." *Psychology and Marketing*. 15: 2: 145-161.

McLaughlin, E. 1991. "Police Accountability and Black People: Into the 1990's." In *Out of Order: Policing Black People*, edited by E. Cashmore and E. McLaughlin, 109-133. London: Routledge.

McLaughlin, E., and J. Muncie. 2001. *The Sage Dictionary of Criminology*. London: Sage.

McLean, A., and A. Leibing, eds. 2007. *The Shadow Side of Fieldwork: Exploring the Blurred Borders between Ethnography and Life*. Boston: Blackwell.

McLean, J. 20-23 May 1997a. "The Future of Women in Policing in Canada—Final Notes." A Presentation Made at the Women in Policing in Canada: The Year 2000 and Beyond—Its Challenges workshop, Canadian Police College, Ottawa, ON.

——. 20-23 May 1997b. "The Effects of the Police Culture on Social Identity." A presentation made at the Women in Policing in Canada: The Year 2000 and Beyond—Its Challenges workshop, Canadian Police College, Ottawa, ON.

McNamara, J. 1967. "Uncertainties in Police Work: The Relevance of Recruits' Back-Ground and Training." In *Police Work*, edited by D.J. Bordua, 163-252. New York: Wiley and Sons.

McNulty, E.W. Fall 1994. "Generating Common Sense Knowledge among Police Officers." *Symbolic Interaction*. 17: 3: 281-294.

Mead, G.H. 1962 [1934]. *Mind, Self, and Society*, edited by Charles W. Morris. Chicago: University of Chicago Press.

Meis Knupfer, A. 1996. *Toward a Tenderer Humanity and a Nobler Womanhood: African American Women's Clubs in Turn-of-the-Century Chicago*. New York: New York University Press.

Merleau-Ponty, M. 1962. "The Body in its Sexual Being." In *The Phenomenology of Perception*, translated by Colin Smith. Boston: Routledge and Kegan Paul.

Messerschmidt, J. 1997. *Crime as Structured Action: Gender, Race, Class, and Crime in the Making*. Thousand Oaks, CA: Sage.

——. 1993. *Masculinities and Crime: Critique and Reconceptualization of Theory*. Landham, MD: Rowman & Littlefield.

Miller, S.L. 1999. *Gender and Community Policing: Walking the Talk*. Boston, MA: Northeastern University Press.

Miller, S.L., K.B. Forest, and N.C. Jurik. 2004. "Lesbians in Policing: Perceptions and Work Experiences within the Macho Cop Culture." In *The Criminal Justice System and Women*, edited by B.R. Price and N.J. Sokoloff, 511-526. New York: McGraw-Hill.

——. 2003. "Diversity in Blue: Lesbian and Gay Police Officers in a Masculine Occupation." *Men and Masculinities*. 5: 4: 355-385.

Miller, S.L., and J. Hodge. 2004. "Rethinking Gender and Community Policing: Cultural Obstacles and Policy Issues." *Law Enforcement Executive Forum*. 44: 39-49.

Millman, M. 1975. "She Did It All for Love: A Feminist View of the Sociology of Deviance." In *Another Voice: Feminist Perspectives on Social Life and Social Science*, edited by Marcia Millman and Rosabeth Moss Kanter, 251-279. Garden City, NY: Anchor/Doubleday.

Milton, C. 1972. *Women in Police*. Washington, DC: Police Foundation.

Ministry of Community Safety and Correctional Services, Ontario. 2004. *Constable Selection System*. Ottawa, ON: Queen's Printer for Ontario. <http://www.mcscs. jus.gov.on.ca/english/police_serv/const_select_sys/overview.html>.

Ministry of the Solicitor General, Ontario. 1986. *Report on the Study of Female Police Officers. Ontario Regional and Municipal Police Forces*. Ottawa, ON: Ministry of the Solicitor General.

Mohanty, J.N. 1997. *Phenomenology: Between Essentialism and Transcendental Philosophy*. Evanston, IL: Northwestern University Press.

Monture-Angus, P. 2000. "The Roles and Responsibilities of Aboriginal Women: Reclaiming Justice." In *Criminal Injustice: Racism in the Criminal Justice System*, edited by R. Neugebauer, 231-274. Toronto: Canadian Scholars' Press.

Moore, H. 20-23 May 1997. "An Historical Account of Women in Policing in Canada." A presentation made at the Women in Policing in Canada: The Year 2000 and Beyond — Its Challenges workshop, Canadian Police College, Ottawa, ON.

Morash, M., and J.R. Greene. April 1986. "Evaluating Women on Patrol: A Critique of Contemporary Wisdom." *Evaluation Review*. 10: 2: 230-255.

Morash, M., and R.N. Haar. 1995. "Gender, Workplace Problems and Stress in Policing." *Justice Quarterly*. 12: 1: 113-140.

Morash. M., and A.L. Robinson. 2 July 2002. "Correctional Administrators' Perspectives on Gender Arrangements and Family-Related Programming for Women Offenders." *Marriage and the Family Review*. 32: 3-4: 83-109.

Morris, A. 1988. "Sex and Sentencing." *The Criminal Law Review*. 163: 167-171.

———. 1987. *Women, Crime and Criminal Justice*. New York: Blackwell.

Myers, G.E. 1995. *A Municipal Mother: Portland's Lola Greene Baldwin: America's First Policewoman*. Corvallis: Oregon State University Press.

Myers, T. 1993. "Women Policing Women: A Patrol Woman in Montreal in the 1910's." *Journal of the Canadian Historical Association/Revue de la Société historique du Canada*. 4: New Series: 229-244.

Naffine, N. 1996. *Feminism and Criminology*. Philadelphia: Temple University Press.

———. 1987. *Female Crime: The Construction of Women in Criminology*. Sydney: Allen and Unwin.

Nagel, I.H., and B.L. Johnson. 1994. "The Role of Gender in a Structured Sentencing System: Equal Treatment, Policy Choices, and the Sentencing of Female Offenders." *Journal of Criminal Law and Criminology*. 85: 1: 181-221.

National Center for Women and Policing. 2005a. "A History of Women in Policing in the United States." Feminist Majority Foundation. <http://womeninpolicing.org/history/index.asp>.

———. 2005b. "Workplace Issues: Pregnancy Issues in Law Enforcement." Feminist Majority Foundation. <http://www.womeninpolicing.org/workplace4~pregnancy.asp>.

——. 2003. "Under Scrutiny: The Effect of Consent Decrees on the Representation of Women in Sworn Law Enforcement." Feminist Majority Foundation. <http://www.womeninpolicing.org/pdf/Fullconsentdecreestudy.pdf>.

——. 2001. "Equality Denied: The Status of Women in Policing: 2001." Feminist Majority Foundation. <http://www.womeninpolicing.org/PDF/2002_Status_Report.pdf>.

——. December 2000. "Recruiting and Retaining Women: A Self-Assessment Guide for Law Enforcement." Feminist Majority Foundation. <http://www.womeninpolicing.org/sag.asp>.

——. 1999. "Equality Denied: The Status of Women in Policing, 1999." Feminist Majority Foundation. <http://www.womeninpolicing.org/Final_1999StatusReport.htm>.

——. 1998. "Equality Denied: The Status of Women in Policing, 1997." Washington, DC: National Center for Women and Policing. <http://www.womeninpolicing.org/status.html>.

National Opinion Research Center (NORC). 2003. *General Social Surveys, 1972-2002: Cumulative Codebook*. Chicago: National Opinion Research Center.

National Research Council. 2004. *Fairness and Effectiveness in Policing: The Evidence*. Washington, DC: National Academies Press.

Neilsen, J.M., ed. 1990. "Introduction." In *Feminist Research Methods*, edited by Joyce McCarl Neilsen, 1-37. Boulder, CO: Westview Press.

Ness, C., and R. Gordon. 13 August 1995. "Beating the Rap." *San Francisco Examiner*, A11.

Neugebauer, R. 1999. "First Nations People and Law Enforcement." In *Interrogating Social Justice: Politics, Culture and Identity*, edited by Marilyn Corsianos and Kelly A. Train, 247-269. Toronto: Canadian Scholars' Press.

——. 1996. "Kids, Cops and Colour: The Social Organization of Police-Minority Youth Relations." In *Not a Kid Anymore*, edited by Gary M. O'Bireck. Toronto: Nelson.

Newell, C.E., P. Rosenfeld, and A.L. Culbertson. 1995. "Sexual Harassment Experiences and Equal Opportunity Perceptions of Navy Women." *Sex Roles*. 32: 3-4: 159-168.

Nichols, D. Summer 1995. "The Brotherhood: Sexual Harassment in Police Agencies." *Women Police*. 29: 2: 10-12.

Nova Scotia Records and Archives Management. 2007. *African Nova Scotians*. <http://www.gov.ns.ca/nsarm/virtual/africanns/archives.asp?ID=33&Language=English>.

O'Connor, M.L. 2003. "Early Policing in the United States — Help Wanted — Women Need Not Apply!" In *It's a Crime: Women and Justice*, 3rd edition, edited by Roslyn Muraskin. Upper Saddle River, NJ: Prentice Hall.

Odem, M.E., and S. Schlossman. 1991. "Guardians of Virtue: The Juvenile Court and Female Delinquency in Early 20th Century Los Angeles." *Crime and Delinquency*. 37: 2: 186-203.

Ogle, R., D. Maier-Katkin, and T. Bernard. 1995. "A Theory of Homicidal Behaviour Among Women." *Criminology*. 22: 2: 173-191.

Orban, C. 1998. "Badges, Bitches, Dykes and Whores: Women in the Occupation of Policing." In *Women, Crime and Culture: Whores and Heroes*, edited by S. McMahon, 267-291. Toronto: Centre for Police and Security Studies at York University.

Ostiguy, L. 20-23 May 1997. "Encountering Barriers in the Police Field: What Female Police Members Must Confront." A presentation made at the Women in Policing in Canada: The Year 2000 and Beyond—Its Challenges workshop, Canadian Police College, Ottawa, ON.

Ottawa Citizen. 23 July 1984.

——. 30 November 1983.

Paget, M.A. 1990a. "Life Mirrors Work Mirrors Text Mirrors Life." *Social Problems*. 37: 137-150.

——. 1990b. "Performing the Text." *Journal of Contemporary Ethnography*. 19: 136-155.

——. 1983. "On the Work of Talk: Studies in Misunderstandings." In *The Social Organization of Doctor-Patient Communication*, edited by Sue Fisher and Alexander Dundas Todd. Washington, DC: Center for Applied Linguistics.

Peel Regional Police. 2008. "New Physical Testing P.R.E.P. (Physical Readiness Evaluation for Police)." <http://www.peelpolice.on.ca/Employment/ecms.aspx/PREP_Notice _JUN16.pdf>.

——. 2007. "Frequently Asked Questions." <http://www.peel police.on.ca/employment/FAQ>.

Perlstein, G.R. 1972. "Certain Characteristics of Policewomen." *Police*. 16: 5: 45-46.

——. 1971. *Exploratory Analysis of Certain Characteristics of Policewomen*. Ann Arbor: University of Michigan Microfilms.

Petchesky, R. 1980. "Reproductive Freedom: Beyond a Woman's Right to Choose." *Signs*. 5: 661-685.

Pierce, J. 1995. *Gender Trials: Emotional Lives in Contemporary Law Firms*. Berkeley: University of California Press.

Pike, D.L. 1992. "Women in Police Academy Training: Some Aspects of Organizational Response." In *Changing Roles of Women in the Criminal Justice System: Offenders, Victims and Professionals*, 2nd edition, edited by I. Moyer. Prospect Heights, IL: Waveland Press.

Plato. 1997. *The Complete Works of Plato*, translated by J.M. Cooper. Indianapolis: Hackett.

Pocket Criminal Code. 2002. *Constitution Act, 1982—Part 1 Canadian Charter of Rights and Freedoms*. Toronto: Carswell.

Pogrebin, M., M. Dodge, and H. Chatman. 2000. "Reflections of African-American Women on their Careers in Urban Policing. Their Experiences of Racial and Sexual Discrimination." *International Journal of the Sociology of Law*. 28: 311-326.

Pogrebin, M.R., and E.D. Poole. 1997. "The Sexualized Work Environment: A Look at

Women Jail Officers." *The Prison Journal.* 77: 1: 41-57.

Policewomen in the News. 2007. "Accomplishments by Women Police Officers in the RCMP." <http://www.sameshield.com/leaders/rcmp.html>.

Pollack, O. 1950. *The Criminality of Women.* Philadelphia: University of Pennsylvania Press.

Pollock, J.M. 2002. *Women Prisons and Crime,* 2nd edition. Florence, KY: Wadsworth.

Poulantzas, N. 1980. *State, Power, Socialism.* London: Verso.

Price, B.R. 1974. "A Study of Leadership Strength of Female Police Executives." *Journal of Police Science and Administration.* 2: 219-226.

Price, B.R. and N.J. Sokoloff. 1995. *The Criminal Justice System and Women: Offenders, Victims and Workers,* 2nd edition. New York: McGraw-Hill.

Prokos, A., and I. Padavic. 2002. "'There Oughtta Be a Law Against Bitches': Masculinity Lessons in Police Academy Training." *Gender, Work, and Organization.* 9: 439-459.

Rafter, N.H. 1985. *Partial Justice: Women in State Prisons 1800-1935.* Boston: Northeastern Press.

Rainguet, F.W., and M. Dodge. 2001. "The Problems of Police Chiefs: An Examination of the Issues in Tenure and Turnover." *Police Quarterly.* 4: 3: 271.

Reaves, B., and L. Bauer. 2003. *Federal Law Enforcement Officers, 2002.* Washington, DC: Bureau of Justice Statistics, US Department of Justice.

Reckless, W.C. 1961. *The Crime Problem,* 3rd edition. New York: Appleton-Century-Crofts.

Reiman, J. 2007. *The Rich Get Richer and the Poor Get Prison: Ideology, Class and Criminal Justice,* 8th edition. Boston: Allyn and Bacon.

Reiter, R. 1975. *Toward an Anthropology of Women.* New York: Monthly Review Press.

Renzetti, C.M. 1993. "On the Margins of the Mainstream (Or They Still Don't Get It, Do They?): Feminist Analyses in Criminal Justice Education." *Journal of Criminal Justice Education.* 4: 219-249.

Rich, A. 1980. "Compulsory Heterosexuality and Lesbian Existence." *Signs.* 5: 531-560.

Riley, D. 1988. *"Am I That Name?" Feminism and the Category of Women in History.* Minneapolis: University of Minnesota Press.

Robinson, G.V. 1993. "Sexual Harassment in Florida Law Enforcement: Panacea or Pandora's Box." Senior Leadership Research Paper. <http://www.state.fl.us/FCJEI/publications.asp>.

Rockwood, E., and A.J. Street. 1932. *Social Protective Work of Public Agencies: With Special Emphasis on the Policewoman.* Washington, DC: Committee on Social Hygiene — National League of Women Voters.

Roth, J.A., J. Roehl, and C.C. Johnson. 2004. "Trends in Community Policing." In *Community Policing (Can it Work?),* edited by Westley G. Skogan. Florence, KY: Wadsworth.

Russell, K.K. 1998. *The Color of Crime: Racial Hoaxes, White Fear, Black Protectionism, Police Harassment and Other Macroaggressions.* New York: New York University Press.

Ryan, G.F. "In Memory of Georgia Ann Robinson — LAPD's First Black Policewoman

1916-1928." *LA City Police* (#13322 Newton Street Division).

Sampson, R.J., and J. Cohen. 1988. "Deterrent Effects of the Police on Crime: A Replication and Theoretical Extension. *Law and Society Review.* 22: 1: 163-189.

Saunders, R.H. 1999. "The Space Community Policing Makes and the Body That Makes It." *Professional Geographer.* 51: 1: 135-146.

Scheurich, J.J., and M.D. Young. 2002. "White Racism among White Faculty: From Critical Understanding to Antiracist Activism." In *The Racial Crisis in American Higher Education: Continuing Challenges for the 21st Century,* edited by W.A. Smith, P.G. Altbach, and K. Lomotey, 221-242. New York: SUNY Press.

Schneider, E.M. 1992. "Particularity and Generality: Challenges of Feminist Theory and Practice in Work on Woman-Abuse." *New York University Law Review.* 67: 520-568.

Schram, P.J., and B. Koons-Witt, eds. 2004. *Gendered (In) Justice: Theory and Practice in Feminist Criminology.* Long Grove, IL: Waveland Press.

Schrom D.N. 1980. *As Equals and as Sisters: Feminism, the Labor Movement, and the Women's Trade Union League of New York.* Columbia: University of Missouri Press.

Schulz, D.M. 2004a. "Invisible No More: A Social History of Women in U.S. Policing." In *The Criminal Justice System and Women: Offenders, Prisoners, Victims, and Workers,* 3rd edition, edited by Barbara Raffel Price and Natalie J. Sokoloff. New York: McGraw Hill.

———. 2004b. *Breaking the Brass Ceiling: Women Police Chiefs and Their Paths to the Top.* Westport, CT: Praeger.

———. 2003. "Women Police Chiefs: A Statistical Profile." *Police Quarterly.* 6: 330-345.

———. 1995. *From Social Worker to Crime Fighter: Women in U.S. Municipal Policing.* Westport, CT: Praeger.

Scripture, A.E. 1997. "The Sources of Police Culture: Demographic or Environmental Variables?" *Policing and Society.* 7: 3: 63-176.

Seagram, B.C., and C. Stark-Adamec. 1992. "Women in Canadian Urban Policing: Why Are they Leaving?" *Police Chief.* 59: 10: 120-128.

Segrave, K. 1995. *Policewomen: A History.* Jefferson, NC: McFarland and Company.

Shankarraman, G. 2003. *Police Resources in Canada, 2003.* Statistics Canada Catalogue No. 85-225-XIE. Ottawa, ON: Minister Responsible for Statistics Canada.

Shaw, C., and H. McKay. 1969. *Juvenile Delinquency and Urban Areas.* Chicago: University of Chicago Press.

Shearing, C. August 1981. "Subterranean Processes in the Maintenance of Power: An Examination of the Mechanisms Coordinating Police Action." *Canadian Review of Sociology and Anthropology.* 18: 3: 283-298.

Shearing, C., and P. Stenning. 1987. *Private Policing.* Beverly Hills, CA: Sage.

Shelden, R. 1981. "Sex Discrimination in the Juvenile Justice System: Memphis, Tennessee, 1900-1917." In *Comparing Male and Female Offenders,* edited by M.Q. Warren. Beverly Hills, CA: Sage.

Sherman, L. 1995. "The Police." In *Crime,* edited by J.Q. Wilson and J. Petersilia. San Francisco: Institute for Contemporary Studies.

———. 1975. "Evaluation of Policewomen on Patrol in a Suburban Police Department." *Journal of Police Science and Administration.* 3: 4: 434-438.

Sherman, L., ed. 1974. *Police Corruption: A Sociological Perspective.* Garden City, NY: Anchor.

Sibley, D. 1988. "Survey 13: Purification of Space." *Environment and Planning D: Society and Space.* 6: 409-421.

Sichel, J., et al. 1978. *Women on Patrol: A Pilot Study of Police Performance in New York City.* Washington, DC: National Institute of Law Enforcement and Criminal Justice.

Silbert, M.H., and A.M. Pines. 1981. "Sexual Child Abuse as an Antecedent to Prostitution." *Child Abuse and Neglect.* 5: 407-411.

Simon, R. 1975. *Women and Crime.* Lexington, MA: D.C. Heath.

Simpson, S.S. 1989. "Feminist Theory, Crime, and Justice." *Criminology.* 27: 605-631.

Sims, B., K.E. Scarborough, and J. Ahmad. 2003. "The Relationship Between Officers' Attitudes toward Women and Perceptions of Police Models." *Police Quarterly.* 6: 278-297.

Singer, M., et al. 1995. "The Psychological Issues of Women Serving Time in Jail." *Journal of the National Association of Social Workers.* 40: 2: 103-113.

Singleton, Jr., R.A., and B.C. Straits. 1999. *Approaches to Social Research,* 3rd edition. New York: Oxford University Press.

Skogan, W.G., ed. 2004. *Community Policing: Can it Work?.* Florence, KY: Wadsworth.

———. August 1996. "The Community's Role in Community Policing." *National Institute of Justice Journal.* 31-34.

———. 1990. *Disorder and Decline.* New York: Free Press.

Skolnick, J. 1966. *Justice without Trial.* New York: Wiley and Sons.

Smart, C. 1995. *Law, Crime and Sexuality; Essays in Feminism.* London: Sage.

———. 1989. *Feminism and the Power of Law.* London: Routledge and Kegan Paul.

———. 1976. *Women, Crime and Criminology: A Feminist Critique.* Boston: Routledge and Kegan Paul.

Smith, D.E. 1990. *The Conceptual Practices of Power: A Feminist Sociology of Knowledge.* Boston: Northeastern University Press.

———. 1987. *The Everyday World as Problematic: A Feminist Sociology.* Boston: Northeastern University Press.

———. 1981. "The Experienced World as Problematic: A Feminist Method." Sorokin Lecture No. 12, University of Saskatchewan, Saskatoon.

Spelman, E. 1988. *Inessential Woman: Problems of Exclusion in Feminist Thought.* Boston: Beacon Press.

Spelman, E.V. 1997. "Woman: The One and the Many." In *Feminist Social Thought: A Reader,* edited by Diana Tietjens Meyers, 161-179. New York: Routledge.

Spelman, E.V., and M. Minow. 1995. "Outlaw Women: An Essay on Thelma and Louise." In *After Identity,* edited by D. Danielsen and K. Engle, 314-331. New York: Routledge.

Spelman, W., and J.E. Eck. 1987. *Problem-Oriented Policing.* Washington, DC: National Institute of Justice (Research in Brief Series).

Stanley, L., ed. 1990. *Feminist Praxis: Research, Theory and Epistemology in Feminist Sociology*. London: Routledge.

Statistics Canada. 2005a. *Income in Canada 2003*. Catalogue No. 75-202-XIE. Ottawa, ON: Statistics Canada.

———. 2005b. "Police Personnel and Expenditures." *The Daily*. Canada: Minister of Industry. <http://www.statcan.ca/Daily/English/051215/d051215d.htm>.

———. 2005c. *Spotlight: Police Officers*. <http://www42.statcan.ca/smr04/2005/01/smr04_02505_04_e.htm>.

Steffensmeier, D.J., and E.A. Allan. 1988. "Sex Disparities in Arrests by Residence, Race, and Age: An Assessment of the Gender Convergence/Crime Hypothesis." *Justice Quarterly*. 5: 53-80.

Steffensmeier, D.J., and M.J. Cobb. 1981. "Sex Differences in Urban Arrest Patterns, 1934-1979." *Social Problems*. 29: 37-50.

Stenson, K. August 1993. "Community Policing as Governmental Technology." *Economy and Society*. 22: 3: 373-389.

Stewart, D., and A. Mickunas. 1974. *Exploring Phenomenology*. Chicago: American Library Association.

Stier, H. March 1996. "Continuity and Change in Women's Occupations following First Childbirth." *Social Science Quarterly*. 77: 1: 60-75.

Stoddard, E. 1979. "Organizational Norms and Police Discretion: An Observational Study of Police Work with Traffic Violators." *Criminology*. 17: 2: 159-171.

Stokes, L., and J. Scott. 1996. "Affirmative Action and Selected Minority Groups in Law Enforcement." *Journal of Criminal Justice*. 24: 1: 29-38.

Storch, J., and R. Panzarella. 1996. "Police Stress: State-Trait Anxiety in Relation to Occupational and Personal Stressors." *Journal of Criminal Justice*. 24: 2: 99-107.

Straus, M.A., and R.J. Gelles. 1986. "Societal Changes and Change in Family Violence from 1975 to 1985 as Revealed by Two National Surveys." *Journal of Marriage and the Family*. 48: 465-480.

Susini, J. 1977. "Femme dans la police. Rouage anonyme de plus, caricature de l'homme ou condition d'emergence d'un type nouveau de personnalite policiere. (L'etonnante absence historique de la femme dans la police?)" *Revue de Science Criminelle et de Droit Penal Comparee*. 3: 651-664.

Sykes, R., and E. Brent. 1980. "The Regulation of Interaction by the Police." *Criminology*. 18: 2: 182-197.

Tappan, P.W. 1947. *Delinquent Girls in Court: A Study of the Wayward Minor Court of New York*. New York: Columbia University Press.

Temin, C.E. 1973. "Discriminatory Sentencing of Women Offenders." *American Criminal Law Review*. 11: 2: 355-372.

Temkin, L.S. 1995. "Justice and Equality: Some Questions About Scope." In *The Just Society*, edited by Ellen Frankel Paul, Fred D. Miller, Jr., and Jeffrey Paul, 72-104. Cambridge: Cambridge University Press.

Texeira, M.T. 2002. "'Who Protects and Serves Me?' A Case Study of Sexual Harassment of African-American Women in One U.S. Law Enforcement Agency." *Gender and Society.* 16: 4: 524-545.

Thacher, D. 2001. "Conflicting Values in Community Policing." *Law and Society Review.* 35: 4: 765-798.

Thomas, B. 1984. "Principles of Anti-Racist Education." *Current: Readings in Race Relations.* Toronto: Canadian Race Relations Foundation.

Thomas, W.I. 1923. *The Unadjusted Girl.* Boston: Little, Brown.

Thompson, J. 1992. *Justice and World Order: A Philosophical Inquiry.* London: Routledge.

Timmins, W.M., and Brad E. Hainsworth. 1989. "Attracting and Retaining Females in Law Enforcement: Sex-Based Problems of Women Cops in 1988." *International Journal of Offender Therapy and Comparative Criminology.* 33: 3: 197-205.

Tong, R. 1989. *Feminist Thought.* Boulder, CO: Westview Press.

Toronto Police Service. 2007. "A History of Policing in Toronto." <http://www.toronto police.on.ca/publications/files/misc/history/4t.html>.

Totten, M. 2000. *Guys, Gangs, and Girlfriend Abuse.* Peterborough, ON: Broadview Press.

Tougas, F., et al. 2005. "Policewomen Acting in Self-Defense: Can Psychological Disengagement Protect Self-Esteem from the Negative Outcomes of Relative Deprivation?" *Journal of Personality and Social Psychology.* 88: 790-800.

Townsey, R.D. 1980. *National Information and Research Center on Women in Policing.* Washington, DC: Police Foundation.

Trojanowicz, R.J. 1983. "An Evaluation of a Neighborhood Foot Patrol Program." *Journal of Police Science and Administration.* 11: 4: 410-419.

Trojanowicz, R.J., and B. Bucqueroux. 1990. *Community Policing: A Contemporary Perspective.* Cincinnati: Anderson.

US Census Bureau. 14 October 2005. *Historical Income Tables — People.* "(Tables) P-10, P-54." Washington, DC. <http://www.census.gov/hhes/www/income/ histinc/incpertoc.html>.

———. 2002. *Women and Men in the United States: Population Characteristics.* Washington, DC. <http://www.census.gov/prod/2003pubs/p20-544.pdf>.

US Department of Justice, Bureau of Justice Statistics. 2000. *Census of State and Local Law Enforcement Agencies.* Washington, DC: US Government Printing Office.

US Department of Labor, Bureau of Labor Statistics. January 2005. *Employment and Earnings.* Vol. 52, No. 1. <http://www.bls.gov/cps>.

US Merit System Protection Board (USMSPB). 1987. *Sexual Harassment of Federal Workers: An Update.* Washington, DC: US GPO.

———. 1981. *Sexual Harassment in the Workplace. Is It a Problem?* Washington, DC: US General Post Office.

Ussher, J. 1992. *Women's Madness: Misogyny or Mental Illness?* Amherst: University of Massachusetts Press.

Van-Maanen, J. July-October 1984. "Making Rank: Becoming an American Police Sergeant." *Urban Life*. 13: 2-3: 155-176.

Van Wormer, K.S., and C. Bartollas. 2000. *Women and the Criminal Justice System*. Boston: Allyn and Bacon.

Vedder, C.B., and D.B. Somerville. 1970. *The Delinquent Girl*. Springfield, IL: Charles C. Thomas.

Vega, M., and I.J. Silverman. 1982. "Female Police Officers as Viewed by their Male Counterparts." *Police Studies*. 5: 1: 31-39.

Villenueve, C. 20-23 May 1997. "Female Troops in the Royal Canadian Mounted Police." A presentation made at the Women in Policing in Canada: The Year 2000 and Beyond—Its challenges workshop, Canadian Police College, Ottawa, ON.

Visano, L. 1998. *Crime and Culture: Refining the Traditions*. Toronto: Canadian Scholars' Press.

Waldfogel, J. April 1997. "The Effect of Children on Women's Wages." *American Sociological Review*. 62: 2: 209-17.

Walker, S., and C.M. Katz. 2005. *Police in America: An Introduction*, 5th edition. New York: McGraw-Hill.

Walker, S.G. 2005. *The New World of Police Accountability*. Thousand Oaks, CA: Sage.

——. 1993. *The Status of Women in Canadian Policing*. Ottawa, ON: Ministry of the Solicitor General—Canada.

——. 1977. *A Critical History of Police Reform: The Emergence of Police Professionalism*. Lexington, MA: Lexington Books.

Walklate, S. 1995. *Gender and Crime*. London: Prentice Hall/Harvester Wheatsheaf.

Walter, N. 1999. *The New Feminism*. London: Virago.

Washington, B. 1981. "Stress and the Female Officer." In *Stress and Police Personnel*, edited by Leonard Territo and Harold J. Vetter. Boston: Allyn and Bacon.

Watters, J.K., and P. Biernacki. 1989. "Targeted Sampling: Options for the Study of Hidden Populations." *Social Problems*. 36: 416-430.

Websdale, N. 2001. *Policing the Poor: From Slave Plantation to Public Housing*. Boston: Northeastern University Press.

Welsh, S. 1999. "Gender and Sexual Harassment." *Annual Reviews Sociology*. 25: 169-190.

Welsh, S., and A. Nierobisz. 1997. "How Prevalent is Sexual Harassment? A Research Note on Measuring Sexual Harassment in Canada." *Canadian Journal of Sociology*. 22: 4: 505-522.

Wertsch, Teresa L. 1998. "Walking the Thin Blue Line: Policewomen and Tokenism Today." *Women and Criminal Justice*. 9: 3: 52-61.

West, C., and D.H. Zimmerman. 1987. "Doing Gender." *Gender and Society*. 1: 125-151.

Westley, W. August 1953. "Violence and the Police." *American Journal of Sociology*. 49: 34-41.

Westmarland, L. 2001. *Gender and Policing: Sex, Power and Culture*. Uffculme, UK: Willan Publishing.

Wexler, J.G. 1985. "Role Styles of Women Police Officers." *Journal of Police Science and Administration*. 12: 7-8: 749-756.

Wexler, J.G., and D.D. Logan. 1983. "Sources of Stress Among Women Police Officers." *Journal of Police Science and Administration*. 11: 1: 46-53.

Williams, C.L. 1989. *Gender Differences at Work: Women and Men in Nontraditional Occupations*. Berkeley: University of California Press.

Wilson, J.Q., and G.L. Kelling. March 1982. "Broken Windows: The Police and Neighborhood Safety." *Atlantic Monthly*. 29-38.

Wilson, S.J. 1996. *Women, Families and Work*, 4th edition. Toronto: McGraw Hill Ryerson.

Wise, S., and L. Stanley. 1987. *Georgie Porgie: Sexual Harassment in Everyday Life*. London: Pandora Press.

Wise, S., and L. Stanley, eds. 1984. "Men and Sex: A Case Study in Sexual Politics." A Special Issue of *Women's Studies International Forum*. 7: 1.

Withrow, B.L. 2006. *Racial Profiling: From Rhetoric to Reason*. Upper Saddle River, NJ: Pearson/Prentice-Hall.

Women's Rights Project—American Civil Liberties Union. 2006. *Women's Rights Project Report: Executive Summary*. <http://www.aclu.org/womensrights/gen/28644pub20070223.html>.

Wyrick, P.A. November 2000. "Law Enforcement Referral of At-Risk Youth: The SHIELD Program." Office of Juvenile Justice and Delinquency Prevention, US Department of Justice.

Zdanowicz, M. June 2001. "A Shift in Care." *Community Links*. 3-5.

Zhao, J., N. He, and N. Lovrich. 2003. "Community Policing: Is It Changing the Basic Functions of Policing in the 1990s?" *Justice Quarterly*. 20: 697-724.

Index